HOW THINGS WORK

IN SPACE

TIME LIFE BOOKS®

Other publications:

AMERICAN COUNTRY
VOYAGE THROUGH THE UNIVERSE
THE THIRD REICH
THE TIME-LIFE GARDENER'S GUIDE
MYSTERIES OF THE UNKNOWN
TIME FRAME
FIX IT YOURSELF
FITNESS, HEALTH & NUTRITION
SUCCESSFUL PARENTING
HEALTHY HOME COOKING
UNDERSTANDING COMPUTERS
LIBRARY OF NATIONS
THE ENCHANTED WORLD
THE KODAK LIBRARY OF CREATIVE PHOTOGRAPHY
GREAT MEALS IN MINUTES
THE CIVIL WAR
PLANET EARTH
COLLECTOR'S LIBRARY OF THE CIVIL WAR
THE EPIC OF FLIGHT
THE GOOD COOK
WORLD WAR II
HOME REPAIR AND IMPROVEMENT
THE OLD WEST

COVER

Strapped into a Manned Maneuvering Unit "jetpack," American astronaut Bruce McCandless became the first human satellite as he flew untethered from the shuttle Challenger *in February 1984.*

HOW THINGS WORK

IN SPACE

TIME-LIFE BOOKS
ALEXANDRIA, VIRGINIA

Library of Congress Cataloging-in-Publication Data

In space
p. cm. — (How things work)
Includes index.
ISBN 0-8094-7862-5
ISBN 0-8094-7863-3 (lib. bdg.)
1. Astronautics—Popular works.
I. Time-Life Books. II. Series.
TL793.I48 1991
629.4—dc20 90-21496
CIP

How Things Work was produced by

ST. REMY PRESS

PRESIDENT	Pierre Léveillé
PUBLISHER	Kenneth Winchester
	Staff for *IN SPACE*
Editor	Pierre Home-Douglas
Art Director	Solange Laberge
Assistant Editor	Christopher Little
Contributing Editor	George Daniels
Research Editor	Fiona Gilsenan
Researcher	Hayes Jackson
Picture Editor	Chris Jackson
Designer	Chantal Bilodeau
Illustrators	Maryse Doray, Nicolas Moumouris, Robert Paquet, Maryo Proulx
Index	Christine M. Jacobs
	Staff for *HOW THINGS WORK*
Series Editor	Carolyn Jackson
Senior Art Director	Diane Denoncourt
Senior Editor	Elizabeth Cameron
Researcher	Nyla Ahmad
Administrator	Natalie Watanabe
Production Manager	Michelle Turbide
Coordinator	Dominique Gagné
Systems Coordinator	Jean-Luc Roy

Time-Life Books Inc. is a wholly owned subsidiary of

THE TIME INC. BOOK COMPANY

President and Chief	Kelso F. Sutton
President, Time Inc. Books Direct	Christopher T. Linen

TIME-LIFE BOOKS INC.

Managing Editor	Thomas H. Flaherty
Director of Editorial Resources	Elise D. Ritter-Clough
Director of Photography and Research	John Conrad Weiser
Editorial Board	Dale Brown, Roberta Conlan, Laura Foreman, Lee Hassig, Jim Hicks, Blaine Marshall, Rita Mullin, Henry Woodhead
PUBLISHER	Joseph J. Ward
Associate Publisher	Trevor Lunn
Editorial Director	Donia Steele
Marketing Director	Regina Hall
Director of Design	Louis Klein
Supervisor of Quality Control	James King
	Editorial Operations
Production	Celia Beattie
Library	Louise D. Forstall
Correspondents	Elisabeth Kraemer-Singh (Bonn); Christina Lieberman (New York); Maria Vincenza Aloisi (Paris); Ann Natanson (Rome).

THE WRITERS

Lydia Dotto is a freelance science writer and former science reporter for Toronto's *The Globe and Mail* newspaper. She is the author of five books and is now working on a sixth—*The Astronaut: How Canadians Will Live and Work in Space.*

Stephen Hart writes about science and technology from his home in the foothills of the Olympic mountains near Port Angeles, Washington.

Gina Maranto is an award-winning science journalist who has written for *Discover, Redbook, The New York Times* and numerous other publications.

Peter Pocock is a freelance writer with a special interest in science and technology. He was a writer and editor for Time-Life Books for 10 years and most recently worked on the *Understanding Computers* and *Voyage Through the Universe* series.

THE CONSULTANTS

Gregory P. Kennedy is Executive Director of the Space Center in Alamogordo, New Mexico. Formerly an Associate Curator at the National Air and Space Museum, he is the author of numerous books and articles on space flight. He is a Corresponding Member of the International Academy of Astronautics and is a Fellow of the British Interplanetary Society.

Dennis Newkirk is the author of *Almanac of Soviet Manned Space Flight* and articles on the Soviet manned space program. He works as a software analyst for E-SYSTEMS, in Falls Church, Virginia.

Andrew Phillips earned a BS from the University of Arizona and an MS from the University of Minnesota in astronomy. He has since worked at the Cerro-Tololo Inter-American Observatory in Chile and is now at the University of Washington in Seattle.

Charles Redmond, manager of NASA's internal communications, has worked in a variety of positions during his 18 years at the space agency, serving as Public Affairs Officer for Space Flight, science public information officer at the Johnson Space Center, Public Affairs Officer for the Office of Space Science, as well as science writer for the Skylab program.

Ken Tapping studied mathematics at University of London and space science at University College London before joining the U.K.'s Radio and Space Research Station. He is head of solar radio astronomy at Canada's Herzberg Institute of Astrophysics.

For information about any Time-Life book, please write:
Reader Information
Time-Life Customer Service
P.O. Box C-32068
Richmond, Virginia
23261-2068

First printing. Printed in U.S.A.
Published simultaneously in Canada.
School and library distribution by Silver Burdett Company, Morristown, New Jersey.

CONTENTS

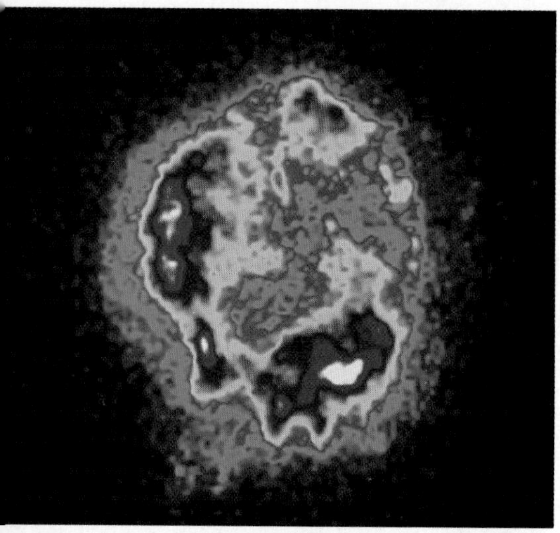

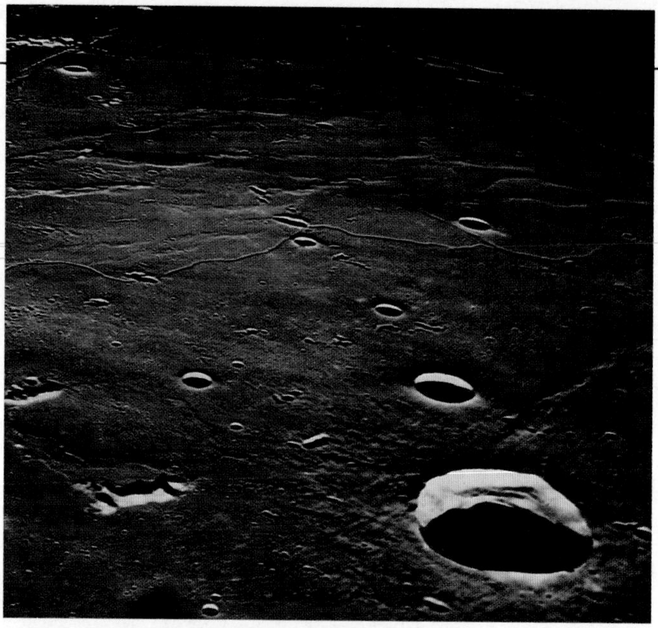

To the Outer Limits

Though the conquest of space began the moment humans first gazed at the stars and wondered how to reach out to them, the technology took centuries to develop. The early impetus was largely military; the Chinese, credited as the first rocket builders, aimed to strike terror in the hearts of their adversaries with their "arrows of fire."

Five centuries later, rockets such as the Congreve—whose "red glare" inspired the *Star-Spangled Banner*—proved more effective and far-reaching. Still, by the turn of the 20th Century, the heavens seemed overwhelmingly remote. Then, in the 1920s, the U.S. scientist Robert Goddard produced a rocket lofted by liquid propellants that provided potent and controllable burns and set the stage for the introduction of more powerful and sophisticated rockets. With the 1957 launch into orbit of the U.S.S.R.'s Sputnik—the world's first artificial satellite—the curtain rose on the Space Age.

The pace in the race to see who could put a man on the Moon was breathtaking. By the end of the 1960s, a mammoth Apollo Saturn V rocket had helped place two Americans on the lunar surface.

The next two decades witnessed the birth of the space shuttle, a reusable rocket that flew against a developmental backdrop of 700 years, and that may have marked the true beginning of the Space Age.

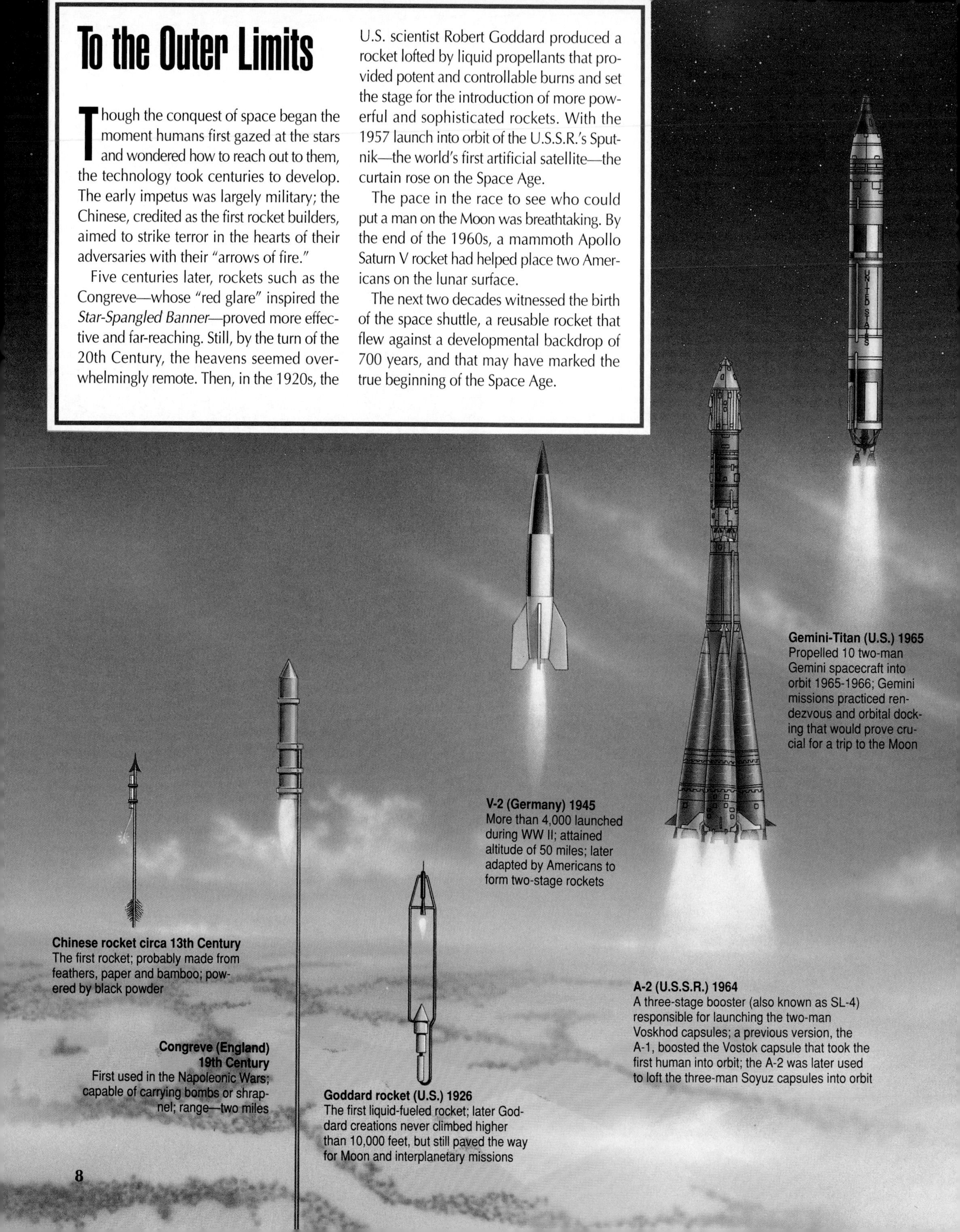
UNITED STATES
Gemini-Titan (U.S.) 1965
Propelled 10 two-man Gemini spacecraft into orbit 1965-1966; Gemini missions practiced rendezvous and orbital docking that would prove crucial for a trip to the Moon
V-2 (Germany) 1945
More than 4,000 launched during WW II; attained altitude of 50 miles; later adapted by Americans to form two-stage rockets
Chinese rocket circa 13th Century
The first rocket; probably made from feathers, paper and bamboo; powered by black powder
A-2 (U.S.S.R.) 1964
A three-stage booster (also known as SL-4) responsible for launching the two-man Voskhod capsules; a previous version, the A-1, boosted the Vostok capsule that took the first human into orbit; the A-2 was later used to loft the three-man Soyuz capsules into orbit
Congreve (England) 19th Century
First used in the Napoleonic Wars; capable of carrying bombs or shrapnel; range—two miles
Goddard rocket (U.S.) 1926
The first liquid-fueled rocket; later Goddard creations never climbed higher than 10,000 feet, but still paved the way for Moon and interplanetary missions

esa
esa
USA
NASA
Discovery
UNITED STATES
UNITED STATES
USA
USA

Ariane-Hermes
(European Space Agency) 1996
Proposed to launch commercial geostationary and Sun-synchronous satellites, and the Hermes manned spaceplane

Space Shuttle (U.S.) 1985
The first reusable spacecraft; first launched in 1981, the shuttle rides into orbit like a rocket, orbits like a spacecraft and lands like a glider

Apollo Saturn V (U.S.) 1969
Apollo 8 tested out the rocket on a trip around the Moon in 1968; in July 1969, Neil Armstrong set his foot down on the Sea of Tranquillity—the first human to walk on the Moon

The pace of the Space Age has been nothing short of astounding. A mere decade after the first satellite rocketed into orbit in 1957, probes had already landed on the desolate plains of the Moon and plumbed the mysteries of planets millions of miles from Earth. That was but a prelude to the grand ventures of the 1970s and '80s, which witnessed soft landings on two of Earth's closest planetary neighbors, Venus and Mars, and interplanetary probes that ventured to the edges of the Solar System—and beyond.

Nowhere was that spirit of adventure better embodied than in the splendid odyssey of Voyager 2, which took advantage of a rare celestial alignment of the gaseous outer planets to leapfrog from planet to planet. In August 1989, Voyager 2 skimmed past Neptune, the last encounter on its grand tour, sending back some astonishingly clear photos of the Sun's most distant progeny, before heading into uncharted interstellar space.

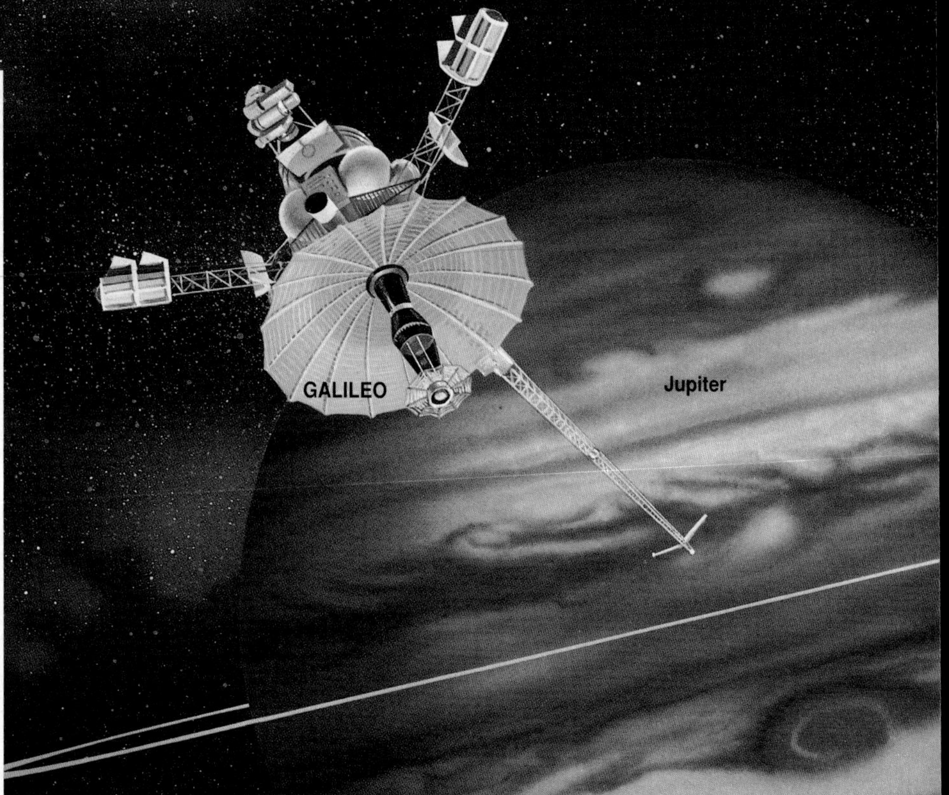
GALILEO
Jupiter

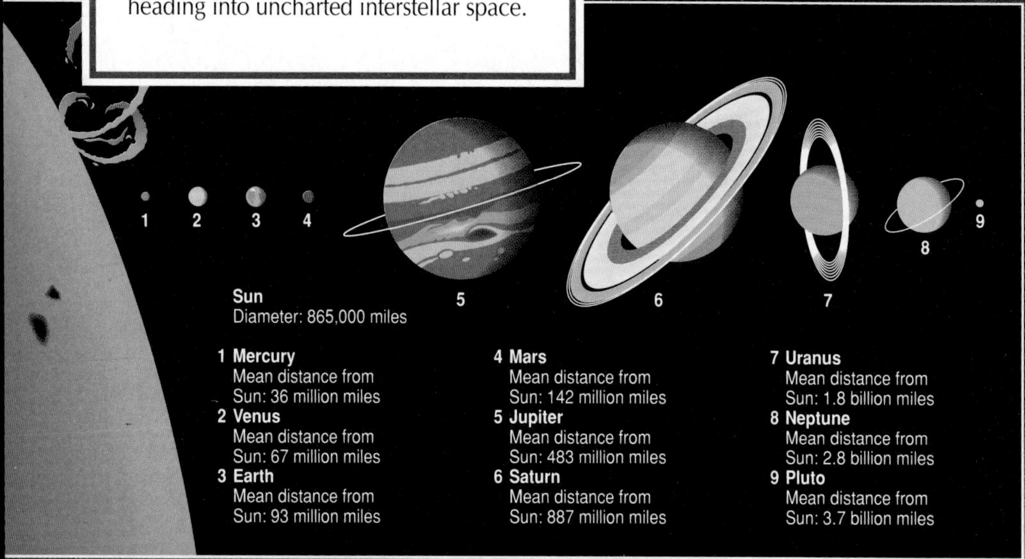
1
2
3
4
5
6
7
8
9
Sun
Diameter: 865,000 miles
1 Mercury
Mean distance from Sun: 36 million miles
2 Venus
Mean distance from Sun: 67 million miles
3 Earth
Mean distance from Sun: 93 million miles
4 Mars
Mean distance from Sun: 142 million miles
5 Jupiter
Mean distance from Sun: 483 million miles
6 Saturn
Mean distance from Sun: 887 million miles
7 Uranus
Mean distance from Sun: 1.8 billion miles
8 Neptune
Mean distance from Sun: 2.8 billion miles
9 Pluto
Mean distance from Sun: 3.7 billion miles

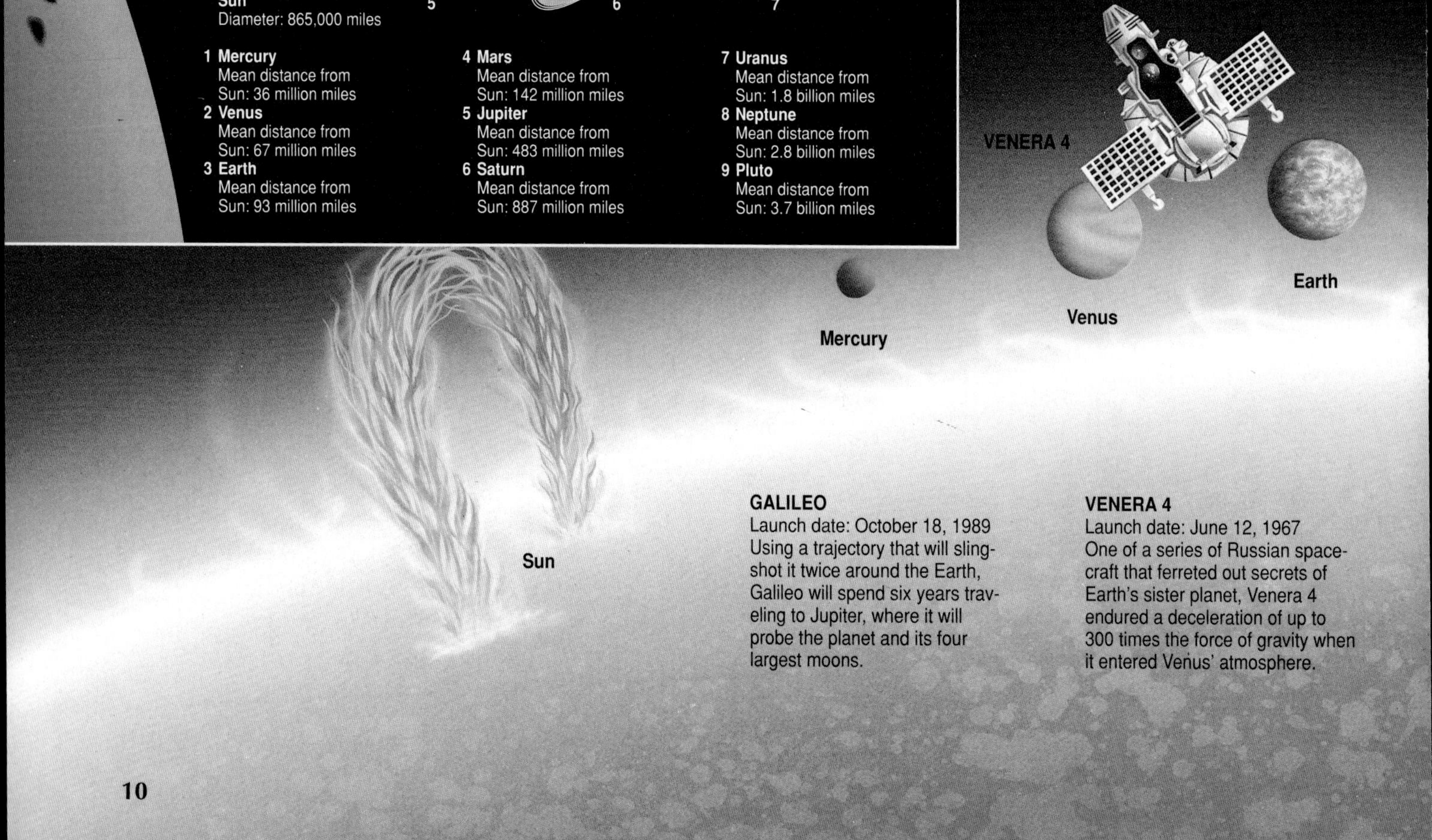
VENERA 4
Mercury
Venus
Earth
Sun

GALILEO
Launch date: October 18, 1989
Using a trajectory that will slingshot it twice around the Earth, Galileo will spend six years traveling to Jupiter, where it will probe the planet and its four largest moons.

VENERA 4
Launch date: June 12, 1967
One of a series of Russian spacecraft that ferreted out secrets of Earth's sister planet, Venera 4 endured a deceleration of up to 300 times the force of gravity when it entered Venus' atmosphere.

PIONEER 11
Saturn
VIKING 1
Mars
Uranus
VOYAGER 2
Neptune
Pluto

VIKING 1
Launch date: August 20, 1975
The first spacecraft to soft-land on Mars, Viking 1 was equipped with a mini laboratory to carry out experiments on the Martian soil.

PIONEER 11
Launch date: April 5, 1973
After using Jupiter's gravitational field for a boost, Pioneer 11 hurtled past Saturn in 1979 and continued on toward the edge of the Solar System.

VOYAGER 2
Launch date: August 20, 1977
Originally intended only to conduct close-up studies of Jupiter and Saturn, Voyager 2 performed so well that scientists reprogrammed the spacecraft to continue its celestial odyssey on to Uranus and Neptune, close to 3 billion miles from Earth.

The universe. The word encompasses everything—all that ever has been and ever will be. The scope of it is so vast, so utterly immense that it numbs the mind's power to comprehend. In just one galaxy, visible from Earth in the clear night sky as a hazy band called the Milky Way, spins the life-sustaining Sun (shown greatly enlarged as a bright spot in the outer spiral of the Milky Way, at right) and its family of nine revolving planets.

To humans on Earth, the range of the Solar System seems overwhelming; light traveling at 186,282 miles per second takes more than four hours to bridge the distance from the Sun to Neptune—along with Pluto, one of the two outermost planets. But size in the universe, like time itself, is relative. If the Solar System were reduced to the size of a plate, the Milky Way would span the continental U.S.

And that is only the beginning. The Sun's home galaxy is, itself, but one infinitesimally small player in the scheme of things—one of billions of galaxies in the universe. Traveling within those galaxies, or occupying remote regions of space, is a catalog of objects that increases as humanity's power to explore improves.

Quasars, pulsars and black holes once graced the names of sci-fi magazines; today, astronomers probe their secrets with an array of astonishingly sophisticated devices—optical telescopes so powerful they can see a lit match from thousands of miles away and radio telescopes sensitive enough to detect cosmic radiation produced when the universe took form billions of years ago.

Supernova
The explosion of a star that signals the end of its life. Before fading away, supernovas can flare so brightly that they can be seen from Earth during the day.

Comet
Composed mostly of ice, methane and ammonia, comets travel through the Solar System in a orbit that can take hundreds of years to make a single circuit.

Pulsar
Also known as a neutron star, a pulsar is a star that has collapsed into a highly dense body that emits radio waves in pulses, varying from every few thousands of a second to every few seconds.

Black hole
Matter so dense that light cannot escape from its enormous gravitational attraction. Black holes are formed by stars that have collapsed. A single spoonful of matter in a black hole would weigh more than the Earth.

Quasar
An incredibly bright luminous body, a quasar—or quasi-stellar radio source—is also extremely remote; some are thought to be receding from Earth at more than 90 percent of the velocity of light.

Nebula
The birthplace of stars, nebulae are, essentially, clouds of dust and gas.

THE VIEW FROM EARTH

The glittering lights of the night sky have struck sparks in the human imagination for millennia. The myriad stars and the hazy band of the Milky Way galaxy wheel slowly across the black dome; bright planets wander among the stars, sometimes joined by the luminous smudges of comets; occasionally a new star appears, flares brilliantly and then fades away. Long before history was recorded, people sought to explain these mysterious lights; societies developed myths and legends about the cosmos and their place in it. Ancient observers imagined that the stars were all attached to an immense, distant sphere. Others believed that various animals populated the night sky in configurations now called constellations. The often fanciful stories coexisted with the practical understanding and application of the great periodic phenomena by which time was counted: day and night, the waxing and waning of the Moon and the cycle of the seasons.

Astronomers, who are counted among the first scientists, have observed and analyzed the movements of stars and planets with increasing precision through the centuries. The invention of the telescope in the 1600s opened the door to a universe that contained far more numerous and stranger bodies than anyone had ever dreamed. Furthermore, astronomers began to put telescopes and other devices to work in the new science of astrophysics, probing the physical and chemical composition of celestial matter. Like the rest of astronomy, it is an observational pursuit. No controlled experiments are possible on objects so remote that their light—traveling at more than 186,000 miles a second—can take billions of years to reach the Earth.

In the last two centuries, astronomers have learned that there is much more to the universe than meets the eye. Everything that exists, from single atoms to distant galaxies, radiates waves of energy. Much of it is invisible, swallowed up or distorted by the life-sustaining atmosphere that girdles the globe. Driven by an ambition to see what cannot be seen from Earth, and propelled by an insatiable

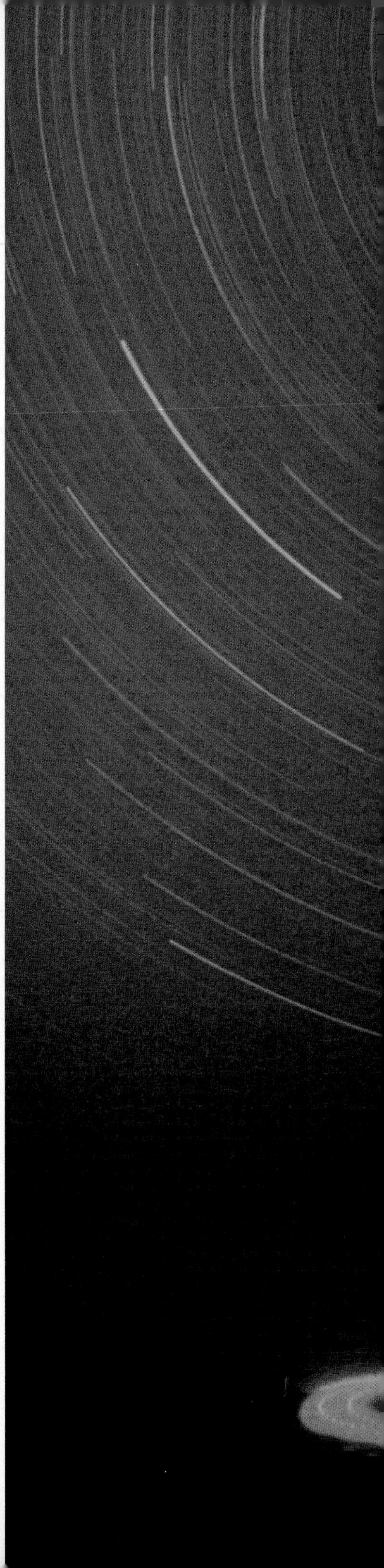

Against the swirling backdrop of stars created by a time-exposure photograph, the observatory housing the Canada-France-Hawaii telescope atop Mauna Kea in Hawaii casts its farsighted gaze on the mysteries of the universe.

curiosity to explore, the human race has begun to leave its earthbound base. The first journeys into space were fleeting affairs, but within a few decades probes were dispatched to the outermost reaches of the solar system. People, too, have ventured into space—to live, to work and to observe the unfolding mysteries of the universe.

ANCIENT EYES

Astronomy was at first a very practical pursuit. Before humans had writing, they had names for the bright bodies of the night sky. Seafarers used them to steer by; nomads relied on them to guide their peregrinations. Farmers matched the phases of the Moon and the passage of the Sun to the times for planting and harvesting. The ancient Egyptians marked the beginning of their crop year when the brightest star in the night sky, Sirius, appeared at a certain hour in the east.

Despite their limited resources, early astronomers proved remarkably clever at measuring the Earth and the heavens. In the third century B.C., the Greek astronomer Eratosthenes calculated the Earth's circumference by comparing the angle of the Sun at two Egyptian cities. Eratosthenes learned that at the summer solstice, the Sun shone directly down a well in Syene, near Aswan. On the same day in another year in the port city of Alexandria, where he served as director of its famous library, Eratosthenes noted that the angle of a shadow cast by the Sun was a little more than seven degrees, or $^{1}/_{50}$th of a circle. Multiplying the distance between the two cities to make a complete circle, the ingenious astronomer came up with a figure for the Earth's circumference. Historians of astronomy disagree about the exact value of that figure, but many now believe that Eratosthenes was within a few hundred miles of the modern measurement of some 25,000 miles.

Another Greek astronomer, Hipparchus, who lived in Asia Minor in the second century B.C., devised a variety of excellent measuring instruments and began to determine the positions and brightness of more than a thousand stars. Hipparchus ranked all the stars according to a brightness scale—the basis of the same scale used by astronomers today. The brightest stars he classified as first magnitude; the dimmest, magnitude six. He also fixed the length of the year with an accuracy to within six minutes, and calculated the mean distance to the Moon as being $29^{1}/_{2}$ Earth diameters—just one-half diameter less than its actual measurement.

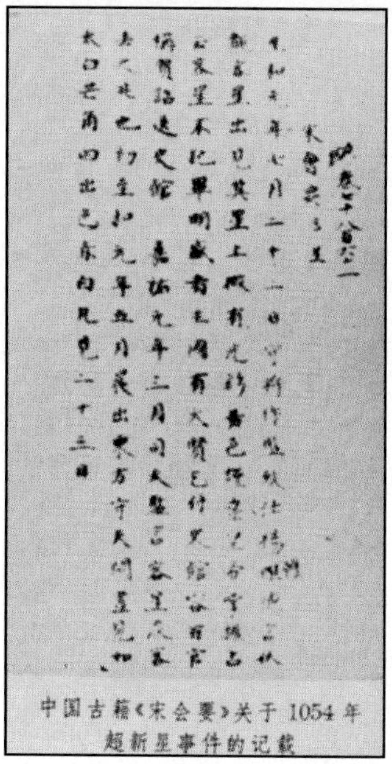
中国古籍《宋会要》关于 1054 年超新星事件的记载

The 1054 supernova was also recorded by Chinese astronomers in a book entitled Sung Hui Yao, *a court record of events during the Sung dynasty.*

Hipparchus' observations provided the basis for a theory that would govern Western astronomy for more than a millennium. In the second century A.D., the celebrated Greco-Egyptian man-of-all-science, Ptolemy, perfected a system that explained the movement of the stars and planets in precise mathematical terms. Ptolemy's cosmos was centered on Earth, with all other celestial bodies moving in complex paths around it. Although the system was extremely complicated, it allowed the future positions of planets to be calculated with reasonable accuracy. Its major elements were accepted by stargazers for more than a thousand years, until Polish Renaissance astronomer Nicholas Copernicus showed that the Sun was, in fact, the center of the solar system. In the early 17th Century German astronomer and mathematician Johannes Kepler further refined Copernicus' theory by demonstrating that Earth and the other eight planets actually move in ellipse-shaped orbits around the Sun.

This burial bowl, created by the Mimbres Indians of southwestern New Mexico, portrays an exploding star known as a supernova, which first appeared in the eastern sky on July 5, 1054. In the center of the bowl is a rabbit curled into a crescent to symbolize the Moon. According to a computer analysis, the sunburst at the rabbit's foot appears in the same relative location as the supernova did to the Moon on July 5, 1054.

During the Middle Ages in Europe, the stars held more meaning for astrologers than anyone else. Still, skywatchers everywhere, baffled by what they saw, felt compelled to record their observations. On July 5, 1054, the Mimbres Indians of what is now southwestern New Mexico saw a new star flare up near the Moon, so bright that it was visible in daylight for 23 days. The Mimbres had no written language, but someone recorded the event pictorially on a ceramic bowl, found by archaeologists hundreds of years later. At the center of the bowl is a rabbit curled into a crescent shape symbolizing the Moon, a well-known lunar deity in Mesoamerican folklore. According to historians, Indians tended to see a "rabbit in the Moon" rather than a "man in the Moon." Near the rabbit's feet the observant Mimbres painted a sunburst with 23 tines.

That blazing light of 1054 was a supernova, a distant star exploding into brief brilliance before it faded away. The same daytime display also was observed in China, where court astrologers noted that "a 'guest star' appeared in the fifth lunar month of the first year of the Tse Ho reign. It was as bright as Venus and was seen in daylight for 23 days." The remnant of that supernova, which took place in the constellation Taurus, can still be seen today as a rapidly expanding cloud of hot, glowing gas known as the Crab Nebula.

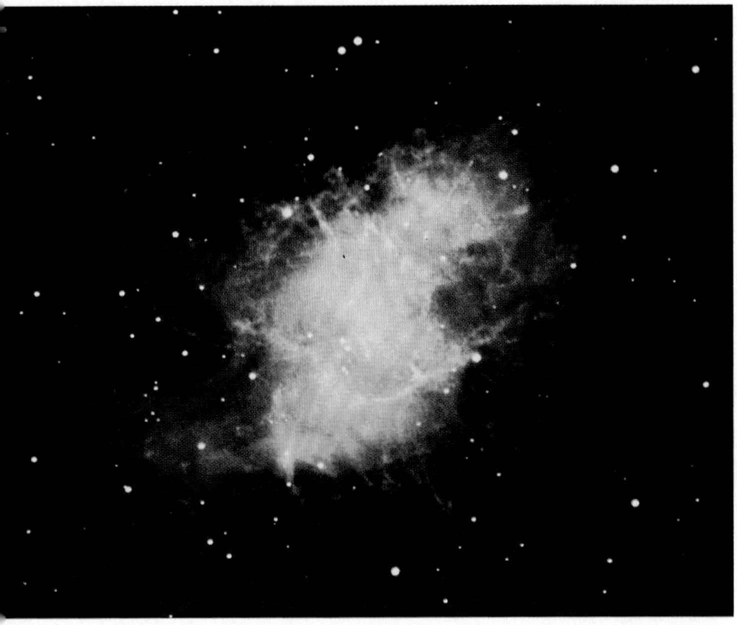

The explosion of the supernova created the diaphanous glow of the Crab Nebula, still visible to astronomers today. During the last 2,000 years, fewer than 20 supernovae in the Milky Way have been recorded by earthbound observers.

NEW VIEWS

Western astronomy was revolutionized by the introduction of the telescope in the 17th Century. The invention is attributed to Hans Lippershey, a Dutch lens maker who in 1608 chanced to hold two lenses in line and aim them at a distant church steeple. One lens, which he held at arm's length, was thicker at the center than at the edges, like an eyeglass. Called a convex lens, it caused light rays to converge. A second lens, which he held close to his eye, was thicker at the edges than the center and caused light rays to diverge—a concave lens. Looking through the two lenses, Lippershey saw that the church suddenly appeared closer and larger. To keep the two lenses held in place he mounted them in a rigid tube, thereby constructing the world's first telescope. Rumors of the invention spread quickly, and by the next year reached the ears of Galileo Galilei, an Italian scientist and mathematician, who immediately made a telescope of his own. Continuing to tinker with a variety of lenses and tube lengths, Galileo developed a device that magnified by a factor of 30.

Galileo's instrument was one of the earliest examples of a refractor telescope—along with a reflector, one of the two principal types of telescopes still used today. In the simplest refractor, light is collected at one end of a tube by a lens known as the object glass or objective, which varies in diameter from a few inches to a few feet. Passing through the objective, the light is bent, or refracted, to a point where the rays converge and come to a focus, known as the focal point. The second lens, the eyepiece, then enlarges the collected image.

The ability of a refractor to magnify is determined by the ratio of the objective lens' focal length—the distance between the lens and where light passing through

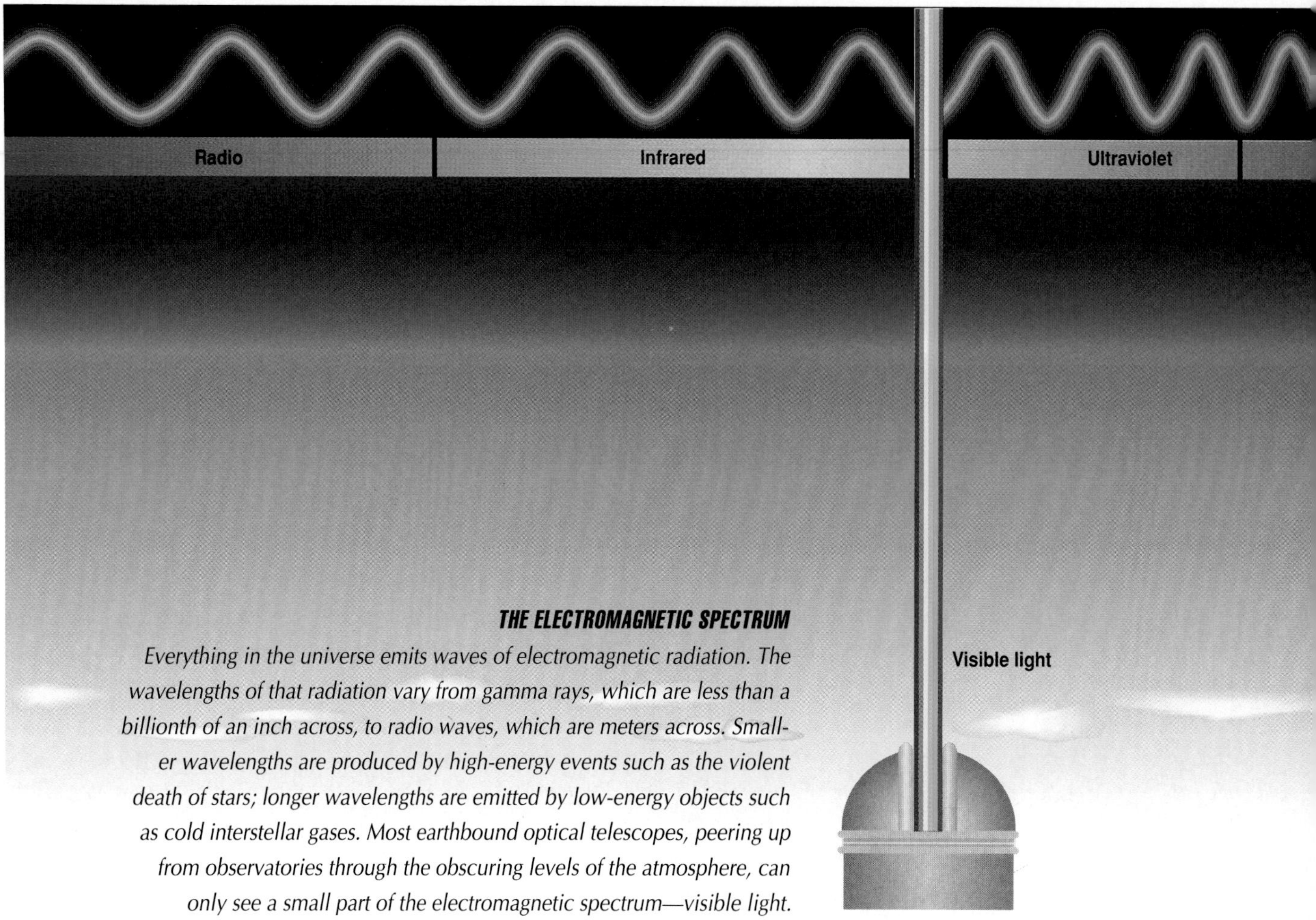
Radio
Infrared
Ultraviolet
Visible light

THE ELECTROMAGNETIC SPECTRUM

Everything in the universe emits waves of electromagnetic radiation. The wavelengths of that radiation vary from gamma rays, which are less than a billionth of an inch across, to radio waves, which are meters across. Smaller wavelengths are produced by high-energy events such as the violent death of stars; longer wavelengths are emitted by low-energy objects such as cold interstellar gases. Most earthbound optical telescopes, peering up from observatories through the obscuring levels of the atmosphere, can only see a small part of the electromagnetic spectrum—visible light.

it comes to a focus—and the focal length of the eyepiece. If, for example, the focal length of the objective lens is 1,000 millimeters and the focal length of the eyepiece is 25 millimeters, the magnification is 1,000 divided by 25—or 40 times. The same sized objective but with an eyepiece featuring a 10 millimeter focal length would produce 100 times magnification.

While Galileo's telescope opened up new worlds, revealing valleys and craters on the moon and satellites circling Jupiter, it still remained blind to most of the universe. Unbeknownst to Galileo, visible light is only one small part of the spectrum of electromagnetic radiation, which ranges from radio waves to gamma rays. Every object in the universe gives off radiation—waves of energy that travel through space at the speed of light. The distance between the crests of each wave is known as the wavelength. Radiation with longer waves—radio waves, for example—have wavelengths measured in meters; gamma rays' wavelengths are less than a billionth of an inch. Neither can be detected by the human eye. Nor can infrared, ultraviolet or X-rays. Visible light is a remarkably narrow window that falls roughly in the middle of the electromagnetic spectrum, with red light having the longest wavelength and blue light the shortest. What Galileo was seeing, therefore, as he turned his telescope towards the heavens, was just the visible light emanating from the Moon, planets and stars—one small piece of the celestial puzzle.

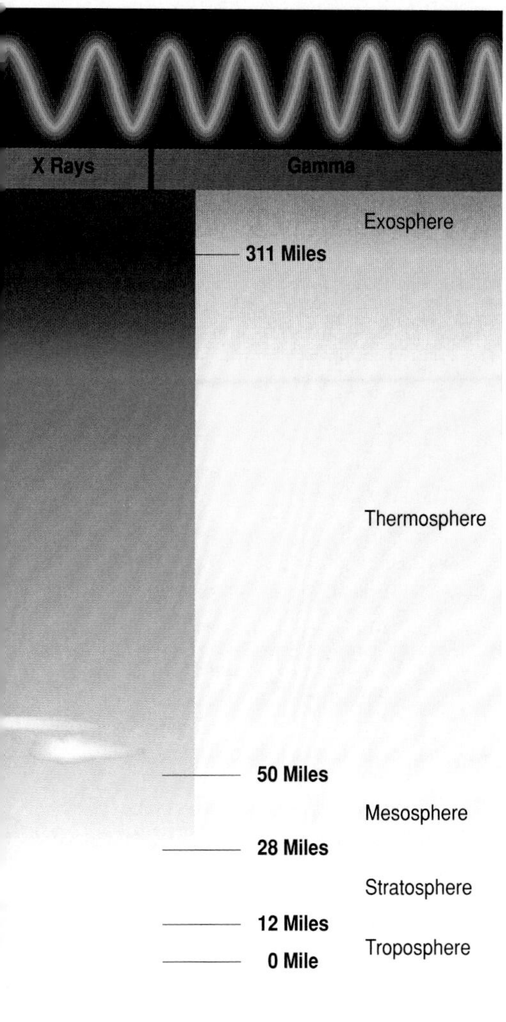
X Rays
Gamma
Exosphere
311 Miles
Thermosphere
50 Miles
Mesosphere
28 Miles
Stratosphere
12 Miles
Troposphere
0 Mile

Despite its ability to magnify an image, the first refractor telescopes were plagued by an inherent problem of design. When light passes through a lens, it is broken down into its rainbowlike range of component colors, each focusing at a slightly different point depending on the wavelength of that color. The shorter blue waves are bent more than the longer waves of red light. This so-called chromatic aberration results in a blurred, falsely colored image. Furthermore, lenses ground to a spherical shape focus light at different points, depending on where the light passes through the lens, causing an additional blurring known as spherical aberration. Because these distortions are less pronounced in long telescopes, astronomers soon began to build increasingly unwieldy instruments. In 1656, Dutch astronomer Christian Huygens made a telescope whose lenses were separated by 210 feet. Too long to be housed in a tube, the device consisted of one lens mounted on a tower and controlled by ropes while the other was aimed from a support on the ground.

Another solution to the problems inherent in glass lenses was to eliminate them altogether. Soon after the introduction of refractor telescopes, it was suggested that mirrors could be used in place of lenses to gather and focus light. Instead of bending light to a focus with a lens and then magnifying the image, a curved mirror could reflect light back to a focal point, and then be magnified by an eyepiece. The first reflector telescope was built in 1668 in England by Isaac Newton, the discoverer of the law of gravity. A brilliant mathematician and an inveterate tinkerer, Newton cast, ground and polished his own mirrors of an alloy of copper, tin and other metals called speculum. He placed a concave-shaped mirror at the lower end of a tube. The upper end was open and pointed at the night sky. The mirror reflected incoming light back to a smaller secondary mirror near the top of the tube. Placed at a 45-degree angle to the primary mirror, the flat secondary mirror then deflected the concentrated light through a hole in the side of the tube to an eyepiece, which in turn magnified the image. Despite the fact that the secondary mirror sits directly in the path of incoming starlight, it merely cuts down, ever so slightly, the amount of starlight that reaches the primary lens—a small price

MAGNIFYING THE HEAVENS

The refractor (left) *was the first type of telescope ever built. It features two lenses: an objective, which gathers light and bends it to a focus; and an eyepiece, which magnifies the image.*

A reflector telescope (middle) *uses a mirror instead of a lens to collect and focus light. A secondary mirror then directs the light to an eyepiece. This model is called a Newtonian reflector after its creator, English mathematician Isaac Newton.*

A second, popular type of reflector (right), *known as a Cassegrain after French astronomer Guillaume Cassegrain who first proposed it in 1672, uses a secondary mirror to bounce light back through a hole in the primary mirror.*

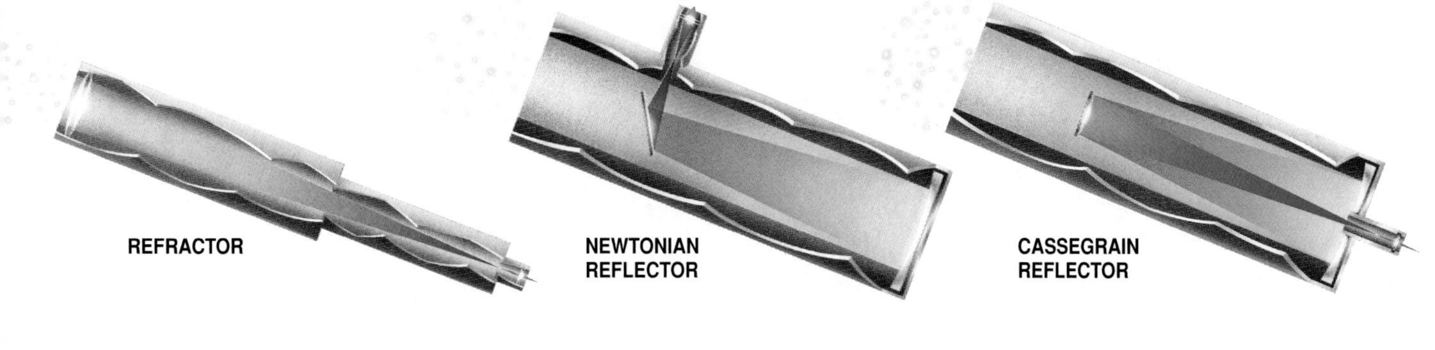
REFRACTOR
NEWTONIAN
REFLECTOR
CASSEGRAIN
REFLECTOR

to pay for the simplicity of the telescope's design. The new instrument was called a Newtonian reflector, in honor of its creator.

Whether a telescope is a refractor or a reflector, it offers several major advantages over the naked eye. An objective lens or mirror eight inches in diameter can gather about a thousand times more light than the pupil of a human eye, which has a diameter of roughly one-quarter inch when adapted to darkness. And by magnifying an image hundreds of times, a telescope allows its user to distinguish two close objects, which the eye would see only as a blur, as being separate and distinct. This ability, called resolution, is calculated in arc seconds or arc minutes. One arc minute equals 1/60 of one degree. (There are 360 degrees in a circle.) An arc second is 1/60 of an arc minute, or 1/3600 of a degree. The unaided human eye can only resolve about two minutes of arc, sufficient, for example, to separate two car headlights at a distance of about two miles. But an amateur astronomer's telescope with a 10-inch mirror can distinguish the same set of headlights as separate orbs from more than 200 miles away.

In the mid-19th Century, European scientists began to develop techniques for making mirrors from glass, covered with a thin coating of silver. As well as being cheaper than speculum metal, glass also was distorted less by temperature changes, and the silver coating offered superior reflective capabilities. By the turn of the century, plans had been laid for a 60-inch glass reflector, which went into operation at California's Mount Wilson Observatory in 1908; it was joined there by a 100-inch reflector 10 years later.

Mount Wilson was one of a growing number of facilities dedicated to the increasingly complex enterprise of skywatching. Observatories had been around for a long time—England's assemblage of megaliths known as Stonehenge, its first stage of construction dating before 2000 B.C., may have been a huge time-keeping device, with all its moving parts in the sky. Priest-astronomers ran the observatory in Babylon almost 3,000 years ago; it may have been the Tower of Babel, the legendary edifice in Genesis whose construction is said to have been interrupted by a cacophony of different languages.

The first modern observatories were founded in the 17th Century —not long after the invention of tele-

MIRROR MOUNTAIN

The steel frame of the Keck telescope (below) *is designed to help support the telescope's 36 hexagonal mirrors. The Keck is located on the dormant volcano Mauna Kea in Hawaii. Workers who pieced the telescope together were ordered to rest for a half an hour during their commute to the work site to help them become acclimatized to the rarefied air on the near-14,000-foot summit.*

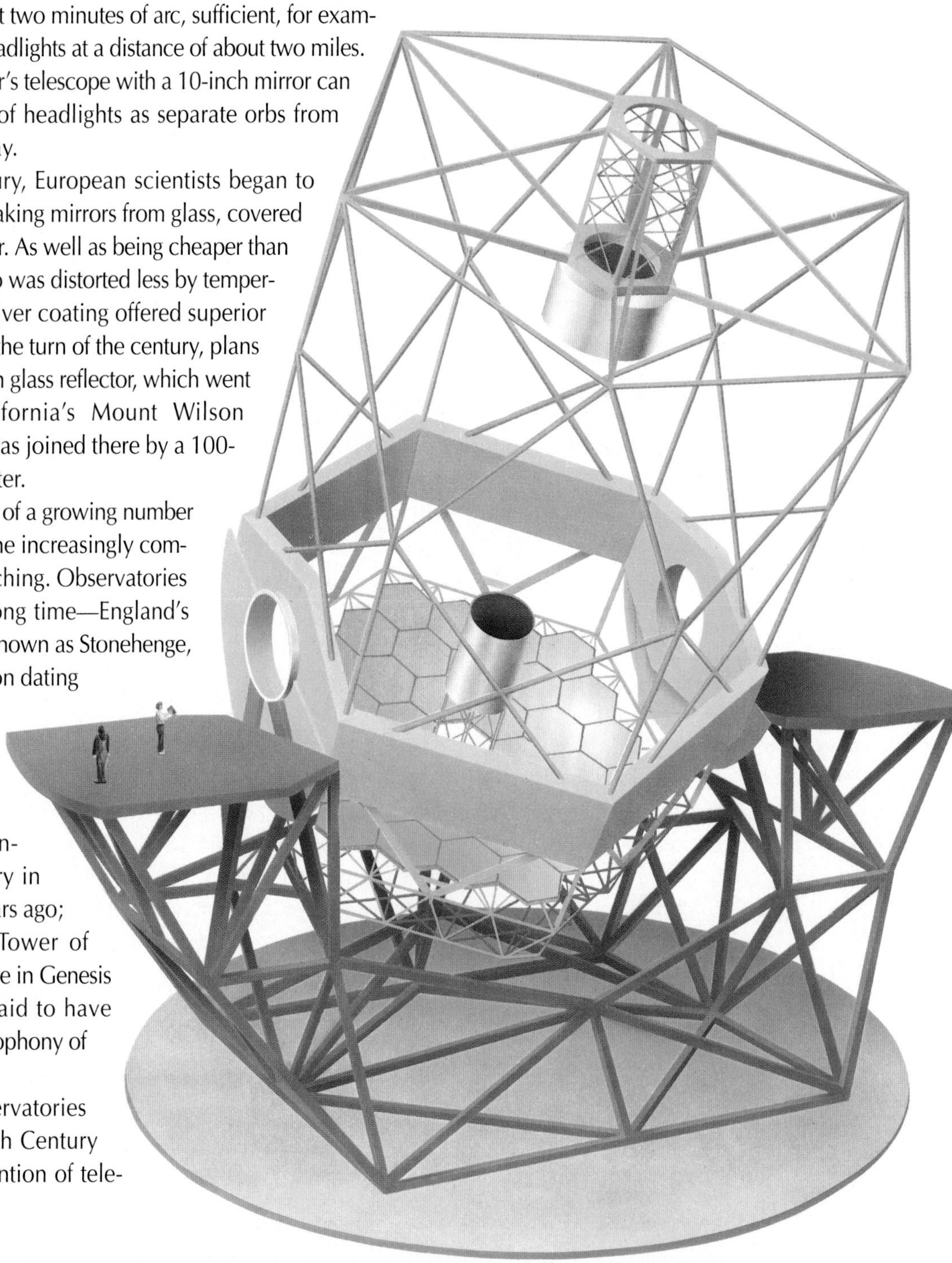

scopes. At first, most were supported by royal subsidies; the French national observatory was built in Paris from 1667 to 1671, although Louis XIV, the Sun King, required such imposing architecture that the finished building was virtually useless for skywatching; its first director, the Italian-born Giovanni Cassini, (who discovered four satellites of Saturn and a division in its rings) could use his telescopes only by taking them out on the grounds. The Royal Observatory at Greenwich, England, founded in 1675, faced the same architectural constraints, and in its early years relied on wealthy patrons and the meager personal means of the court-appointed Astronomer Royal to provide equipment.

But as the scientific revolution took hold in Europe and the United States, astronomical observatories gained increasing support from public and private sources. New facilities were located not in capital cities, but in places where the air was clear and dry. The observatories of today most often are situated on the remote tops of mountains, far away from any urban skyglow, which can seriously interfere with a telscope's performance by reducing the darkness of the night sky, much as a mist or fog reduces visibility for night drivers.

To keep Keck's 36 individual mirror segments aligned to within one-millionth of an inch, the telescope's designers have created an elaborate support system for each mirror that includes a flexible central disk and radiating arms with a series of pins embedded in the mirror. Computer-controlled adjustments can be made twice a second.

Light pollution poses one of the most serious threats to astronomers and has severely hampered the performances of telescopes such as Palomar Mountain's mammoth Hale telescope, whose builders could scarcely have envisioned how the sprawl of Los Angeles would one day encroach on their isolated mountain aeries. It also has resulted in city ordinances designed to reduce ambient light. Tucson, Arizona, for example, situated 50 miles from a collection of telescopes perched on 6,875-foot Kitt Peak, requires all homeowners to install shades above any outdoor lights of more than 150 watts and has banned the use of mercury-vapor streetlights. Hawaii has passed similar laws to protect the mountain summit that many consider to be the pinnacle of the world's vantage points for the stars—the extinct volcano Mauna Kea. At nearly 14,000 feet, the cinder cone sits perched above 35 percent of the Earth's distorting atmosphere, and offers close to 300 crystal-clear nights a year.

Clustered around Mauna Kea's summit sits a growing family of telescopes. The newest member features a novel mirror design that may revolutionize the way reflector telescopes are built. Instead of relying on a single-piece main mirror, the

Keck telescope features a honeycombed-mosaic of 36 hexagonal segments, each about 6 feet across. Held together in a near-perfect curve by a complex computer program, the 880-pound segments function as one gigantic 390-inch single mirror. Each individual mirror is supported by 36 metal rods, thin as pencil lead, which are attached to three whiffletrees. (The term traces its roots to 19th-Century stagecoach drivers, who used horizontal crossbars—whiffletrees—to harness a team of horses. The bars could pivot to accommodate the different pulling power of individual animals and keep a wagon from veering off track.) The Keck's whiffletrees allow the mirror segments to move sideways in the plane of the mirror, but restrain it in the direction perpendicular to the mirror. Each segment also has a centrally located "flex disk" that restrains the mirror from sideways motion, but allows motion perpendicular to the mirror. Operating in unison, these mechanisms allow the segments to be supported rigidly without applying any distorting forces.

Sensors around the perimeter of each segment provide information about the motion of each mirror relative to its neighbors. This information allows a computer to keep the mirror segments in their desired location by moving them infinitesimal amounts twice a second in response to any position errors measured by the sensors. These adjustments are made by three actuators attached to the back of each segment through the whiffletrees.

The task of building Keck's segmented mirror was complicated by the fact that, although the telescope's 36 mirrors have to work together as a single, symmetrical concave surface, each of its segments is actually asymmetrical. The challenge of grinding the mirrors has been compared to that of a potter who, instead of turning a bowl on a wheel, had to shape many small pieces of clay and fashion them together into a smoothly curving surface. The problem for Keck's builders was solved by using "stressed mirror polishing," which alters the manufacture of the mirror segments from an asymmetrical, or aspherical, surface to a simpler spherical polishing task. The three-inch-thick mirrors are installed in a jig with levers that bend the glass while opticians grind a spherical impression. When it is released from the jig the glass then springs back into its stress-free state and the spherical surface distorts to the desired aspherical form. Without this technique, the whole task could well take a year for each segment; with it, the Keck's mirrors are each polished in about six weeks.

The glass for the mirrors is created from a special glass-ceramic called "Zerodur," which resists expansion and contraction caused by temperature variations. Ordinary glass is, technically, a liquid; Zerodur, however, also contains crystallized silica molecules, which are induced to grow in the glass by a carefully controlled heating and cooling process. The "liquid" glass and the silica crystals react oppositely to temperature variation, virtually canceling out expansion and contraction. Manufactured in Mainz, Germany, Zerodur represents a thirtyfold improvement over the Pyrex used in the Hale telescope's 200-inch mirror at Palomar Mountain.

The Keck telescope will serve as the most effective magnifying glass ever turned on the heavens from Earth, powerful enough to see a street light on the Moon or a match lit 10,000 miles away. It will also represent the most sophisticated earthbound time machine ever constructed. Just as sunlight is actually light that left the Sun eight minutes ago, bridging the 93-million-mile gap at 186,282 miles a second, so the starlight that astronomers observe through telescopes emanated

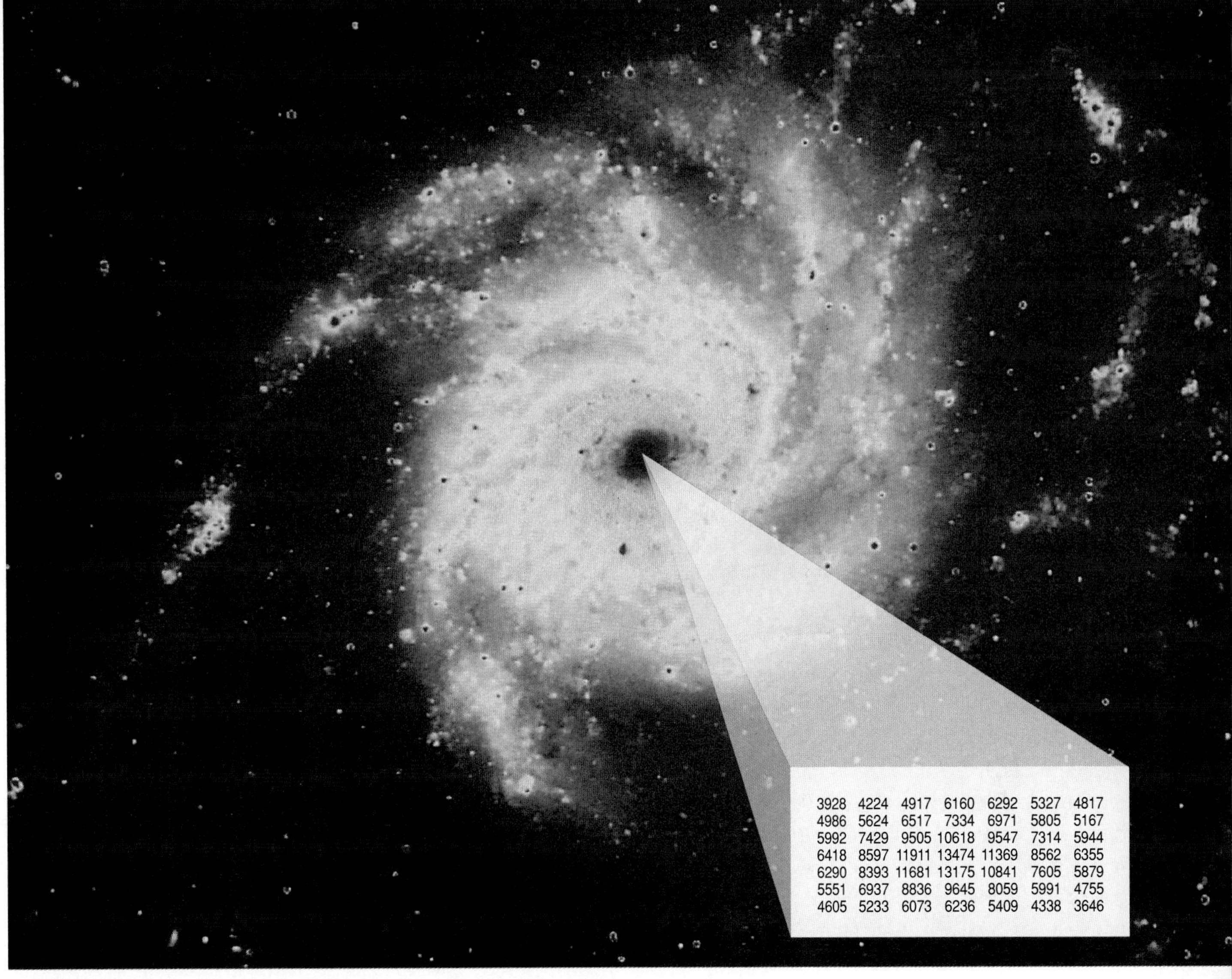

3928	4224	4917	6160	6292	5327	4817
4986	5624	6517	7334	6971	5805	5167
5992	7429	9505	10618	9547	7314	5944
6418	8597	11911	13474	11369	8562	6355
6290	8393	11681	13175	10841	7605	5879
5551	6937	8836	9645	8059	5991	4755
4605	5233	6073	6236	5409	4338	3646

This photograph of the M101 Galaxy (the M stands for the Messier Catalog, a system of numbering heavenly bodies developed by French astronomer Charles Messier in the 18th Century) was taken with a telescope equipped with a Charge Coupled Device (CCD). The 49 numbers below the photograph are the numerical values of the central 49 (7-by-7) electronic picture elements—or pixels—that created that part of the image. The entire photograph contains more than two million pixels. Color was added by assigning hues depending on the intensity of the light.

from their sources often millions of years ago. The distance that light travels in a year—six trillion miles—is called one light-year. The Keck promises to look farther than any telescope on Earth, up to 12 billion light-years into space, to observe stellar objects and events that occurred when the universe first took form.

Scientists' ability to record images produced by the Keck telescope will be greatly enhanced by a revolution in miniaturization that swept the electronics industry several decades ago, resulting in a device that has made photography virtually obsolete for astronomers. Introduced in 1970, the Charge Coupled Device, or CCD, is a chip of silicon about the size of a postage stamp that transforms light falling on its surface into an electrical charge. The chip is divided into thousands of tiny sections, called picture elements, or pixels. The amount of the charge in each pixel is directly proportional to the amount of light striking there, so a computer can read the output of a CCD and use it to construct an image.

A sophisticated CCD can pack several million pixels into a single image or picture. An electronic counting device measures the charge on each pixel and assigns a specific numerical value, depending on its brightness. An image can then be generated on an "image display"—basically a TV monitor—by a computer that assigns a gray level scale, ranging from black to white, for each number. Sophisticated CCDs, like the one used to take the photograph above, can register more than 32,000 levels of grayness. Most image displays, however, only produce 256 levels of grayness. That number is convenient because it represents the maximum number that can be generated by the most common counting unit used by computers, called a byte. The astronomer therefore reconfigures his numbers to fit that range. A zero corresponds to pure black; 255 is pure white. All other values are intermediate shades of gray. The result is a pattern of dots that forms an image, much like the halftone photographs in a newspaper—or in this book.

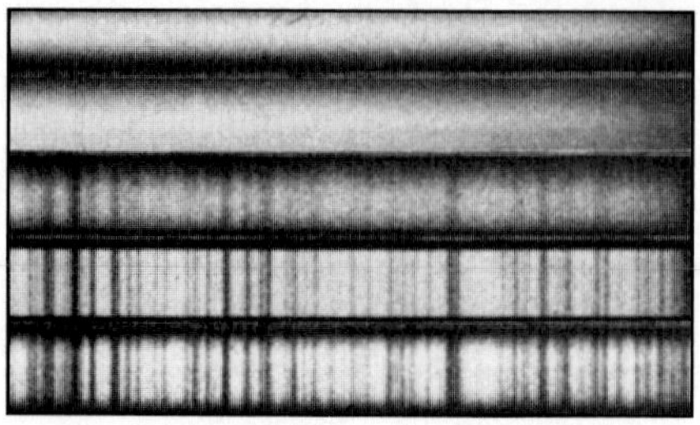

Astronomers now use a diffraction grating instead of a prism to break down starlight into its constituent colors: The one below breaks down the blue light of a laser. Light striking a diffraction grating can then be photographed. The resulting spectra (above), *with their telltale absorption lines, reveal the different characteristics of a star, including its temperature. The top spectrum is of a star with a suface temperature of 36,000° F.; the spectra below it are of increasingly cooler stars. The cooler temperatures allow atoms to capture light of more wavelengths—therefore more absorption lines appear.*

STARLIGHT'S HIDDEN MEANING

The increasingly powerful telescopes that plumbed the depths of the cosmos were only one aspect of the emerging technology of astronomy. Another instrument, called the spectroscope, allows astronomers to determine a variety of characteristics of celestial bodies by analyzing their light. Like many advances in astronomy, this one can be traced to Isaac Newton, who found in the course of his optical experiments in 1665 that a triangular glass prism breaks sunlight into the colors of the rainbow, which he called a spectrum. The phenomenon, called dispersion, arises because the colors are bent at different angles, depending on their wavelengths, as they pass through the prism.

Another English scientist, William Wollaston, discovered in 1802 that if the light of the Sun passed through a narrow slit before entering the prism, the resulting spectrum was crossed by seven dark lines: two in the red, three in the yellow-green and two in the blue-violet. A decade later, Joseph von Fraunhofer, a Bavarian optician, took Wollaston's work a step further. He combined a small telescope with a prism to create the spectroscope, which he used to examine minutely one color after another. The instrument enabled Fraunhofer to study the Sun's spectrum in greater detail than his predecessor, permitting him to count and label 576 lines, mapping their exact positions in the spectrum. Fraunhofer's meticulous labors were recognized by naming the lines after him.

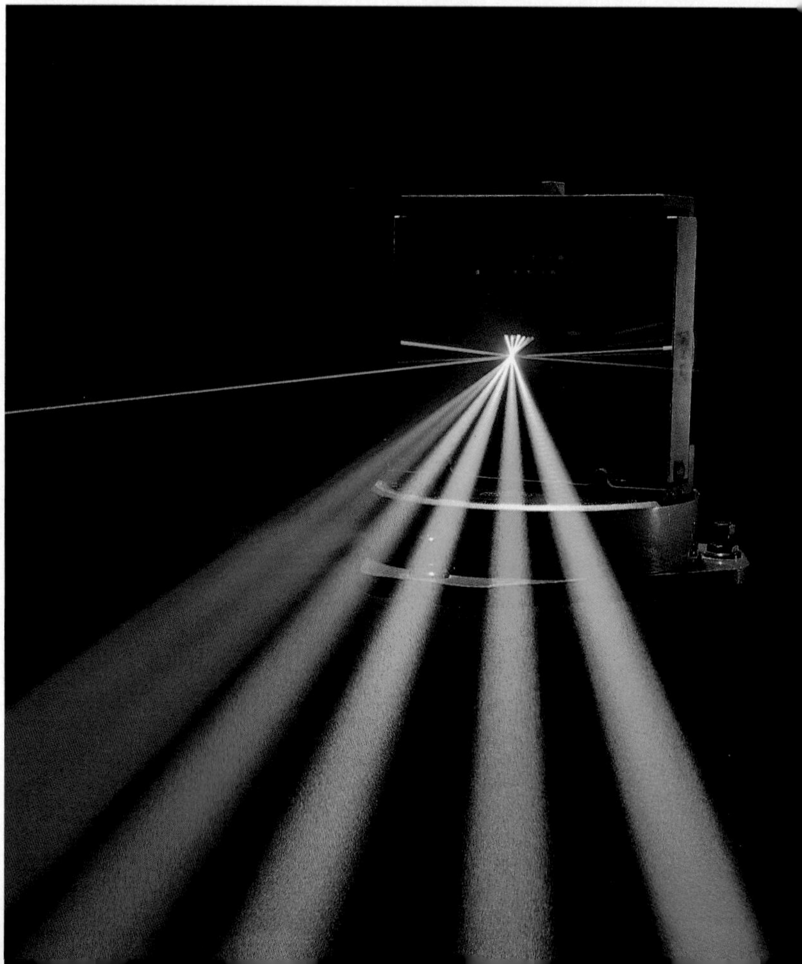

The meaning of the Fraunhofer lines, however, remained unknown until 1859, when two German scientists teamed up to solve the problem. Chemist Gustav Kirchhoff was using a Bunsen burner, invented by his coworker Robert Bunsen, to analyze the spectra produced by various materials when they were heated to incandescence. Viewing the light through a spectroscope, Kirchhoff discovered that each chemical element emits a characteristic pattern of narrow, bright-colored lines. He then demonstrated that the elements also absorb sunlight in exactly the same patterns, producing the dark Fraunhofer lines. Both types of lines, as scientists have since discovered, are as distinctive as a human fingerprint. Seen through a spectroscope, each element creates its own unique spectral signature.

The unlocking of starlight's secrets has been aided by atomic theory. Atoms consist of a central nucleus of protons and neutrons, with electrons revolving around it. According to the quantum theory, first for-

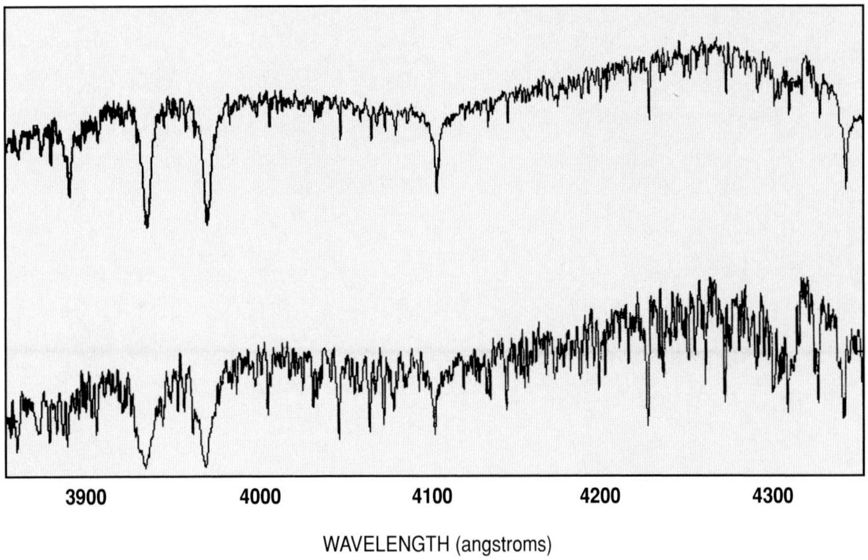
3900
4000
4100
4200
4300
WAVELENGTH (angstroms)

By scanning the brightness of a spectrum, a computer generates a graph that indicates, with dips, where the absorption lines are located. In the two spectra at right, the strong dips at 3933 angstroms and 3968 angstroms indicate the presence of calcium. (One angstrom is one ten-millionth of a millimeter.) The presence of hydrogen is shown by the patterns at 4101 A and 4340 A. The absorption lines are much deeper in the lower spectrum, indicating that it contains more of the "heavy elements"—those with an atomic weight greater than helium.

mulated in the early 20th Century, each of the atomic orbits represents a specific energy state. If an electron jumps from a higher to a lower orbit, energy is given off; if it moves from a lower energy orbit to a higher one, energy is absorbed.

Fraunhofer lines are absorption lines. They mark where light has been absorbed as the electrons of different elements shift orbits. By comparing the spectrum of a star with one of known elements on Earth, the composition of the star can be determined. A spectrum of sodium in a laboratory, for example, shows two lines in the yellow part of the spectrum. Two similar lines in the same position of the Sun's spectrum prove that sodium is also one of its constituent elements.

Spectroscopy is now conducted at every major observatory. Keck project scientist Jerry Nelson calls it "the bread and butter of optical astronomy." But prisms have been superseded by diffraction gratings, pieces of optical glass etched with fine, evenly spaced grooves that disperse starlight into different wavelengths of light. Diffraction gratings, unlike prisms, absorb very little light, and can therefore produce a clearer, brighter spectral image. Spectroscopes, too, have been replaced; spectra are now recorded using CCDs.

New applications of spectroscopy have resulted in once-unimagined revelations, including the speed of a star's rotation, the strength of its magnetic field and even the temperature of its surface. Spectroscopy also has helped astronomers determine the speed a star is moving toward or away from Earth, which has profoundly altered our understanding of the origins of the universe. The birth of that discovery came in 1868, when English astronomer William Huggins used a spectroscope-equipped telescope to test the Doppler effect, a theoretical concept developed 20 years earlier by Austrian physicist Christian Doppler.

The Doppler effect alters the wavelengths of light depending on whether an object is moving toward or away from an observer. If, for example, a star is traveling toward the Earth, its light waves are compressed. Since the wavelength of blue light is shorter than the wavelengths of other visible light, the result is a shift of color—and Fraunhofer lines—toward the blue end of the spectrum. If, on the other hand, the star is receding, the waves are stretched and shifted toward the red end of the spectrum. In the same manner, sound waves can be stretched or

The Gravity of the Matter

It all began, most astronomers now believe, roughly 15 billion years ago, when the universe was compressed into a region smaller than an atom. An unimaginably colossal explosion sent a cloud of energy and matter a trillion times hotter than the Sun spraying outwards. As the universe expanded, it also cooled. Stars and galaxies coalesced and the cosmos slowly took form.

Billions of years after the Big Bang, the universe continues to expand. But can it—will it—expand forever? The answer depends not only on the rate of expansion, but also on gravity itself. If the combined gravitational attraction of all the matter in the universe is strong enough, expansion will eventually slow down, stop and give way to contraction. Everything will collapse in on itself in a "Big Crunch" that will mark the end of the universe—or, as some cosmologists suggest, the end of one cycle and the beginning of another in an unending tale of cosmological birth and rebirth.

Gravity is a function of matter. More matter means more mutual attraction between all the constituent bodies of the universe. If scientists could simply add up all the matter in the universe, they could compute whether there is enough gravity to restrain and then reverse the expansion. Some astronomers now believe that the universe is largely composed of "dark matter," nonluminous objects such as black holes—matter so dense that even light cannot escape from its clutches—and the virtually massless subatomic particles known as neutrinos.

Only when scientists are able to detect and measure all this dark matter will they be able to determine whether there is enough matter to "close" the universe. Physicists have devised a critical number—5 x 10^{-30} grams of matter for every cubic centimeter of space—by which they think they can calculate the possible future of the universe. If the universe contains less matter than this number it will remain "open" and expand forever.

Following the stupendous cosmic explosion known as the Big Bang, the universe began an expansion that still continues 15 billion years or so later.

compressed. The sound of the horn of an approaching car rises higher in pitch as its sound waves are shortened. After the car passes and begins going away, the sound waves are lengthened and the pitch drops.

When Huggins focused on Sirius, the Dog Star, he found that its Fraunhofer lines shifted slightly to the red. According to a mathematical formula, the shift meant that the star was moving away from the Earth at a speed of 30 miles per second. Applying the technique to several other stars, he found similar velocities, although some stars were approaching the Earth rather than receding.

The same held true for distant galaxies. In 1912 American astronomer Vesto Slipher, analyzing the dim light of the giant spiral galaxy in the constellation Andromeda, concluded that the star system was approaching Earth at 186 miles a second, the highest speed then known for any celestial body. Over the next few years, Slipher measured the velocities of 15 spiral galaxies, of which all but two were moving away from Earth, some at speeds of more than 600 miles per second. For years, no one knew quite what to make of Slipher's findings. For one thing, no one was then certain that the spirals were actually separate entities from the Earth's home galaxy, the Milky Way. But in 1924 Edwin Hubble, a Rhodes Scholar and former boxer, developed a technique for determining the distance to the Andromeda spiral. He declared that it was 900,000 light-years away—a galaxy in its own right, far beyond the boundaries of the Milky Way.

Working with the 100-inch reflector atop Mount Wilson, Hubble went on to measure the distance to many other galaxies, and then began to correlate his findings with the speeds produced by Slipher and others. He discovered that there was a direct relationship between a galaxy's distance and velocity: The farther away a galaxy is, the faster it is moving away. The rate at which that recessional velocity changes with distance, known as the Hubble constant, is measured in units called parsecs—one parsec being equal to 3.26 light years. Though that value has not been determined precisely, the current belief is that the speed is roughly 50 miles per million parsecs—or megaparsecs.

Published in 1929, Hubble's findings radically challenged the existing concept of a static universe. If galaxies were rushing apart, the universe must be expanding. Furthermore, the rate of expansion provided a clue to the age of the cosmos, since theoretically it could be extrapolated back to the moment when expansion began, at the beginning of space and time. Estimates of the age of the universe—recalculated many times since Hubble's time—now range from 15 to 20 billion years.

"There are some things of which the human race must remain forever in ignorance," French philosopher Auguste Comte once said, "for example the chemical constitution of heavenly bodies." But Comte, writing in 1844, proved a poor soothsayer. Spectroscopy has succeeded in bringing the heavens into the laboratories of astronomers on Earth, making it possible to dissect and analyze objects millions, and sometimes billions, of light-years distant.

More accurate than Comte's statement were the words inscribed on the grave of Joseph von Fraunhofer: "Approximavit sidera"—He brought the heavens closer.

TUNING IN TO THE COSMOS

Although the visible portion of the electromagnetic spectrum has yielded a wealth of information, modern astronomy relies on far more than light rays to learn about the cosmos. But of all the other kinds of electromagnetic radiation, only radio waves—and a narrow band of the infrared—readily pierce Earth's atmosphere, allowing extensive observations from the ground. This fact was discovered by accident in the 1930s, when Karl Jansky, an American communications engineer, tried to find the source of static that interfered with ship-to-shore radiotelephone calls.

One of the sources Jansky detected with his rotating antenna of wood and metal seemed to move with the stars; it was focused near the constellation Sagittarius, in the direction of the center of the Milky Way galaxy. Coming at a time of rapid developments in optical astronomy, Jansky's discovery was largely ignored, and for years, the only research on celestial radio sources was performed by Grote Reber, an electronics engineer who built an antenna in the yard of his home near Chicago. In 1944 Reber capped seven years of research by producing a map of radio sources in the Milky Way. But he was untrained in astronomy and was unable to explain their origins.

Reber's antenna was the prototype for the most widely used type of radio telescope today. A 31-foot parabolic dish, it featured a surface of steel sheets screwed to a wooden support structure. The radio waves falling on the metal surface were reflected to the focus of the dish, much as the mirror of a reflector telescope focuses light waves. But whereas an optical telescope forms an image that can be recorded by a Charge Coupled Device or observed through an eyepiece, a radio telescope creates an electrical signal that is amplified and then analyzed by a sophisticated computer. The result is a map of a radio source that records the brightness of each point much as a topographical map, using contour lines, charts areas of equal height.

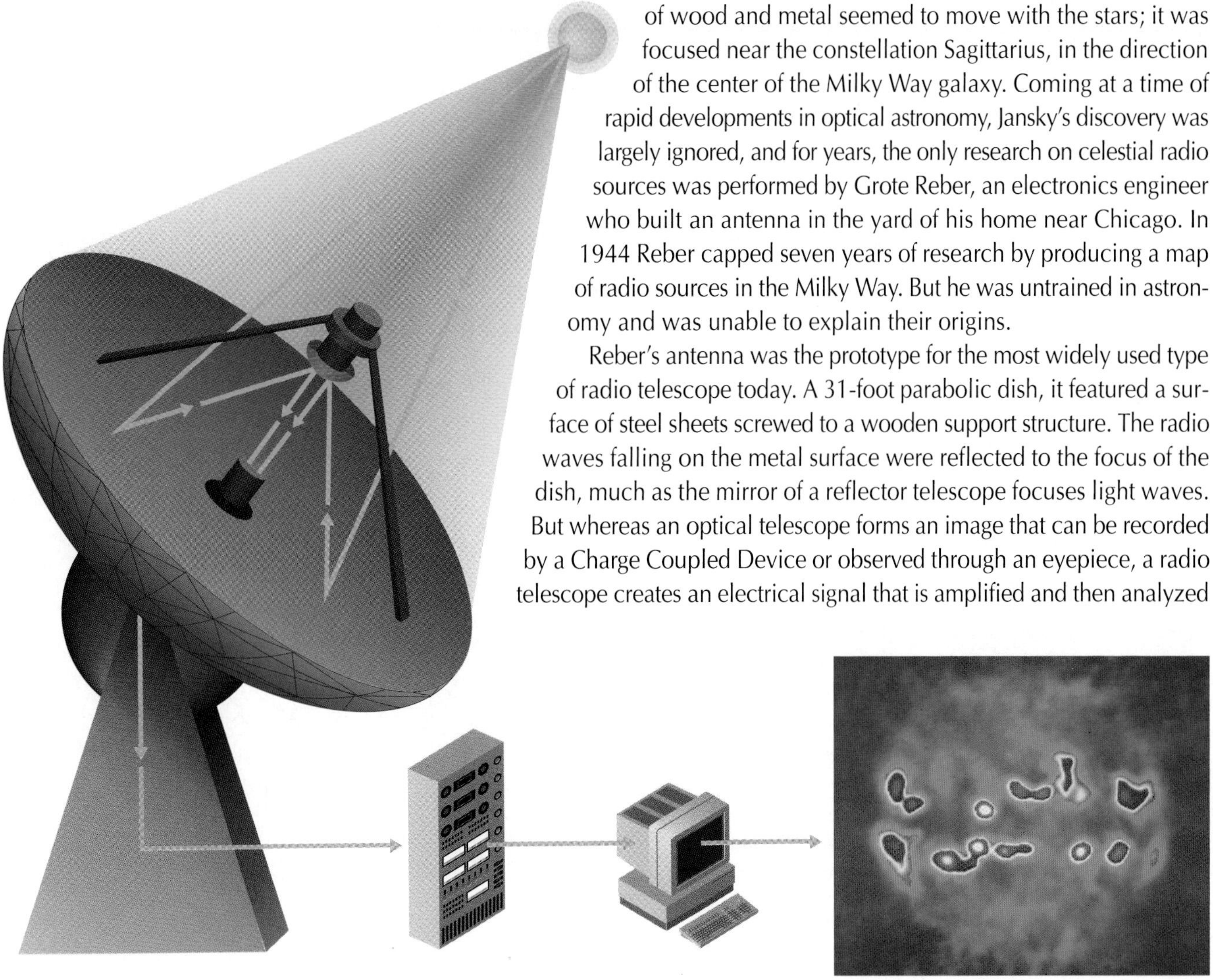

DISHING IT IN

A radio telescope's dish collects radio waves from a small area of the sky, focusing them onto an antenna which produces an electric signal. After amplification and electronic processing, the intensity of the signal is recorded. To map radio waves coming from the Sun, for example, scientists measure radio energy received from each point of the solar disk, and combine the data. The result is a radio image like the one shown above right.

One of radio astronomy's first major discoveries came in 1951, when three different research teams detected radiation with a wavelength of 21 centimeters in the radio band, evidence of cool atomic hydrogen clouds in the Milky Way. A map of the clouds, published in 1958, confirmed the suspicion that the Milky Way is a spiral galaxy, like the one pictured on page 23. Other early discoveries included the detection of quasars, the most powerful radiation sources in the sky (now understood to be very remote, violently active galaxies). Nevertheless, the first radio telescopes were capable of far less resolution than optical telescopes. A tele-

The largest single-site radio telescope in the world, the Very Large Array (VLA), consists of 27 telescopes spread out along the arms of a giant Y in the New Mexico desert. Railroad tracks allow operators to reconfigure the array, spreading the antennas out for extremely high resolution, or drawing them closer together for wide-angle observations.

scope's resolving power is proportional to the ratio of its diameter to the wavelength it detects. An optical telescope with a mirror several feet in diameter is millions of times bigger than the wavelength of visible light. The wavelength of radio waves, however, may be many feet. To offer the same resolution as an optical telescope, its radio counterpart would have to be miles in diameter. The largest radio telescope ever built, 1,000 feet across, was assembled in 1963 by draping nearly 40,000 perforated aluminum panels in a natural limestone hollow among the tropical hills near Arecibo, Puerto Rico. The Arecibo telescope's immobility limits it to scanning only a narrow swath of the sky as the Earth rotates. And although its size allows it to detect very weak signals, its resolution is only on a par with the human eye.

Brute size, however, was not the only way to achieve better resolution. During the 1950s, British and Australian radio astronomers devised a technique known as interferometry (the term refers to the inference pattern caused by overlapping

waves) that allowed two radio telescopes hundreds or thousands of feet apart to operate effectively as a single antenna having a "diameter" equal to the distance between the two telescopes. Astronomers further discovered that if one of the telescopes was fixed and the other movable, the latter could be shifted to cover all the ground around the fixed telescope that would be covered by one imaginary large telescope. Using more than one movable telescope, this procedure, known as aperture synthesis, can produce an image that would otherwise require an enormous single dish. One of the most arresting examples of aperture synthesis came into being on a desert plain in New Mexico during the 1970s. The Very Large Array (VLA) deploys 27 antennas, each 82 feet in diameter, in a pattern shaped like the letter Y. Nine antennas are positioned at intervals along each of the three arms of the Y. Signals from the antennas are transmitted to a central building, where a computer synchronizes signal reception in order to compensate for the slight differences in the distance between each dish and the celestial source. The signals are then combined and analyzed.

The VLA took more than a decade to complete, slowed by frustrating funding delays and construction difficulties. But by 1980 the entire array was operating 24 hours a day, performing like a single telescope 21 miles across. Its images offer powers of resolution comparable to the largest earthbound telescopes in the optical range. The VLA has detected thin filaments of radio emission from the center of the Milky Way, probed the atmospheres of the outer planets of the solar system, and discovered powerful radiation coming from cool interstellar clouds, where new stars are forming. It has examined quasars and other active galaxies, finding jets of high-energy electrons spurting from them at nearly the speed of light. Astronomers theorize that these jets are powered by supermassive black holes, objects so dense that even light cannot escape their gravity. Matter falls toward a black hole, swirling into a vortexlike disk where violent forces blast a small fraction of the matter back into space, forming jets. An image of such a disk would help transform black holes from theory to reality, but here the VLA simply is not equal to the task. Any possible disk would be hundreds of times smaller than the VLA can make out at the extreme distance of quasars, some of which are receding from Earth at 90 percent of the speed of light.

In an effort to make out such details, astronomers sometimes combine a number of widely spaced telescopes using a technique called very long baseline interferometry (VLBI), which removes the need for an array of radio telescopes to be connected together; with VLBI, separate radio telescopes merely have to observe the same celestial object at the same time. Signals from radio dishes separated by thousands of miles are recorded, along with special timing signals, on magnetic tape. The tapes are then merged at a central facility, where they are synchronized. The timing is extremely precise, requiring the use of atomic clocks accurate to within one second in a million years. The result is virtually a hundredfold improvement in resolution over the VLA, and has spurred the development of a dedicated Very Long Baseline Array (VLBA). The 10 telescopes of the VLBA, spread across North America, Hawaii and Puerto Rico, will probe the very hearts of quasars and other cosmic mysteries in unprecedented detail. Eventually, they may be joined by an orbiting telescope, producing a telescope with a "diameter" larger than the Earth itself, capable of discovering yet more of the secrets of the universe.

Heaven on Earth

Every year, 12 million people around the world recline in dome-topped theaters and gaze at the star-spangled night sky. The stars and planets that flash across the ceiling emanate from the floor, where a dumbbell-shaped mass of metal, glass and wiring projects its heavenly show upward. It is this Zeiss projector that distinguishes each theater it graces as a planetarium.

In fact, this "projector" is actually 160 small projectors supported on a metal framework. Together, they accurately reproduce the planets and their motions, star configurations, constellations, eclipses, comets, the Milky Way galaxy and other astronomical wonders. The large ball, called a "star carrier," at each end of the framework houses 32 small projectors that reproduce stars of varying brightness. One carrier projects 4,500 northern hemisphere stars; the other, 4,500 southern hemisphere stars. A seven-foot-long truss connecting the star carriers contains the Sun, Moon and planetary projectors. Projectors designed to reproduce rarer astronomical phenomena are attached to the truss exterior.

Invented by Walter Bauersfeld at the Carl Zeiss optical works in Jena, Germany, in 1919, the Zeiss planetarium projector so accurately depicted the night skies that it quickly earned the reputation as "the wonder of Jena." Bauersfeld's intricate design was light-years ahead of the clumsy revolving globe planetaria that had preceded it—sphere-shaped rooms that rotated around starry-eyed audiences sitting on a central fixed platform to watch the supposed motion of the skies. Rotation came courtesy of large gears that were first powered by water and later by electricity.

Bauersfeld and his colleagues perfected the idea of geared rotation, but applied it to projectors rather than the room. Today's models rotate at different speeds to portray the diurnal and annual motion of the skies, whisking viewers from beneath North Pole skies to the beaches of Fiji, from prehistoric times to the present—all in a matter of minutes.

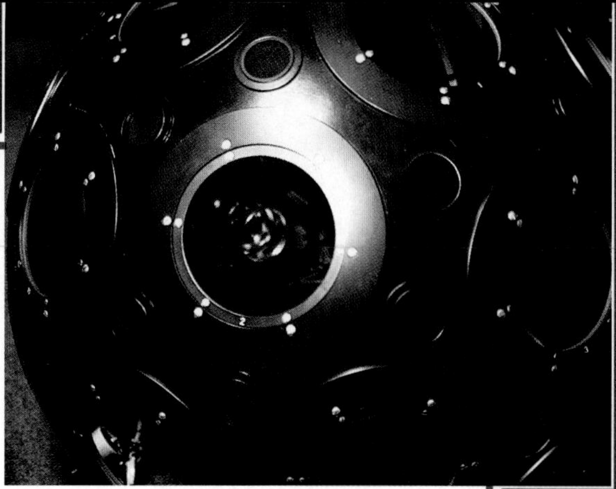

Each star projector aperture, fitted with a special slide containing hundreds of minute perforations, emits pinpoints of light calibrated to reproduce actual star brightness and position. As the projection nears the screen's horizon, a mercury-filled level signals the aperture shutter to close like an eyelid, preventing the light from shining below the screen.

A console, normally located behind the audience, directs the $2.5-million projector. Shows are mostly narrated live, but computers can be programmed to provide a fully automated show.

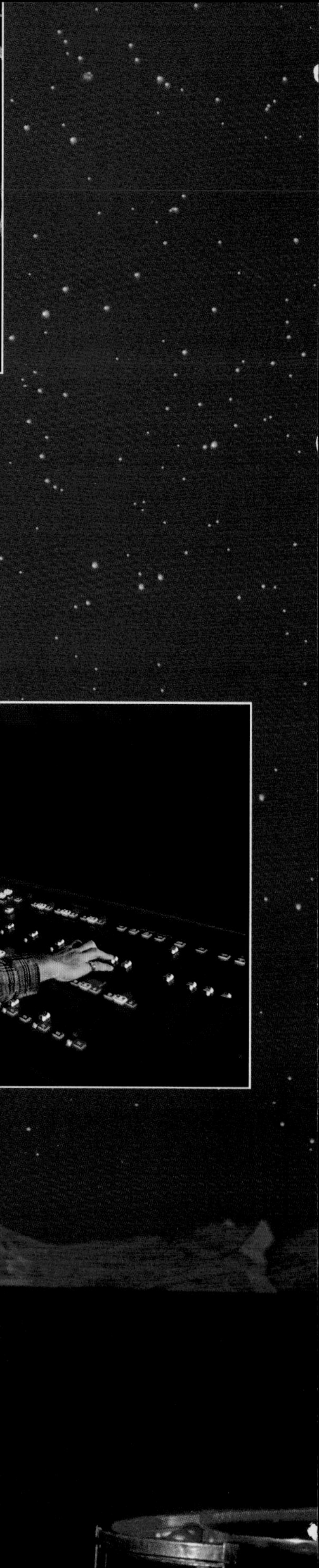

The Zeiss VI projector may look ungainly, but equal division of weight perfectly balances the three-ton machine on a horizontal beam set at the dome's horizon, usually 10 feet high.

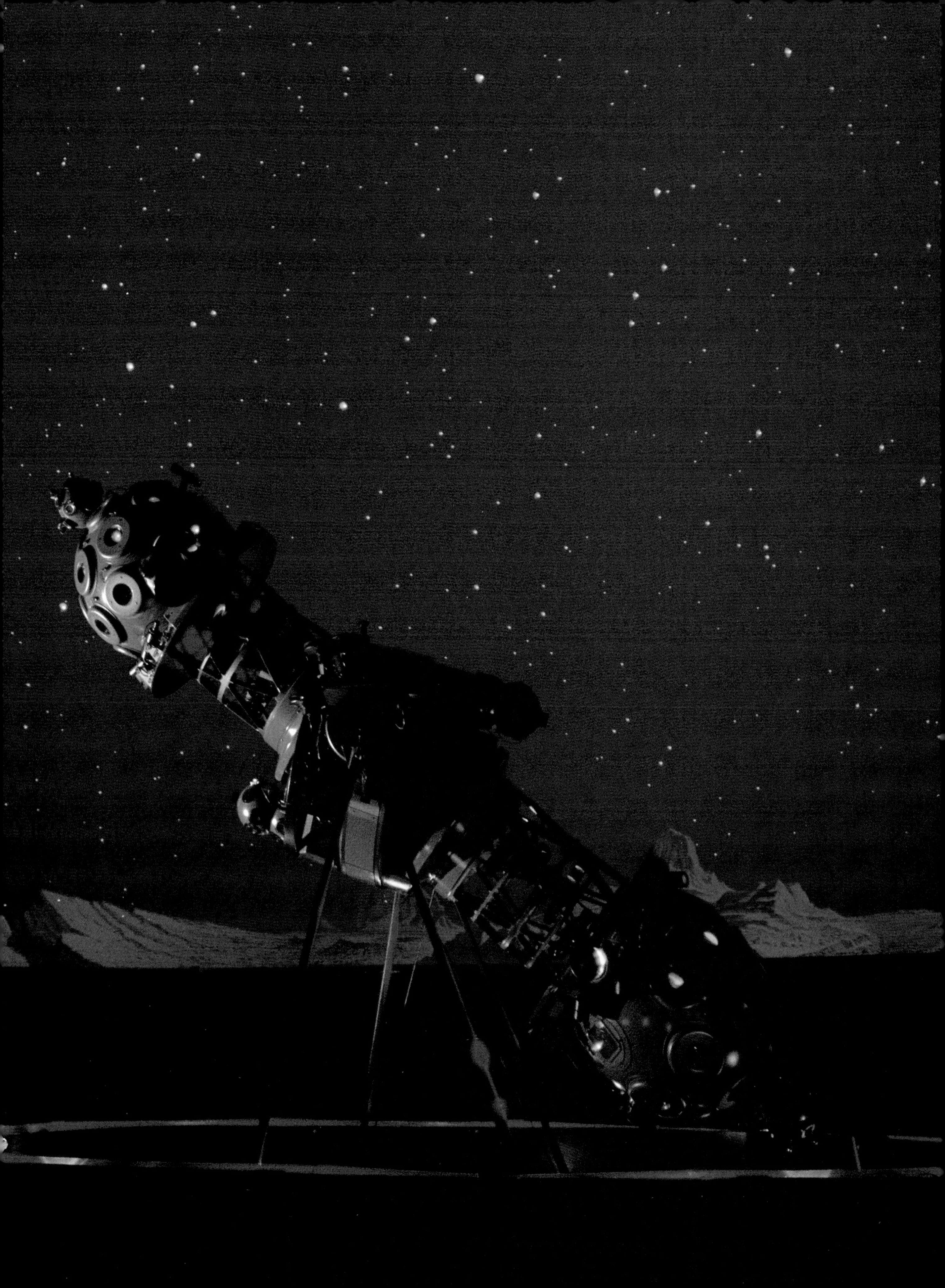

PROBING THE PLANETS AND BEYOND

Racing past Neptune in August of 1989 at more than 60,000 miles per hour, a tiny spacecraft tracks the huge planet with cameras and other instruments, collecting data on a tape recorder for later transmission to Earth, 2.8 billion miles away. Twelve years after its blastoff, Voyager 2 is passing the last station on its grand tour of the Solar System, a trip that has already taken it from Earth to Jupiter, Saturn and Uranus on one of the most productive interplanetary missions ever launched. At each planet it has gathered information impossible to discover by other means; now it is adding the last dramatic strokes to its rich picture of the outer planets. Transmitted back to Earth at the speed of light, each of the millions of bits of information Voyager gathers takes more than four hours to reach its home planet, where they are reconstituted to provide vivid images of Neptune and its environs. Tenuous rings of charcoal-dark particles scatter the dim light of the distant Sun. Vast storms, one the size of Earth itself—known as the Great Dark Spot—mark its blue, cloud-layered atmosphere, where winds blow as strong as 1,200 miles per hour. On Triton, the planet's largest moon, huge geysers of nitrogen gas and dust particles erupt miles into a thin atmosphere before falling back to a craggy surface of nitrogen and methane ice. The satellite's southern hemisphere displays a huge ice cap rimmed with blue, implying fresh frost—and an atmosphere in continuous flux.

Dozens of other spacecraft have investigated the cosmos for more than three decades. Primitive at first, these robotic explorers have grown increasingly sophisticated: Some have even reached the surfaces of other planets, landing softly, sampling their soil and sending back astonishingly clear images of alien worlds. Others have looked farther away, capturing the faint radiation from stars and galaxies—often at the outer edges of the universe—that largely would be obscured by Earth's distorting atmosphere. And many spacecraft have turned their gaze toward home, extending this new perspective on the cosmos to the very surface of Earth itself.

With the Sun only a faint light almost three billion miles away, Voyager 2 sweeps past the mesmerizing blue world of Neptune, the last stop on the spacecraft's grand tour of the outer planets.

SPACEWARD BOUND

Voyager 2 and its cousins—the hundreds of satellites and space probes that have been launched since Sputnik 1 in 1957—have been sent into space by powerful rockets. These massive vehicles, the products of centuries of development, have brought to fruition the dreams of farsighted writers and theoreticians who began to look at the heavens as a destination in the late 1800s. Ever since Isaac Newton in the mid-17th Century described the gravitational links between the Sun, the planets and their moons, scientists have understood the principle of an orbiting body. A satellite is simply an object attracted by the gravity of another body, but traveling at a velocity that keeps it from falling to the surface of that body. For example, a rock thrown from a cliff travels a considerable distance horizontally while it is falling to the ground below; its descent follows a curved trajectory. If the stone were thrown fast enough, the curve of its descent would match the curvature of the Earth; in effect, the ground would be falling away from the stone at the same rate that the stone was dropping, and the stone could circle the Earth. At the Earth's surface, however, "fast enough" is about 18,000 miles per hour—at which speed any ordinary stone would burn up in seconds due to air friction. Therefore artificial satellites must be pushed to altitudes where atmospheric resistance is negligible.

The rockets that finally made artificial satellites possible were a far cry from the "fire arrows" first introduced on the battlefields of China around the 13th Century. Those primitive weapons were little more than tubes packed with black powder, yet they embodied the same principles that guide the design of modern space rockets. The fundamental rule of rocketry is Newton's Third Law of Motion, which states that for every action there must be an equal and opposite reaction. Air rush-

From a control shack in the New Mexico desert in the 1930s, American inventor Robert Goddard—builder of the first liquid-fueled rocket—peers through a telescope at a launch tower 1,000 feet away.

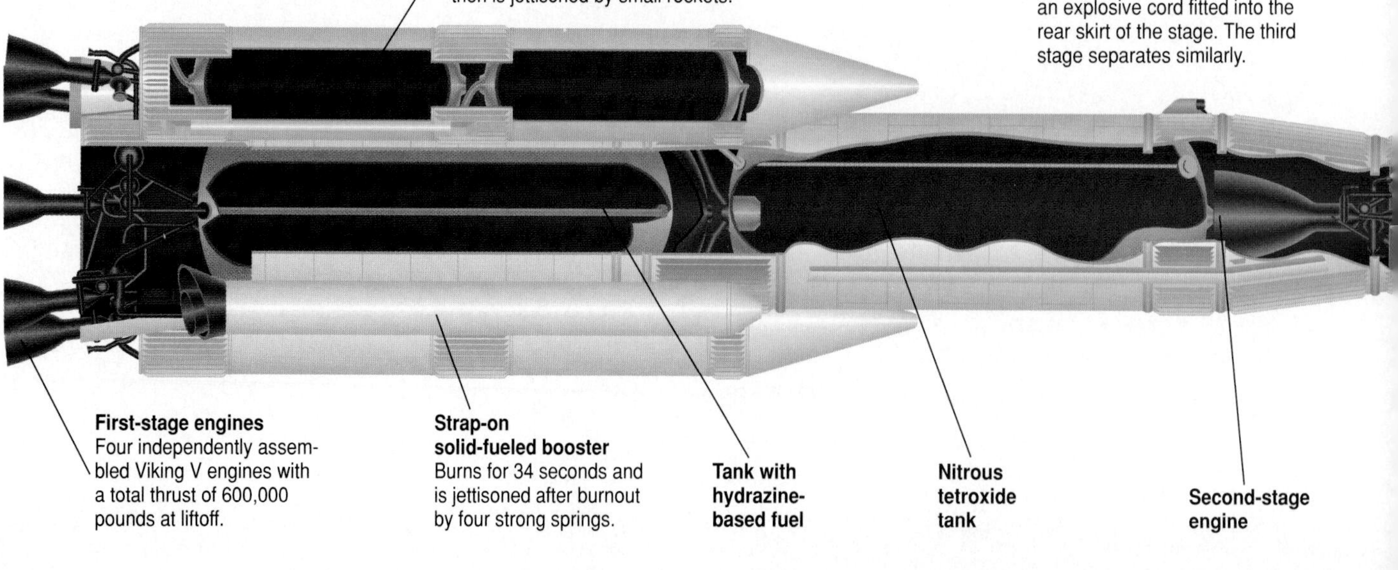

FIRST STAGE
Burn time is 205 seconds, consuming one ton of fuel per second.
Strap-on liquid-fueled booster
Burns as long as 143 seconds and is released from the rocket after burnout by an explosive device and then is jettisoned by small rockets.
SECOND STAGE
Separates from the first stage by an explosive cord fitted into the rear skirt of the stage. The third stage separates similarly.
First-stage engines
Four independently assembled Viking V engines with a total thrust of 600,000 pounds at liftoff.
Strap-on solid-fueled booster
Burns for 34 seconds and is jettisoned after burnout by four strong springs.
Tank with hydrazine-based fuel
Nitrous tetroxide tank
Second-stage engine

ing out of an inflated balloon propels the balloon in the opposite direction. In a rocket motor, burning fuel produces expanding exhaust gases, which are discharged to the rear; the force this produces, called thrust, pushes the rocket forward. Thrust is measured in pounds. A pound of thrust will lift a pound of rocket. A jet engine generates thrust by burning fuel mixed with air that it sucks from the atmosphere; a rocket, however, carries all its propellants within: a combustible fuel and an oxidizer that allows it to burn. With no need for oxygen, rocket motors are uniquely suited for propulsion in the near-vacuum of space.

Until the 20th Century, all rockets relied on solid propellants similar to the black powder that powered the earliest Chinese missiles. But in 1903, the Russian mathematician Konstantin Tsiolkovsky revolutionized the field of rocketry by publishing the results of years of theoretical work, conducted while Tsiolkovsky made his living as a schoolteacher. Tsiolkovsky showed that rocket motors burning fuels such as kerosene mixed with liquid oxygen could achieve far higher performance than solid fuel motors. By maximizing the velocity of the exhaust gases from the combustion of liquid propellants, Tsiolkovsky suggested, rocket designers could even increase thrust to the levels required to carry rockets into Earth orbit.

Tsiolkovsky was far ahead of his time, but as techniques for producing and handling liquefied gases progressed, a new generation of rockets was born. The first liquid-fueled rocket was launched in 1926, the brainchild of Robert H. Goddard, an American physicist and inventor. Goddard's first effort looked like a plumber's nightmare, but it incorporated many of the essential elements of a modern liquid-propellant rocket: tanks for fuel and oxidizer (in this case, gasoline and liquid oxygen); a motor with a combustion chamber where the propellants were mixed and burned; an exhaust nozzle that directed the flow of the hot expanding gases; a system for circulating the frigid liquid fuels around the motor to cool it before entering the combustion chamber to burn; and a gyroscopic guidance system that steered either by turning vanes in the exhaust or by swiveling—or gimballing—the engine itself. Unlike almost all of its successors, though, Goddard's first rocket

ANATOMY OF A ROCKET

The Ariane 4 rocket, workhorse of the European Space Agency (ESA), is far more sophisticated than earlier liquid-fueled rockets. Still, it displays many of the same features: multiple stages, separate tanks for fuel and oxidizer, and engines that can swivel to steer the missile. Ariane is designed to carry as many as three satellites at once into orbit.

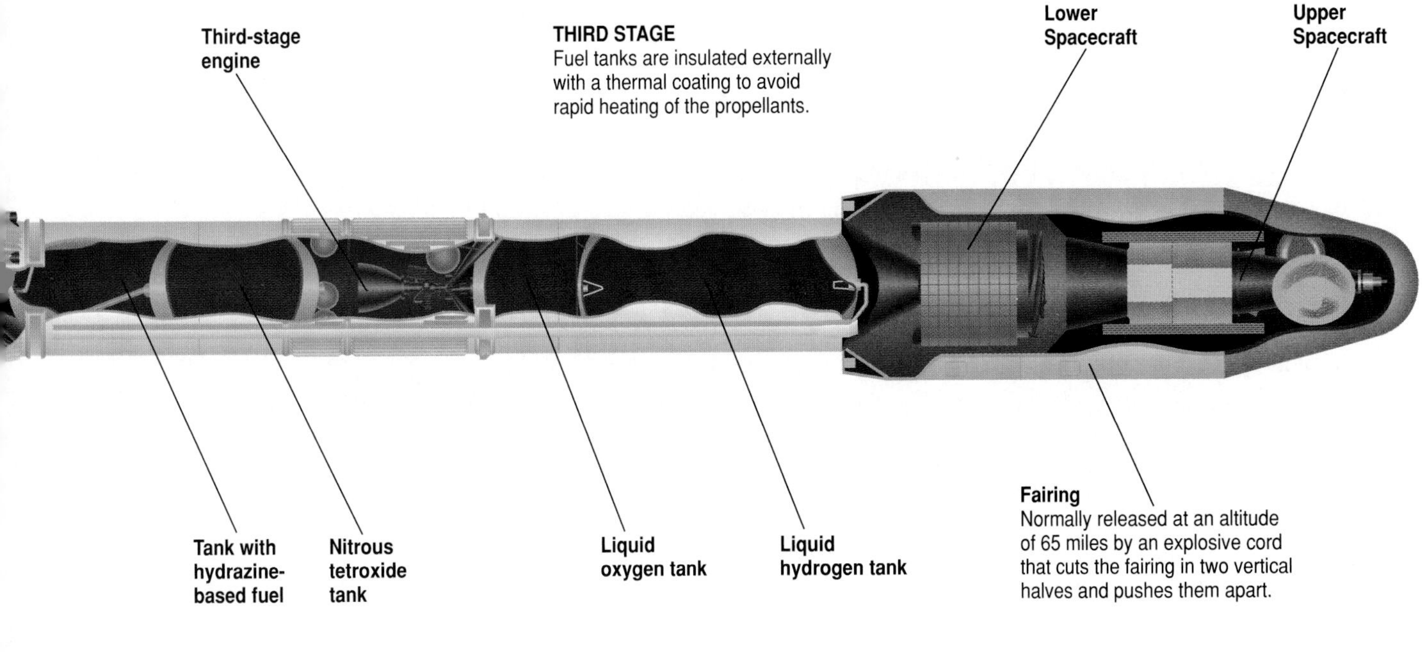
Third-stage engine
THIRD STAGE
Fuel tanks are insulated externally with a thermal coating to avoid rapid heating of the propellants.
Lower Spacecraft
Upper Spacecraft
Tank with hydrazine-based fuel
Nitrous tetroxide tank
Liquid oxygen tank
Liquid hydrogen tank
Fairing
Normally released at an altitude of 65 miles by an explosive cord that cuts the fairing in two vertical halves and pushes them apart.

had its motor mounted above the fuel tanks; the fuel lines doubled as the structure of the rocket, which had no outer skin. To prevent the hot gases from igniting the fuel tank, an asbestos cap served as a deflection shield.

Despite efforts to pare weight, the rocket barely had enough power to fly; it rose 41 feet before crashing 184 feet away, but was deemed a success nonetheless. After subsequent tests, Goddard gained enough funding to set up a research facility in the New Mexico desert. There during the 1930s, a succession of rockets validated myriad design improvements and reached ever greater speeds and altitudes.

A new impetus for advancing rocket design was provided by the Second World War. Under the leadership of Wernher von Braun—the man who would later help develop the Saturn V Moon rocket—a team of German scientists created the single-stage V-2 rocket. By the end of 1942, the stubby-shaped missile reached an altitude of 53 miles. (None of Goddard's 1930s' rockets ever rose more than 10,000 feet.) Before the Allies succeeding in destroying the V-2's production site, more than 4,000 had been launched, killing and wounding thousands in London alone.

While the new liquid-fueled creations offered a quantum leap in rocket propulsion they also have their drawbacks. Modern rockets generally rely on cryogenic propellants—liquefied gases that must be stored at extremely low temperatures. (Liquid hydrogen, for example, boils at only a few degrees above absolute zero—-459° F.—the temperature at which there is a complete absence of heat.) Creating and storing such fuels is expensive and technically difficult. So while rocket designers further refined the liquid-fueled design they also explored new solid propellants. Poured into the rocket casing, these propellants congeal to form a rubbery composite of fuel and oxidizer called the grain. Because the grain burns in place, the rockets have no need for tanks, pumps or combustion chambers. Requiring little preparation for launching, solid propellant rockets have become predominant in many military applications and, in fact, two solid-fuel motors also help propel each U.S. space shuttle into orbit. Still, in addition to their weight-efficient design, liquid propellants have one overriding attribute: By controlling the flow of propellants, a rocket can be throttled up or down, or even stopped and then restarted as necessary. A solid-fuel booster, on the other hand, cannot be shut off or throttled once it is ignited, and is therefore unsuitable for maneuvering a craft in space.

The system that controls the thrust and steers the rocket must cope with a trajectory that changes second by second. Not only does the missile slowly shift from its vertical launch position to enter orbit horizontally; it also is buffeted by winds and turbulence on its way through the atmosphere, culminating at a point known as Max Q, which usually occurs as the rocket passes through the sound barrier. To keep track of the rocket's exact position and speed, the inertial guidance system employs three devices called accelerometers, positioned at right angles to each other, to measure changes of velocity in three dimensions. The accelerometers are mounted on a platform, stabilized by a gyroscope, that maintains a fixed orientation regardless of the motion of the rocket. A computer continually analyzes the signals from the accelerometers, translates them to determine position and speed, and issues the appropriate commands to the control system.

Most satellite boosters are not single-stage rockets. Instead they are assembled in as many as four stages, each with its own motors that take over when the previous stage runs out of fuel and is jettisoned. Staging is economical: Rather than

A WORLD OF ORBITS

Satellites use different orbits for different reasons. An elliptical orbit allows a satellite to make scientific measurements at varying altitudes. A polar orbit permits the entire Earth to be mapped as the planet revolves beneath a satellite. Inclined a few degrees beyond a polar orbit, a Sun-synchronous orbit allows a satellite to take pictures with the sunlight always hitting the Earth from the same angle. Launched into an orbit 22,300 miles above the equator, a satellite will always remain in the same position relative to the Earth, traveling at the same speed that the planet rotates. Known as a geosynchronous orbit, it is favored by weather and communications satellites. The latitude of a launch site affects the orbit that a satellite assumes. U.S. satellites launched from Florida's Cape Canaveral have a lesser angle, or inclination, with the equator than those launched in Russia from higher latitudes. Satellites launched from near the equator, like those sent aloft aboard Ariane from French Guiana, will remain in an equatorial orbit unless shifted by course-correcting nudges of attitude-control thrusters.

using the most powerful motors and large amounts of fuel to drag the dead weight of empty fuel tanks, successive stages can be smaller, with just enough power to push the remaining stages toward orbit. The job of the booster rockets is done when the spacecraft has enough altitude and velocity to stay in orbit. The final velocity required is a function of altitude: At 200 miles, it must be traveling 17,244 miles per hour; at 22,300 miles, only 6,444 miles per hour. Up to a few hundred miles above the Earth, the fast-moving satellite will encounter enough friction with the tenuous atmosphere to drag it slowly downward; a satellite in an orbit 100 miles up can last only a few weeks. At higher altitudes, however, atmospheric drag disappears entirely, so that a satellite will continue its orbit indefinitely.

Satellite orbits are elliptical; a so-called circular orbit, which maintains a relatively constant distance from Earth is, technically, just one type of ellipse. Putting a satellite into an elliptical orbit requires that it be released from the rocket at an angle that carries it away from Earth. As the satellite moves into space, gravity slows it. When it reaches the highest point of its orbit—the apogee—the satellite is moving at its lowest speed. The continuing tug of Earth's gravity pulls it back toward the planet, at increasing speed, until it reaches maximum velocity at the low point of its orbit—the perigee. A highly elliptical orbit, called eccentric, is desirable for some kinds of satellites: A communications satellite, for example, can travel slowly over a specific region for a large part of its orbit. There are many other kinds of special orbits, each with its own advantages, generally based on the inclination, or the angle at which the orbit is tilted in relation to Earth's equator. In a polar orbit, with a 90-degree inclination, the satellite travels over both the North and South Poles; the Earth revolves slowly under the satellite, allowing it to see almost the whole surface of the planet every 14 days. A geostationary, or geosynchronous orbit, by contrast, places the satellite directly above the equator (an inclination of 0 degrees), at an altitude of 22,300 miles. At this height the satellite takes exactly 24 hours to circle the Earth, which spins once on its axis in the same period; the result is that the spacecraft stays above the same place on Earth. Other orbital inclinations, in combination with the altitude and period of the orbit, produce various coverage patterns: Sun-synchronous satellites, for example, with an inclination of about 98 degrees, pass over each region at the same time of day.

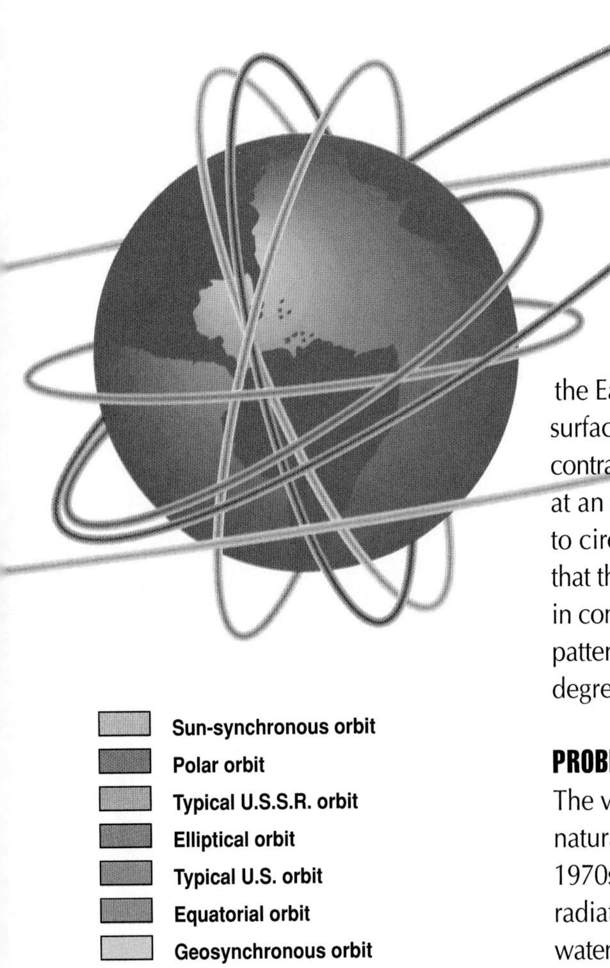
Sun-synchronous orbit
Polar orbit
Typical U.S.S.R. orbit
Elliptical orbit
Typical U.S. orbit
Equatorial orbit
Geosynchronous orbit

PROBING PLANET EARTH

The variety of orbits allow satellites to perform myriad functions, from detecting natural resources to charting the course of life-threatening storms. Since the early 1970s scientists have been studying Earth through space-based sensors. They detect radiation reflected or emitted by any feature. Every substance—desert sand, river water or a blade of grass—has its own characteristic pattern of radiation in different bands of the electromagnetic spectrum. The sensors record data and transmit it to ground stations, where scientists analyze it for clues to the makeup of Earth.

The first of the so-called Earth resources satellites was Landsat 1, launched in 1972. It carried a multispectral scanner (MSS) that measured the intensity of two bands of visible light and two of near-infrared, which indicate the amount of heat

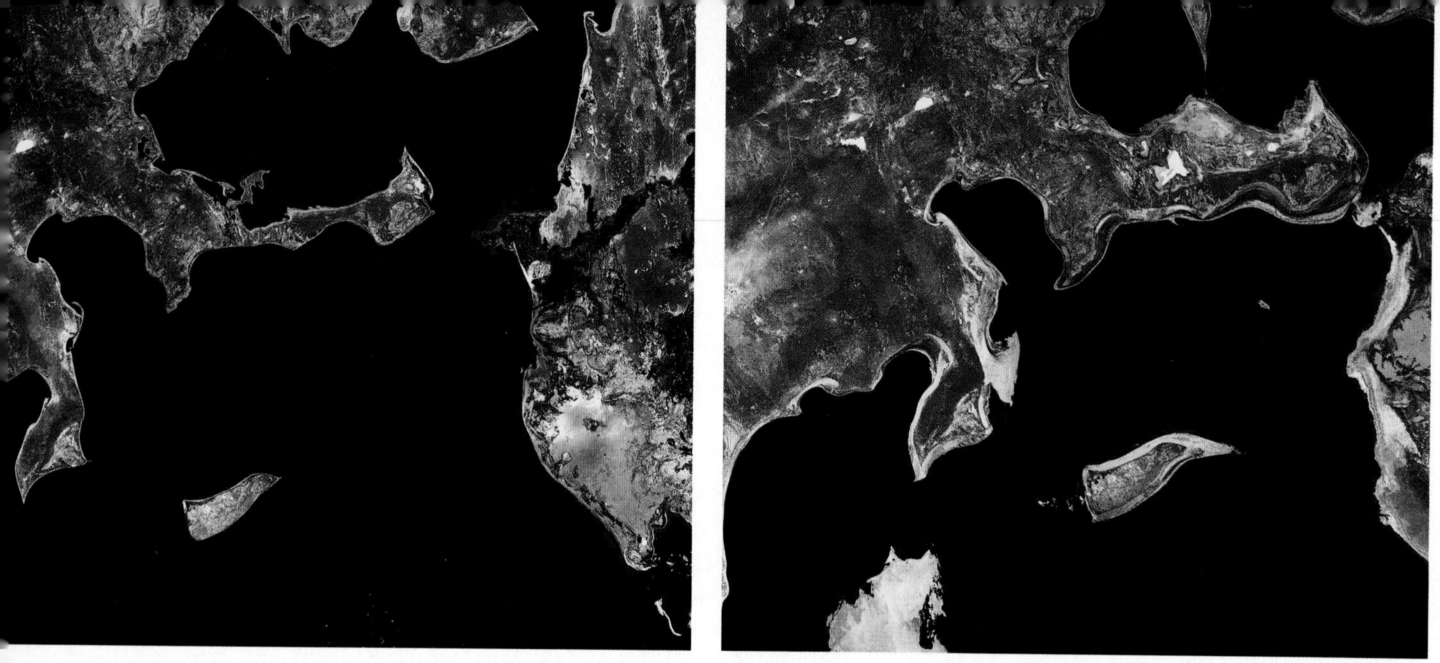

radiating from an object. The radiation was directed to the MSS sensors by a mirror that scanned the ground below 13 times each second, taking in the scene in parallel swaths 115 miles long, like someone walking along a path while sweeping it with a broom. By comparing and combining the simultaneous images created in each of four radiation bands, scientists could analyze surface features with great precision, making out features about the size of a football field.

Launched into a Sun-synchronous orbit at an altitude of 570 miles, Landsat 1 made one rotation every 103 minutes, with each crossing of the equator occurring at 8:50 a.m. local time. Because it always passed over any given point at the same hour of the day, Landsat could take its pictures with the sunlight always striking the Earth from the same angle, making it easier to detect changes in the landscape. The satellite was programmed to provide information to researchers in fields as diverse as geology, oceanography, agriculture and urban studies, and proved an immediate success. It detected a forest fire raging unseen in the Alaskan wilderness, mapped land-use patterns in the eastern U.S., charted the extent of flooding along the Mississippi River and pinpointed archaeological sites in Central America and Afghanistan. In 1975 it was joined in Sun-synchronous orbit by a virtually identical satellite; others in the Landsat series followed every few years.

Those launched during the 1980s carried improved instruments, including one called a Thematic Mapper, which registers radiation from the surface in seven spectral bands. In addition to allowing more subtle analysis of color, the Thematic Mappers provide much better resolution, showing objects as small as 100 feet across and detecting the type of crops in a field and the species of trees in a forest. These eyes in the sky are far more sensitive than human vision. In the case of diseased crops, Landsat can detect the differences in infrared radiation given off as a result of a plant's changing use of water—even before it alters the chlorophyll that produces visible evidence of disease. Landsats have discovered previously uncharted lakes and islets, pointed out oilfields in Sudan, mapped routes for railroads and pipelines, and revealed tin and uranium deposits in Brazil and Australia.

Even greater precision was achieved with the launching in 1986 of a French satellite named SPOT I, which could make out features as small as 35 feet across. Even before the satellite's equipment was fully tested, its sensors became the world's eyes on the Chernobyl nuclear

Circling the globe every 90 minutes in a Sun-synchronous orbit, Landsat 6 (opposite), *scheduled to be launched in mid-1991, will be capable of mapping all of the Earth between 81° N. and 81° S. latitude every 16 days. At its orbital altitude of 438 miles Landsat 6 will survey terrain that an airplane, flying only a few miles above the ground, would take years to cover. Among the many tasks that Landsat satellites have performed since they were first launched in 1972 was mapping precisely the shrinkage of the Aral Sea in the U.S.S.R., caused by poor irrigation practices on tributary rivers. The photo above left was taken in 1973; a photo taken in 1989* (above right) *shows the silting up of hundreds of square miles of what was once open water.*

reactor in the Soviet Union, site of a distastrous explosion in May 1986 that threatened much of Europe with radioactive fallout. In fact, SPOT's high-resolution images provided the news media with near-spy satellite-quality pictures of naval bases, missile sites and radar facilities, in addition to its more regular duties of mapping and mineral prospecting. Landsat 5, however, may have provided the most unusual information: Researchers with Hiroshima's Forestry Experimental Station used Landsat images to look for *matsutake,* a rare mushroom prized by Japanese gourmets. The tasty fungus grows on dying red pines, which produce a spectral signature that signals search areas for mushroom hunters.

Other downward-looking satellites focus on the Earth's atmosphere rather than the surface, searching for changes in the weather. The first experimental weather satellite, TIROS 1, launched in 1960, trained television cameras toward Earth and recorded images on a tape recorder for later broadcast as the satellite passed over ground stations. The 23,000 pictures it sent back in the few short weeks of its life radically changed how meteorologists looked at the world, showing that clouds massed and moved in ways no one had imagined. During the next five years, nine additional TIROS satellites went into orbit, half of them augmenting their cameras with infrared sensors to study the atmosphere's energy content (TIROS is an acronym for Television and Infrared Observation Satellite.) The success of the first TIROS missions led the U.S. to develop an entire system of operational satellites that, combined with Soviet, French and Japanese satellites, now keeps a continual watch on the world's weather.

The system includes satellites in Sun-synchronous orbits, each watching weather patterns around the globe, and other spacecraft in geostationary orbits, each monitoring a single region. Instead of carrying

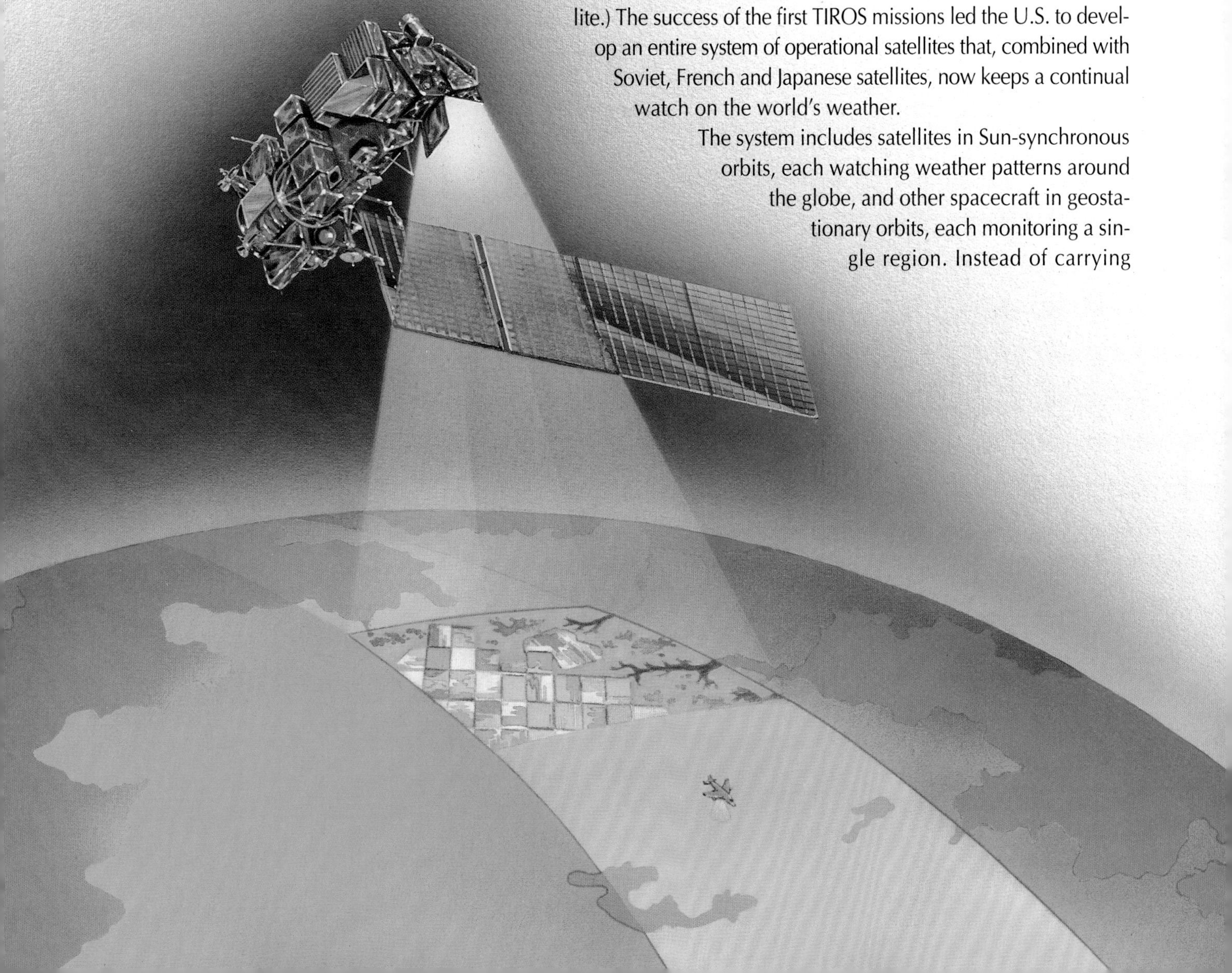

television cameras, they record images with devices called radiometers, which measure the changing levels of radiation reaching a small detector as the instruments scan the scene below. The readings are translated into images, with a maximum resolution of about one-half mile. Because the radiometers measure infrared energy as well as visible light, they can produce cloud images even at night, although with substantially reduced resolution. Infrared readings also provide data about the temperature of land, oceans and clouds. The Sun-synchronous satellites carry another kind of instrument called a sounder, which uses measurements of radiation, primarily in the infrared region, to compute temperatures in the atmosphere at various altitudes up to about 25 miles.

A familiar sight to television watchers, satellite weather photos help to predict weather days in advance. The photos are created from composite images taken by satellites in Sun-synchronous and geostationary orbits.

Some of the data, like that from the original TIROS, is stored on tape for later transmission to the ground. Many of the images, however, are broadcast directly to 2,000 receiving stations around the world; these are the "satellite maps" that show up on television news shows, providing information about weather developments in vast regions such as oceans, deserts and polar areas, where conventional reports are sparse. The cloud formation maps reveal storm systems, fronts, jet streams and high-level winds; the pictures also show important properties of the surface, including the extent and condition of sea ice and the area of snow cover. All of these factors are vital components of the detailed atmospheric models that meteorologists use for developing weather forecasts and are the basic data that help scientists understand long-term global climactic changes like the greenhouse effect, a phenomenon in which heat is trapped near the surface of a planet by atmospheric gases and clouds.

Perhaps the most significant contribution that weather satellites make, however, is in providing early warning of dangerous tropical storms. Originating in the oceans, hurricanes, typhoons and cyclones have frequently ravaged coastal regions, sometimes causing appalling loss of life. But now, spotted from orbit as they develop, and tracked on a daily, sometimes hourly basis, these storms no longer catch coastal residents unaware. Some weather satellites incorporate another life-saving feature: equipment that picks up distress calls from aircraft and ships on a special radio frequency. The signals are relayed to ground stations, where they are analyzed to determine the location of the original transmission.

THE TROUBLE WITH HUBBLE

While the majority of satellites placed in Earth orbit focus their attention on the world below them, others far above the obscuring mantle of the atmosphere gaze out on the mysteries of the universe. Most electromagnetic radiation is absorbed before it reaches Earth's surface, including ultraviolet, infrared, X-rays and gamma rays; even the visible light that gets through is distorted as though seen from underwater. The first astronomical satellites were launched in the 1960s, mainly to observe ultraviolet and gamma ray sources. By the early 1970s, plans were under way to orbit a large optical telescope, which would carry a variety of detectors and be able to detect smaller and dimmer objects than any earthbound instrument. Nearly 20 years later, the Hubble Space Telescope was launched, but unfortunately, a flaw in the optics restricted its ability to see what it had been sent to see.

The Hubble's long gestation was a consequence of protracted debates about its cost (the final price tag was $1.6 billion), and the complex systems required to deal with the harsh environment of space. The reflector telescope—a Cassegrain design *(page 19)*—was designed as a barrel-shaped tube 14 feet across and 43 feet long with a primary mirror 94.5 inches in diameter at its heart. The spacecraft would experience 500° temperature extremes as it moved from darkness to daylight and back during each 90-minute orbit, so it had to be made of a material that would not expand or contract with temperature changes. The structure that holds the primary and secondary mirrors and the focal plane (where images are focused) is a special graphite-epoxy truss that allows the distance between the mirrors to vary by no more than .0001 inch. Other elements of the telescope have thermostats and heaters to allow active control of their temperatures. In addition, onboard equipment had to be designed to operate so smoothly that no vibrations would compromise the instrument's precise aim.

The Hubble's aiming mechanism was one of the greatest engineering challenges. The problem is common to all photography: If a camera moves during a long exposure, the resulting image will be blurry. The Hubble would sometimes require hours of focus on a very dim object, locking onto it and then holding the image perfectly still by slowly turning to compensate for the telescope's movement through space. The design specifications called for the most precisely aimed instrument in the history of astronomy, able to lock on a target for 24 hours without

THE DISAPPEARING OZONE

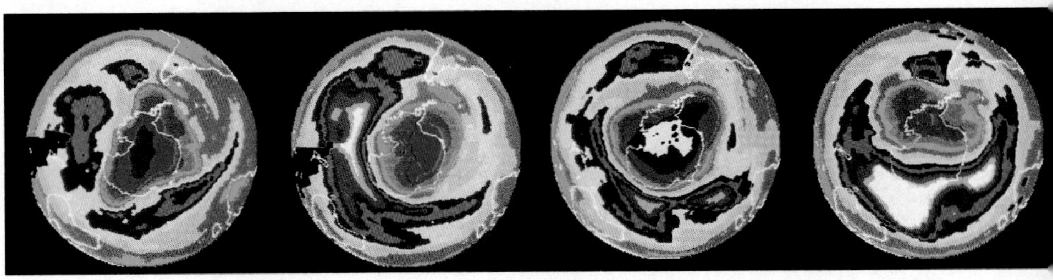

1985 1986 1987 1988

The maps at right chart the total ozone distribution in the Southern Hemisphere for October 2 over a four-year period. Ozone, a three-atom molecule of oxygen, shields Earth from harmful ultraviolet radiation, which can cause skin cancer, immune deficiencies, and even harm crops and marine life. A 1 percent decrease in ozone results in a 2 percent increase in ultraviolet radiation that reaches the Earth.

The photographs show that the areas of lowest ozone (purple) in 1986 and 1988 covered less area than the gaping ozone holes observed in 1985 and 1987, which covered nearly the entire Antarctic continent. High concentrations of ozone are indicated by red, orange and white. Although readings are seasonal and fluctuate from year to year—the result of atmospheric dynamics— scientists have noted a downward trend in ozone amounts in Earth's atmosphere over the last decade.

Damage to the ozone layer has been linked to the use of chlorofluorocarbons (CFCs), which have many applications, especially as refrigerator gases and in aerosol cans. Once the normally stable CFCs enter the stratosphere they break down into their constituent elements; chlorine is released, which destroys ozone.

NASA employs a Nimbus 7 satellite to keep track of the depletion. Equipped with a Total Ozone Mapping Spectrometer, it circles Earth in a Sun-synchronous orbit. As the Sun appears, the satellite can measure the light filtering through the ozone and deduce ozone concentrations.

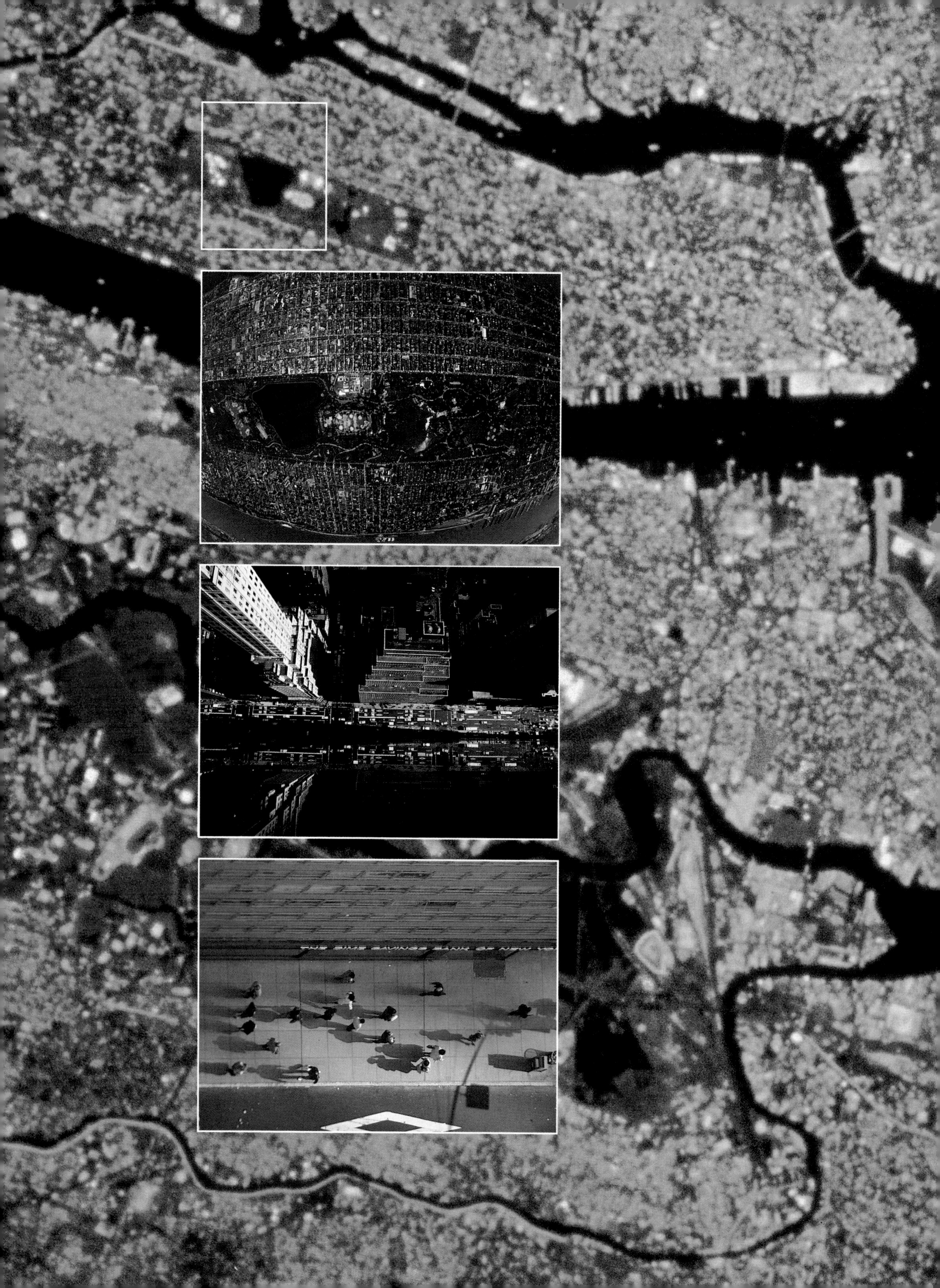

Spies in the Sky

It was an inevitable outgrowth of the Space Age. With America and the Soviet Union's newfound ability to rocket far-seeing satellites into space, came the all-too-human urge to turn them on each other for some unneighborly spying.

Peeping into someone else's backyard from space started as early as 1960. Earth-imaging satellites were souped up with high-resolution optics and placed into strategic orbits. With the right click of a shutter, the hard truth about an enemy's defense facilities could be exposed.

The first successful American spy satellites were propelled into space aboard a Lockheed Agena orbiting rocket stage. Photographs of Soviet missile bases, for example, were snapped automatically from altitudes ranging from 50 to 150 miles high. The exposed film was then ejected earthward in a reentry capsule over the Pacific Ocean near Hawaii. At a predetermined altitude, an aircraft would swoop by and snatch the capsule—descending by parachute—from the air. If the aircraft missed, the capsule would plunge into the ocean and float just below the surface, awaiting recovery by ship.

The Soviets operated similarly. Their first photoreconnaissance satellites were sent aloft aboard unmanned Vostok spacecraft, programmed to self-destruct at the slightest failure. By 1964 the Soviets' space spies were orbiting Earth for eight days at a time before retro firing the reentry capsule and returning it to Soviet soil.

Top-secret films still drop from the sky—though rarely—and usually bear close-up exposures of single objects or small areas. Outfitted with powerful optics of classified design, these close-up cameras can photograph an object as small as a grapefruit. But the need for this level of detail is not always necessary—nor practical, considering the cost involved in retrieving film that may not even live up to expectations.

Beaming images directly to ground stations via TV signals is more typical of photoreconnaisance missions today. Instead of relying on film, satellites use a Charge Coupled Device *(page 23)*, which registers images digitally. This information is then beamed to ground stations, where the images are reconstructed on computer. If something in the image is unclear but piques military curiosity, a film-bearing close-up camera can be programmed to zoom in for a better look during a later orbit.

Photoreconnaissance is not the only method of spying in space. There are infrared detectors that are sensitive to the exhaust plumes of active missiles, for example. And radio-receiving satellites are used to eavesdrop on clandestine radio communications. The latest known American space sleuth is a radar-imaging satellite called Lacrosse, which can see through the darkness and clouds that obscure Soviet skies for much of the year. This satellite beams microwaves through the dark or cloudy skies to the ground below. The microwaves hit the ground and the satellite's huge radar antenna records the intensity of each return signal. A computer image can then be constructed from the recorded signals.

Set against a background photo taken by a SPOT satellite, the three inset photos at left simulate a spy satellite's ability to zoom in on details (in this case New York City) from space. Actually, spy satellites often provide even better powers of resolution—capable of photographing an object as small as a grapefruit from Earth orbit.

deviating by more than two millionths of a degree—the width of a hair seen from a mile away. The movements are driven by so-called reaction wheels, heavy spinning disks that impart a turning force to the spacecraft when their speed of rotation changes. That speed is controlled by varying the voltage to the disk's electrically driven motor, under the control of the onboard attitude-control computer. As the telescope turns—about as fast as the minute hand of a clock—sensitive gyroscopes report position changes to an onboard computer 40 times per second. These gyros, sensitive enough to detect movement of as little as seven hundred-millionths of a degree, work in tandem with sensors in a fine guidance system, providing data to the attitude control computer which "drives" the rotation wheels.

To point the telescope roughly in the right direction the attitude control computers provide coordinates in the sky. Then the fine guidance sensors take over the task of finding the target, a job that usually takes about 20 minutes. The sensors view the sky through three portals in the focal plane (dubbed "pickles" because they are arranged around the imaging area of the focal plane, which is the shape and size of a dinner plate), searching for guide stars that will center the observation target on one of the telescope's five instruments. These guide stars are drawn from a catalog of 19 million objects whose positions have already been precisely determined. Two of the three pickles are given coordinates of candidate guide stars; one searches in a spiral pattern until it finds a star with the correct brightness. When

After years of delay, the Hubble space telescope was finally lofted into a 380-mile-high orbit aboard the shuttle Discovery *in April 1990. The craft's robotic arm then lifted the $1.6-billion instrument and deposited it in orbit.*

the first guide star is found, one of the two other sensors carries out a similar search. A third sensor is not necessary for any one search, but three are provided on Hubble to enable the telescope to cover a sufficiently wide area of the sky. If the relative positions of the two stars do not match the catalog information, the search resumes. In essence, the fine guidance sensors work by geometry. A set of guide stars is selected that fits into any two of the three pickles through which the fine guidance sensors look. The guide stars are selected by identifying the target star and then using a computer to identify the two guide stars which—together with the target star—constitute a triangle of known proportion.

After the telescope has locked onto its target the observation can begin. Images are recorded by one of two instruments, the wide field/planetary camera (WFPC) and the faint object camera; the former takes in relatively large sky areas, while the latter focuses much more narrowly, to make out very distant objects. Two spectrographs analyze radiation in the visible and ultraviolet bands, and a high-speed photometer precisely measures the brightness of an object in a particular spectral band, detecting fluctuations on a time scale of microseconds.

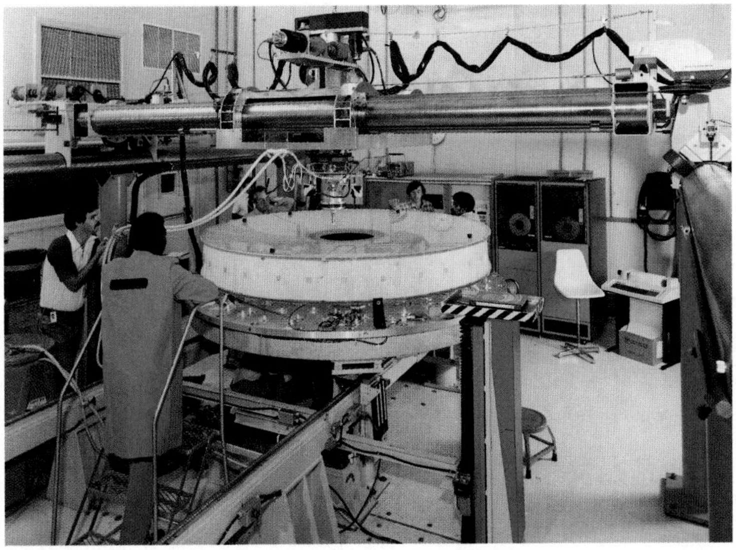

Hubble engineers did not realize, as they ground the telescope's 94.5-inch main mirror (above), *that though they were creating a perfectly smooth mirror it was ground to the wrong curvature. The result was a spherical aberration—light reflecting from different points of the mirror did not focus at the same point. An "all-up" test—one that would have checked all of the telescope's optical components—was rejected as not worth the $100-million cost. In fact, a problem as basic as spherical aberration could have been detected easily, but it was considered inconceivable that such a mistake could have been made and a test was never conducted.*

The Hubble's optical system also presented engineers with an awesome task. Perfect optics concentrate incoming light into a small spot; the fineness of its focus is limited only by the wave nature of the light itself. Because light entering the Hubble would be undistorted by the atmosphere, the designers decided to attempt such perfection that would require a surface on the primary mirror smoother than had ever been achieved on such a large piece of glass. Furthermore, the mirror would have to weigh three-quarters less than a conventional mirror, to keep down the launch weight of the spacecraft, and would have to be thermally stable, to eliminate shape changes as the telescope moved between sunlight and darkness.

After much testing, scientists determined that the mirror could be made from special, low-expansion glass assembled in an "egg-crate" structure, with a honeycomb of slender glass slats fused between two relatively thin plates. The assembled blank was then heated and allowed to sag over a mushroom-shaped mold. A year of grinding shaved away 200 pounds of glass and smoothed out the irregularities left by the mold. For the final polishing, the blank was transferred to a bed of 138 pushrods, adjusted so that they bent the glass into the shape it would take when weightless in space. A computer analyzed maps of the surface, made by bouncing laser beams through a device called a null corrector, and then guided a small polishing disk to remove glass, millionths of an inch at a time, to bring down the high spots. The resulting surface was so smooth that if it were enlarged to the size of the Gulf of Mexico, the highest waves would be less than a fifth of an inch. Then the surface was coated with an extremely thin layer of aluminum, giving it superb reflective abilities at both visible and ultraviolet wavelengths. Finally, a thin protective coat of magnesium fluoride was added.

Although the mirror was finished in 1981, nine years passed before the Hubble made it into space—the result of a lengthy assembly and testing process, and the disruption of space shuttle launches following the *Challenger* accident in 1986. But just two months after launch, with a set of coarse-focusing exercises completed, the Hubble's ground controllers tried to bring the bright star Iota Carina into fine focus with the the WFPC, and discovered—to their horror—that the fuzzy image could not be sharpened, no matter how they manipulated the mirrors. In the investigations that followed, NASA discovered that the shape of the primary mirror was flawed because of an optical error in the null corrector used in the grinding and polishing process. Smooth as it was, the mirror had the wrong curve, which created a spherical aberration in the telescope. In the words of one NASA scientist, the Hubble's mirror was "perfectly wrong."

Although the spectrographs, which do not require precisely focused light, could perform some of their planned experiments, the cameras aboard the Hubble would not, as hoped, provide spectacular views of the universe. But because the Hubble is designed so that astronauts can periodically replace its instruments, there is still hope that Hubble will help unlock the secrets of the universe. During a repair mission tentatively scheduled to be performed in 1993, a space shuttle will sidle up to the Hubble. A team of astronauts will leave the craft and perform an Extravehicular Activity (EVA), during which they will install new cameras—sliding them in along guide rails. Each camera will include small curved mirrors about the size of a nickel that will produce the right "prescription" to cure Hubble's astigmatism.

Since the Hubble began transmitting pictures, they have been relayed to Earth, along with the telescope's other findings, on a system specifically developed to handle satellite data communications. The Tracking and Data Relay Satellite System (TDRSS) uses radio receivers and transmitters aboard two satellites—TDRSS East and TDRSS West—in geosynchronous orbit to maintain almost constant contact with as many as 24 spacecraft at a time, including space shuttles. Before the advent of TDRSS in 1983, satellites in low orbits were typically in touch with the ground only about 15 percent of the time, despite a far-flung network of ground stations. Data-gathering spacecraft like TIROS had to record information and then transmit it in bursts during the few minutes that a receiving station was in view below. But the Hubble and other scientific spacecraft generate far too much data to handle in such a sporadic way; a TDRSS satellite can move the entire contents of a 20-volume encyclopedia in just one second.

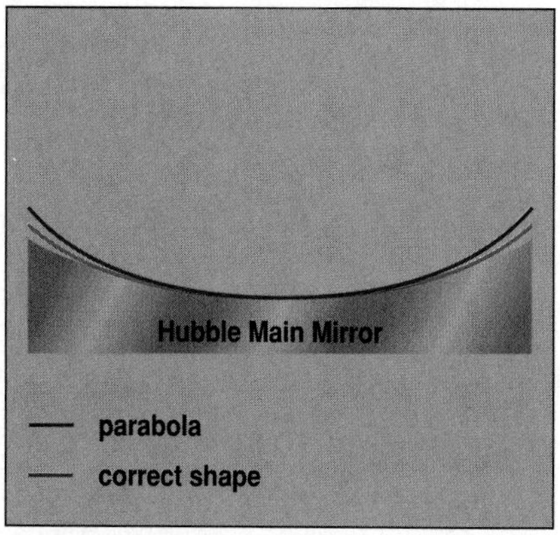
Hubble Main Mirror
parabola
correct shape

THE WRONG CURVE

Hubble's main mirror should have been ground to the shape indicated by the red line. In fact, it was two microns off—less than the thickness of a sheet of paper. The mistake was caused by a faulty optical tool used to guide the grinding process. A measuring rod that should have provided the proper spacing between mirrors and a lens in a device called a null corrector had been inserted backward. As a result, the spacing was off by 1.3 millimeters. To make the telescope's mirror appear correct when viewed through the instrument, technicians ground it to the wrong curvature.

X-RAY EYES

The Hubble is the first of the so-called Great Observatories, a series of U.S. orbiting astronomical facilities designed to examine the universe in many portions of the electromagnetic spectrum. Other planned spacecraft are the Gamma Ray Observatory, the Space Infrared Telescope Facility and the Advanced X-ray Astrophysics Facility. By surveying radiation of different wavelengths, each of the observatories will contribute to a multifaceted picture of the cosmos, revealing objects and events that would otherwise remain impenetrable mysteries. Infrared radiation, for example, is a signature of vast clouds of dust and gas, warmed by the radiance of stars forming within them. High-energy radiation such as X-rays, emitted when substances are heated to millions of degrees, is an indicator of tumultuous processes—supernova explosions of massive stars, and the violent swirling of hot gases that, some scientists believe, are sucked into a black hole.

Until the first X-ray detector soared briefly above the atmosphere on a rocket in 1948, astronomers had no idea how much information they could glean from this portion of the electromagnetic spectrum. In the early 1970s, they began to assemble a map of the X-ray sky, using two years' worth of data beamed down from a small satellite named Uhuru. Its instruments located 339 X-ray sources, with most of the brightest appearing to be part of the Milky Way. Some of the strongest emitters appeared to be binary stars, locked in a close, whirling embrace by their mutual gravitation. Astronomers theorized that one member of each pair must be an extraordinarily dense, massive object—either a neutron star or a possible black hole. Gas sucked from its partner, accelerating as it approached the compact object, would reach such velocities that internal friction would heat it to the point of releasing energy as X-rays.

In 1978 another satellite, dubbed the Einstein Observatory to honor the centennial of the great physicist's birth, began beaming back images of X-ray sources with resolution comparable to that provided by ground-based optical telescopes. The pictures were the product of an ingenious new type of telescope, one of the first with the ability to focus an X-ray emission from a source into an image. The Einstein telescope used a principle known as grazing-incidence reflection, in which X-rays strike smooth surfaces at very shallow angles. The telescope mirrors were sets of concentric tubes, the largest about two feet in diameter, with slightly tapered and curved profiles. Parallel X-rays entering the tube at one end grazed against the sides and converged on a focal plane 11 feet away. Einstein detected objects

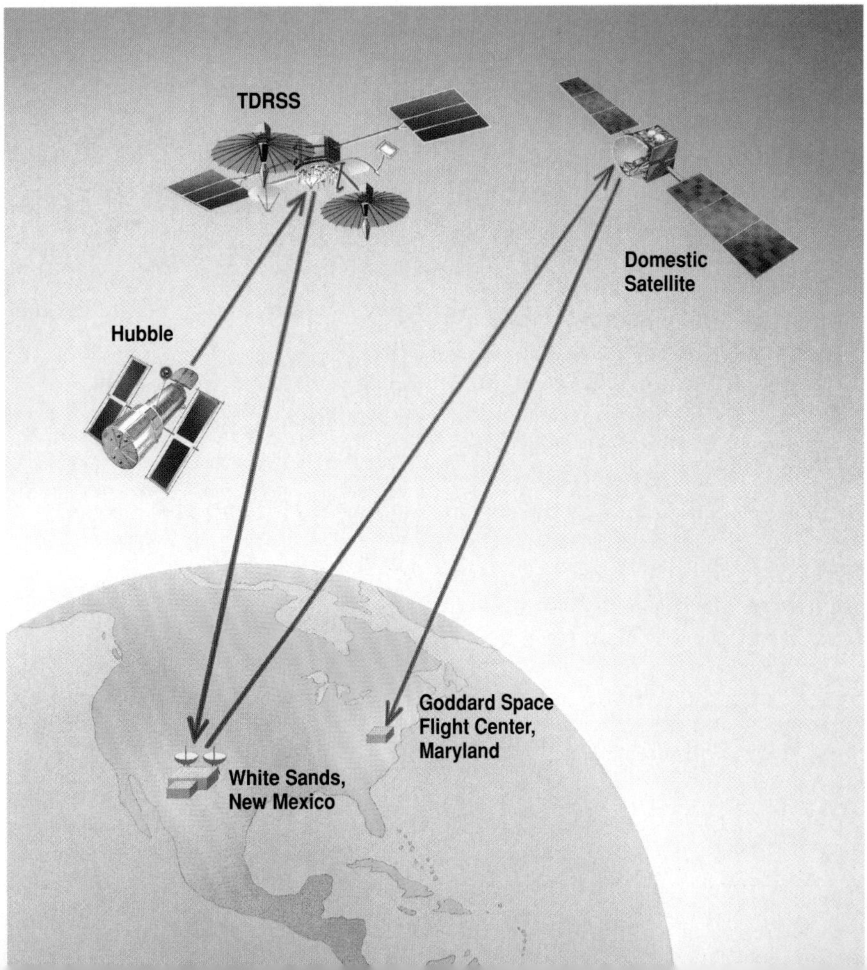
TDRSS
Domestic Satellite
Hubble
Goddard Space Flight Center, Maryland
White Sands, New Mexico

STAYING IN TOUCH

The Tracking and Data Relay Satellite System (TDRSS) allows spacebound instruments like the Hubble telescope and spacecraft such as the shuttle to transmit data back to Earth even when no tracking station on the ground is directly in range. Riding 22,300 miles high in a geosynchronous orbit, TDRSS receives information from the lower-orbiting Hubble telescope, and relays that information to a ground station in White Sands, New Mexico. Then, the data is relayed back up to a domestic satellite—also in geosynchronous orbit —which in turn transmits to NASA's Goddard Space Flight Center in Maryland. From there, the information is routed to the appropriate scientific organization.

Cleaner than Clean

Scrupulousness is not a luxury in satellite construction; it is a necessity. Minute particles of dust or even residues from fumes can infiltrate the inner workings of a satellite and jeopardize its ability to function in space. Moreover, planetary and interplanetary landers and probes can ill-afford to transport earthly bacteria to the very environments they seek to explore—but not taint.

Satellites are assembled in a "clean room," which relies on a sophisticated ventilation system to purge the air of dust particles and fumes produced during assembly. One of the room's walls, or its floor, constantly withdraws air from the room into an exterior duct containing particle-extracting filters. That duct extends around the outside of the room and connects with the opposite wall or ceiling, through which purified air is returned.The air circulating in the cleanest of clean rooms—called a class one—contains one or less particle larger than 0.5 microns per cubic foot of air. (One micron is equal to one millionth of a meter.) By comparison, a cubic foot of air in an air-conditioned office contains 500,000 to a million such particles.

A satellite's dirtiest enemy is not the air but its own maker. To combat the bacteria and particles humans carry with them, a cleansing and clothing ritual is mandatory for all clean room workers before they enter. Bodies are decked out in bunny suits, hands are slipped into rubber gloves, heads are topped with caps, booties are donned and, depending on the satellite, masks may be required. Then the engineers enter a powerful air shower to eliminate remaining dust.

Each satellite component, too, is fussed over before it enters the main clean room. Built and tested in smaller, less-clean rooms, components and subsystems are cleaned with alcohol or pressurized liquid freon and bagged before being brought to the satellite. Once built, a satellite is chemically cleaned again, bagged and sealed in its dust-free home, ready for a new life in space.

Clone-like workers in clean-room garb hover around a marine observation satellite built by NEC. Increased amounts of filtered air are injected back into the clean room to increase pressure. Higher pressure prevents entry of dirty outside air.

Stress Tests

Long before it makes its snail's-pace trip to the pad to face a bolt-rattling launch, a satellite has undergone testing that simulates, as much as is possible, the rigors it will face.

The sound vibration from liftoff alone can shake a satellite to pieces. The average liftoff sound level is 140 decibels; by way of comparison, a level of 130 decibels generally causes physical pain to humans. To test for sound stress, a satellite is placed inside an acoustic chamber that can dole out these ear-piercing decibels. By studying the spacecraft after its acoustic shakedown, engineers learn how to provide adequate protection.

Aerodynamic pressures encountered when the rocket plows through the atmosphere can produce another range of threatening vibrations. To test their effects, a satellite is fastened to a pad called an exciter that shakes a satellite back and forth at precisely controlled levels.

To simulate the extreme temperatures of space, a cylinder called a thermal-vacuum chamber is used. Its inner shroud is filled with liquid nitrogen to simulate temperatures as low as -320° F. Heating panels, also inside the shroud, create temperatures as high as 300°F. As well, infrared lamps are used to mimic the Sun's direct rays. When the highs or lows are reached, which can take as long as two days, the satellite is put through its paces and commands are tested. Also taken into account are the effects of the spacecraft's self-generated heat, a product of its independent power system. Protected by up to 22 layers of Mylar insulation, a satellite can suffer as much from its own heat as from the searing Sun unless this heat is dissipated.

With such testing complete, the satellite that journeys from Earth is no stranger to the punishing environment of space.

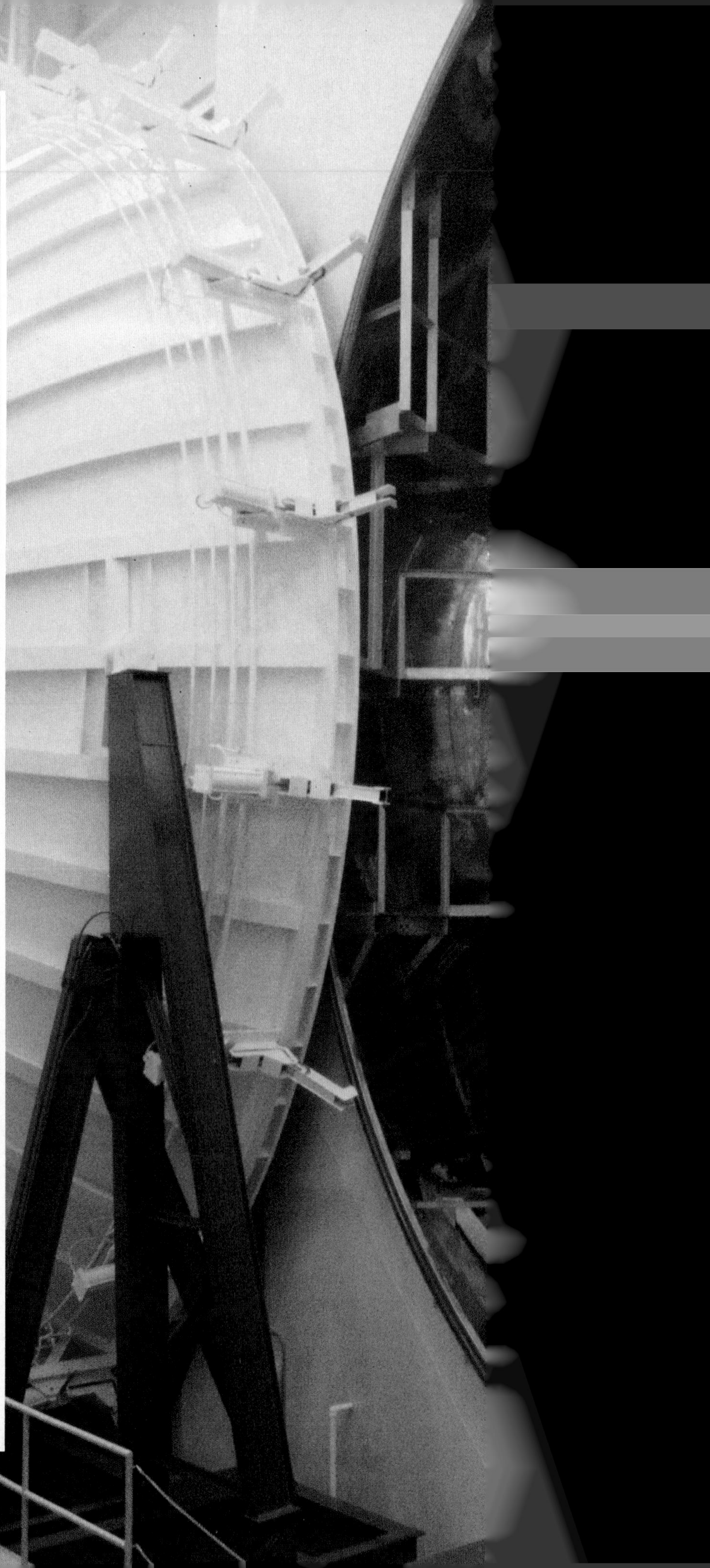

Workers at GE Astro Space stand next to a spacecraft inside a 35-foot-tall thermal-vacuum chamber, designed to test the effects of space's extremes of temperature on satellites.

a thousand times fainter than those found by Uhuru, making more than 5,000 observations in two and a half years and compiling a catalog of images that included distant clusters of galaxies filled with clouds of invisible hot gas, and the brilliant radiance of quasars, violently active galaxies more than 10 billion light years from Earth. Even after Einstein went dark in 1981, plunging back into the atmosphere, scientists continued to mine its rich lode of data for years. And in 1990, a new X-ray telescope went into space aboard Rosat, a West German spacecraft named for Wilhelm Roentgen, the discoverer of X-rays. Rosat's 33-inch telescope began its scientific mission with a complete survey of the celestial sphere, a process that would take six months to complete. Scientists expect that this first true image of the entire X-ray sky will turn up as many as 100,000 radiation sources. Many of these will then be investigated in detail during the remainder of the telescope's life in orbit, likely to be at least two years.

LUNAR LANDSCAPES

As a host of satellites and orbiting observatories have shown, the knowledge that can be gleaned from their unique vantage point is almost inexhaustible. Still, it cannot make up for the information that can be learned by visiting a foreign world physically and sampling its atmosphere or soil. Having mastered the technology to put a satellite in orbit, science had taken one giant step toward the planets. Once a spacecraft is in orbit, only a slight additional push in the right direction is needed to provide escape velocity—25,055 miles per hour—the speed required to break free of Earth's gravitational pull.

The nearest celestial neighbor is the Moon—240,000 miles distant—making it an obvious focus for early space exploration. Centuries of study from a distance had spawned a variety of theories about its origin. Some scientists believed that the Moon had once been the site of considerable volcanic activity, which might have created many of the craters that pock its surface. Others disputed this "hot Moon" theory, contending that the Moon's appearance was determined entirely by billions of years of meteor impacts. Between the extremes of hot and cold was a warm theory, which held that some lunar features were relics of ancient volcanic activity, but that most craters were due to impacts whose widely strewn rubble covered most of the surface. Such issues could be settled only by examining close-up pictures, and by placing instruments on the Moon and sampling its soil.

In 1959, just 15 months after putting the first satellite into Earth orbit, the USSR launched its Luna 1 probe. The first spacecraft to escape Earth's gravity, Luna 1 was intended to crash onto the lunar surface, but missed its target by a few thousand miles, instead going into orbit about the Sun. It was followed less than a year later by the successful Luna 2, which carried Soviet pennants when it hurtled to a crash landing near the Sea of Serenity, and Luna 3, which passed behind the Moon and returned pictures of the far side, never before seen from Earth. The technological achievements of these early lunar missions outstripped their scientific contributions. Simply getting an instrument package across the gulf between Earth and its natural satellite required highly accurate navigation and control systems. These first steps led to increasingly sophisticated remote explorations, including the voyage of Luna 9, the first successful soft lander. At the end of its flight in 1966, a 220-pound instrument package was slowed by retrorockets as it neared the sur-

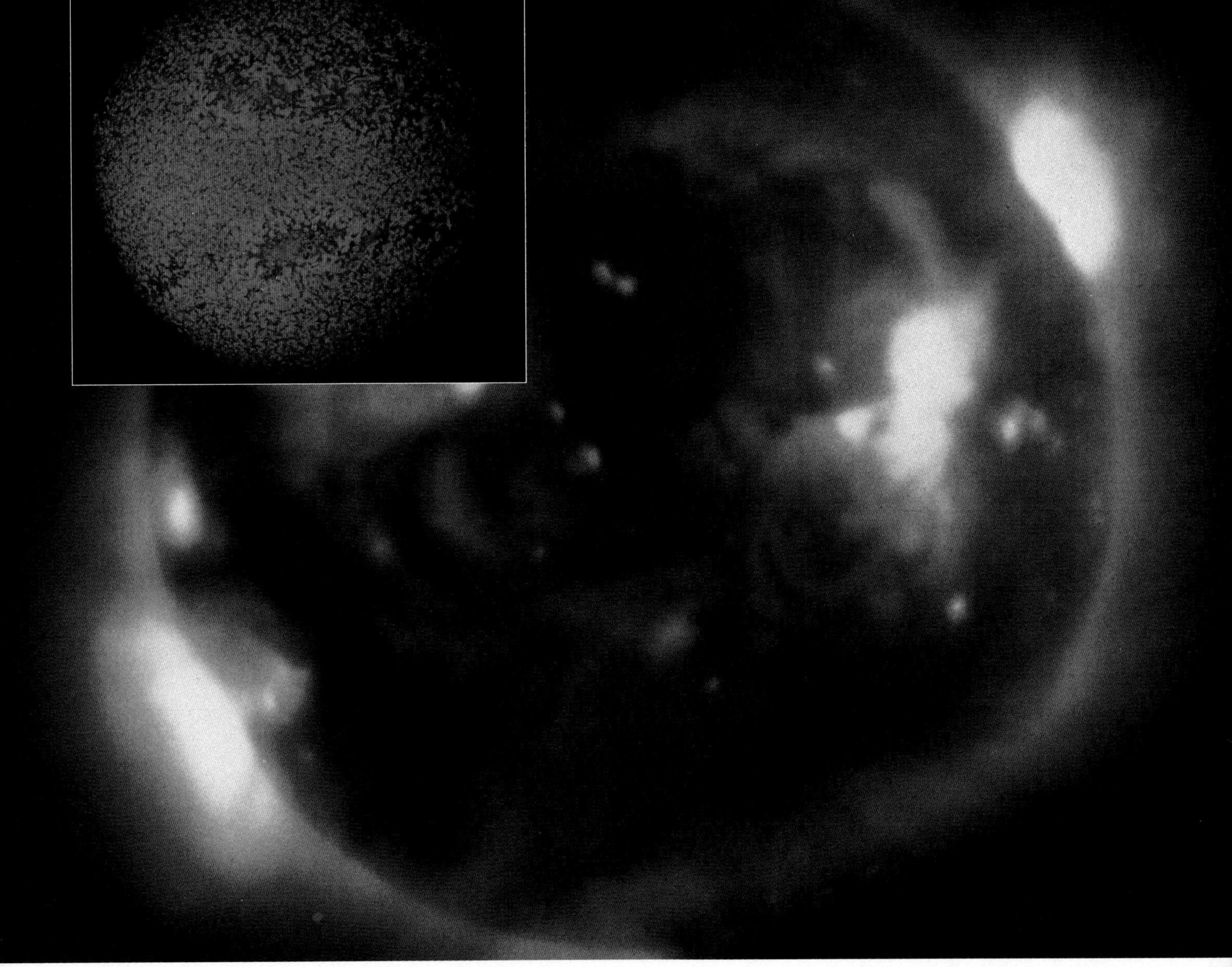

An X-ray image of the Sun taken from the Skylab space station in 1973 reveals the hottest portion of the solar atmosphere, known as the corona, which has a temperature of several million degrees F. The corona's characteristic radiation is X rays—just as yellow light is characteristic of the 11,000° layer called the photosphere as shown in a photograph taken in the visible part of the electromagnetic spectrum (inset).

face of the Ocean of Storms. After it hit, the asymmetrical weight of the egg-shaped capsule rolled it upright; automatically, four spring-loaded stabilizers opened like the petals of a flower. Soon the spacecraft began surveying the lunar landscape, sending back panoramic views of its surroundings—the first television pictures from the Moon's surface—before falling silent three days later.

Within the next two years more than a dozen automated explorers, Soviet and American, took the measure of the Moon. The American Surveyor missions made soft landings, transmitting thousands of photographs and assessing the suitability of the lunar surface for the manned space vehicles that would follow. A series of five Lunar Orbiters photographed the entire surface, giving American space scientists detailed information about potential landing sites.

The most impressive remote control lunar exploration, however, took place after the first Americans walked on the Moon in 1969—and before the Russians finally abandoned plans for their own manned lunar landing. It was conducted by a new generation of Soviet Luna spacecraft, and had its first success with the flight of Luna 16 in September 1970. Less than an hour after touchdown, the probe extended an automatic drill and began boring into the soil. It penetrated a little more than a foot, then withdrew, holding a three-ounce sample that it deposited in a spherical capsule. A day later, the upper stage of the vehicle blasted off from the Moon, leaving the landing platform behind; a three-day direct flight brought it back to Earth with a trajectory so accurate that no course correction was required. Nearing the end of its journey, the sample capsule blazed through the atmosphere before descending by parachute to the plains of Kazakhstan. At relatively low cost, and with no direct human control, Soviet scientists had acquired their own lunar sample—albeit a very small one.

Two months later, in November 1970, Luna 17 achieved a new milestone in remote exploration. After a flight similar to that of Luna 16, it touched down in the Sea of Rains, a semicircular appendage of the vast, flat region known as the Sea of Storms. But instead of picking up samples, Luna 17 let down two sets of ramps and turned loose the 8-foot-long Lunokhod 1, the first wheeled vehicle to venture across the surface of the Moon. The 8-wheeled rover, which weighed about as much as a small car, rolled 20 yards from the landing stage and stopped to give its operators time to analyze the situation. The five members of the control team, a quarter-million miles away, sat before television consoles displaying views of the Moon from Lunokhod 1's two cameras. Commander, driver, engineer, radio operator and navigator worked together to steer the machine toward its objectives while avoiding steep slopes and craters that could trap it or flip it on its back. Their job was complicated by a five-second communication lag, the time it took for signals to cover the round trip between Earth and Moon. Lunokhod 1 incorporated safety devices to keep it from plunging into trouble on its own: Special sensors would halt it if it began to tilt too much in any direction. Each of its eight spoked wheels could maneuver in two forward and reverse speeds. (A ninth wheel served as an odometer/speedometer.) By running the wheels on one side at a faster speed than the other side, Lunokhod's controllers could turn their lunar buggy.

The Soviet moon rover was more than a rolling robotic camera. Its wire-mesh wheels supported a bathtub-shaped body that housed a variety of instruments and communication equipment. High-resolution cameras mounted on its sides sent back detailed images when the vehicle was stopped. A device for soil analysis used X-rays to determine the relative abundance of various metallic elements. A cone-shaped penetrometer determined the mechanical properties of the soil by measuring the resistance as it pushed into the surface and rotated. A small X-ray telescope scanned the heavens as part of a feasibility study for installing larger instruments on the Moon on a permanent basis. A French-built laser reflector mounted on the front of the vehicle provided a target for laser pulses from Earth *(page 102)*. Power for the experiments came from batteries and solar cells mounted on the underside of a lid that covered the vehicle's main body. During the lunar day—half a month long—the lid remained open, allowing the solar cells to charge the batteries. When the rover was parked during the pitch-black lunar night, the lid was closed to protect the cells and insulate the instrument compartment.

Designed to operate for 90 days, Lunokhod 1 crawled over lunar valleys and plains for 11 months before the radioactive isotope that kept its equipment warm during the long nights finally gave out. During that time it had traveled more than

CCCP

The Soviets relied on an unmanned rover known as Lunokhod (above) *to roam about the lunar surface. Two remotely controlled vehicles trekked over the charcoal-gray lunar soil in 1970 and 1971. Each Lunokhod—Russian for Moon Rover—landed aboard a Luna spacecraft, which carried folding ramps that allowed the eight-wheeled vehicle to roll down onto the Moon's surface and embark upon its exploration.*

6 miles, returning 25,000 photographs, performing 500 mechanical tests and 25 chemical analyses of the soil. In February 1971 the rover even observed an eclipse of the Sun by the Earth, with the temperature dropping by nearly 450° F. in just a few hours. But even before Lunokhod 1 fell silent, more automated probes were on their way to the Moon. Luna 18 crashed when it landed on rough terrain; Luna 19 spent a year in orbit, sending back photographs and measuring various properties of the Moon's surface and vicinity. The next two spacecraft in the Luna series were another soil return mission, in the same mountainous region that claimed Luna 18, and an improved robotic vehicle, Lunokhod 2, which covered more than 23 miles over terrain broken by steep slopes and valleys. These missions went so smoothly that the greatest problem occurred on Earth in the recovery of Luna 20's soil samples. The capsule plunged to Earth during a driving blizzard, and was seen falling toward the Karakingir River. At the last moment, a gust of wind blew the capsule into a snowdrift on an island, where it rested for a day before the gale-buffeted recovery team could reach it.

ON TO VENUS

Experience with lunar landers helped Soviet space scientists mount a formidable effort to investigate Earth's nearest planetary neighbor, Venus. Bright enough in Earth's sky that it is sometimes visible even by day, Venus had long been a target for astronomers. But until the 20th Century, they were thwarted by the planet's thick blanket of yellow-white clouds; almost the only facts known about Venus were its size (nearly that of Earth) and its distance (24 million miles, at perigee—its closest approach). Far beyond the reach of early manned spacecraft, the planet could only be known through robot probes. In 1961, the Soviet Union began a series of exploratory missions that would continue for a quarter-century, totaling 18 by 1985; five American spacecraft visited the planet during the same period. When the American Magellan probe reached Venus in 1990 to begin the comprehensive radar mapping of the surface, its controllers could draw on an impressive volume of knowledge about the planet.

The early Venera missions (Venera is the Russian word for Venus) were far from successful. Radio contact with Venera 1, launched in February 1961, was lost inexplicably when the craft was only one-fifth of the way to Venus. Venera 2 also failed to return data, although it flew within 15,000 miles of its target in late February 1966. A few days later, Venera 3—which also had lost its communication link to Earth—became the first spacecraft to reach a planet when it smashed into Venus after a journey of three-and-a-half months.

The first closeup data came from an American probe, Mariner 2, which sailed within 22,000 miles of Venus in December 1962. Its infrared detectors discerned a layered structure in the blanket of clouds, and temperatures near the surface reaching 750° F. Magnetometers aboard the probe detected no sign of a magnetic field around the planet—a discovery that surprised mission designers. Scientists had presumed that the planet possessed an iron core; electrical currents generated by the Venus' rotation should therefore have produced a magnetic envelope. Astronomers concluded the planet spins too slowly to create such a field.

Further efforts had to wait until Venus reached a favorable point in its orbit around the Sun—a short period known as the launch window, which recurs every 19 months. Venera 4 and Mariner 5, arriving almost simultaneously in October 1967, made the wait worthwhile. The Soviet craft ejected an 843-pound instrument capsule, which entered Venus' atmosphere and deployed a parachute. For 94 minutes, the capsule transmitted data about atmospheric temperature, pressure, density and composition; then the signals were snuffed out at an altitude of 15 miles. The

Despite metal-melting heat and crushing atmospheric pressure, Venera 14 succeeded in transmitting photographs from a low-lying basaltic basin on the surface of Venus in March 1982. The spacecraft's spiky foot and a color gauge are visible in the foreground of this composite photograph, formed from three images transmitted through color filters.

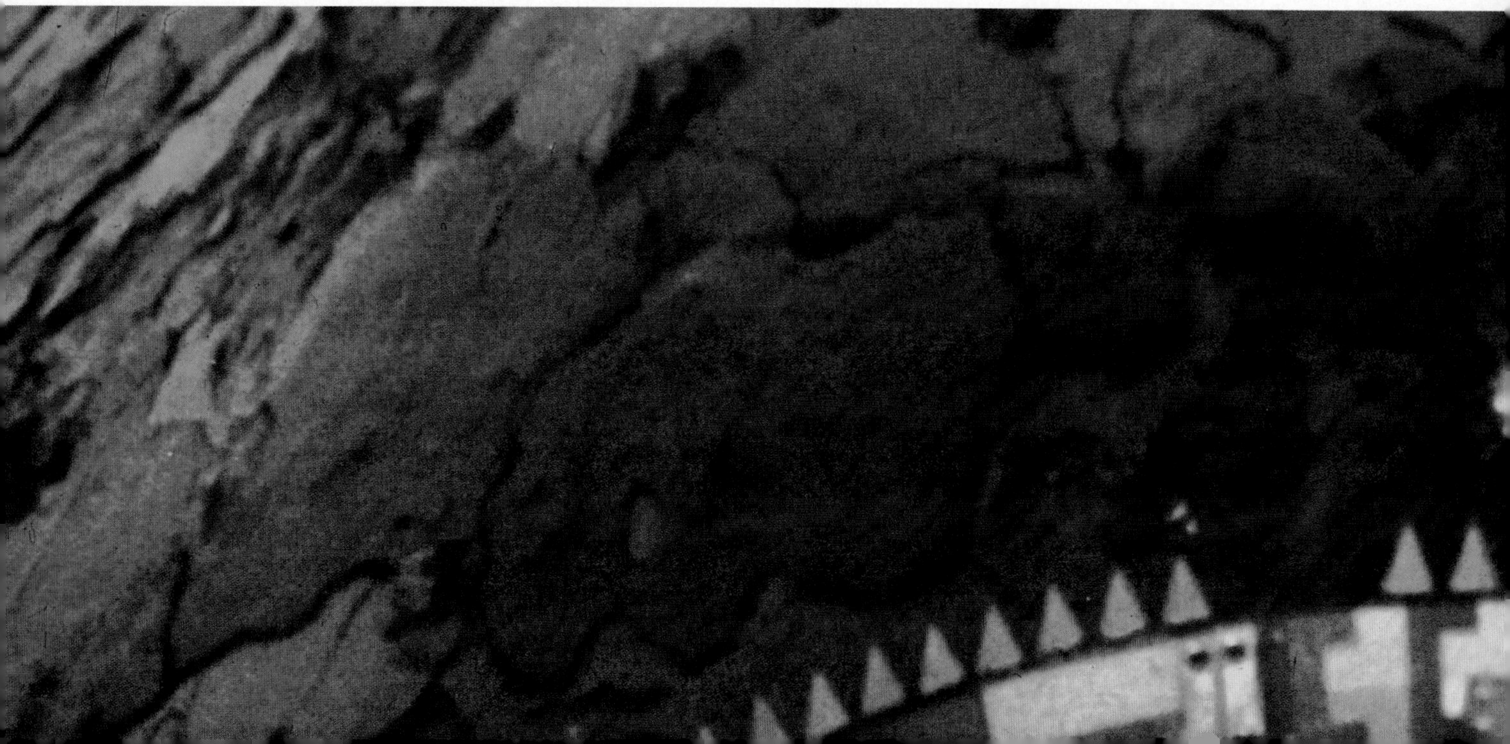

The hermetically sealed, insulated compartment of Venera 7's descent module was designed to protect the craft from the hostile Venusian atmosphere. Three days before landing, the temperature inside the lander was reduced to 15° F. to further prevent the craft from overheating before it had a chance to reach the planet's surface.

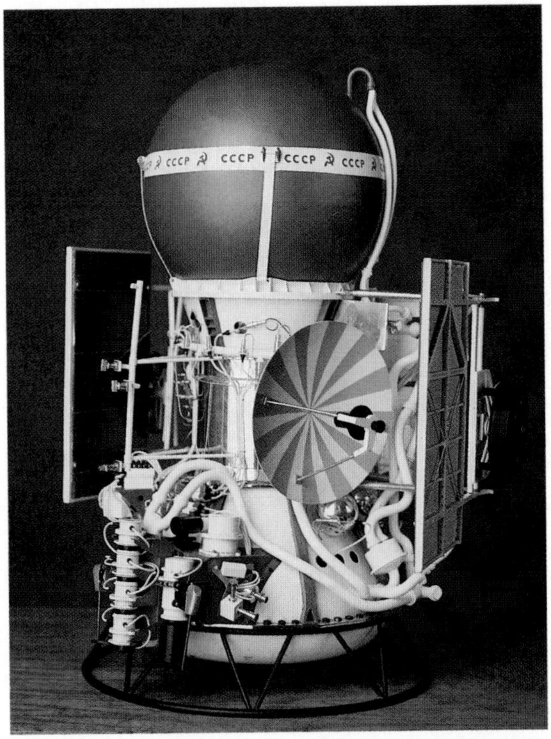
CCCP CCCP CCCP CCCP

data indicated that the clouds were as hot as 525°, and that the atmosphere, almost entirely carbon dioxide, had a surface pressure at least 15 times that of Earth's. Meanwhile, Mariner 5 came within 2,100 miles as it flew by the planet, measuring ultraviolet radiation, magnetic field and other phenomena.

After three more Venera probes investigated the Venusian atmosphere, a stronger and better-insulated Venera 7 made a soft landing in 1970. It recorded a temperature of 880°—hot enough to melt tin and lead—and an atmospheric pressure equivalent to a depth of 3,000 feet in an Earth ocean. Venera 8 in 1972 carried more instruments, detecting traces of ammonia in the atmosphere and measuring wind speeds that ranged from 225 miles per hour at altitudes above 30 miles to less than 2 miles per hour for the last few miles above the surface. (Since Venus' atmosphere is extremely heavy, these low winds actually are equivalent to much stronger Earthly winds.) Radiation detectors found uranium, thorium and potassium in the soil. But it was data from Venera 8's light sensors that aroused the greatest interest: The first mission to land on the day side found it dimly illuminated by sunlight despite the thick cloud cover. If they could get a camera to that hellish place, scientists finally might see the face of Venus.

The opportunity came in 1975, with the descent of Venera 9 and 10. Each spacecraft consisted of an orbiter that would examine the clouds with several different instruments and a sophisticated new lander that would relay data back up to the orbiter. The descent vehicle incorporated an expendable heat shield to protect the instrument capsule for part of its plunge, and a system of parachutes and aerodynamic brakes allowed a faster descent through the cloud layers, ensuring more time on the surface before the intense heat took its toll. The main addition to the instrument package was a camera that could snap a panoramic view of the surface; spotlights were added to illuminate the dim scene expected. They proved unnecessary. The single black-and-white view that Venera 9 returned before its instrument suc-

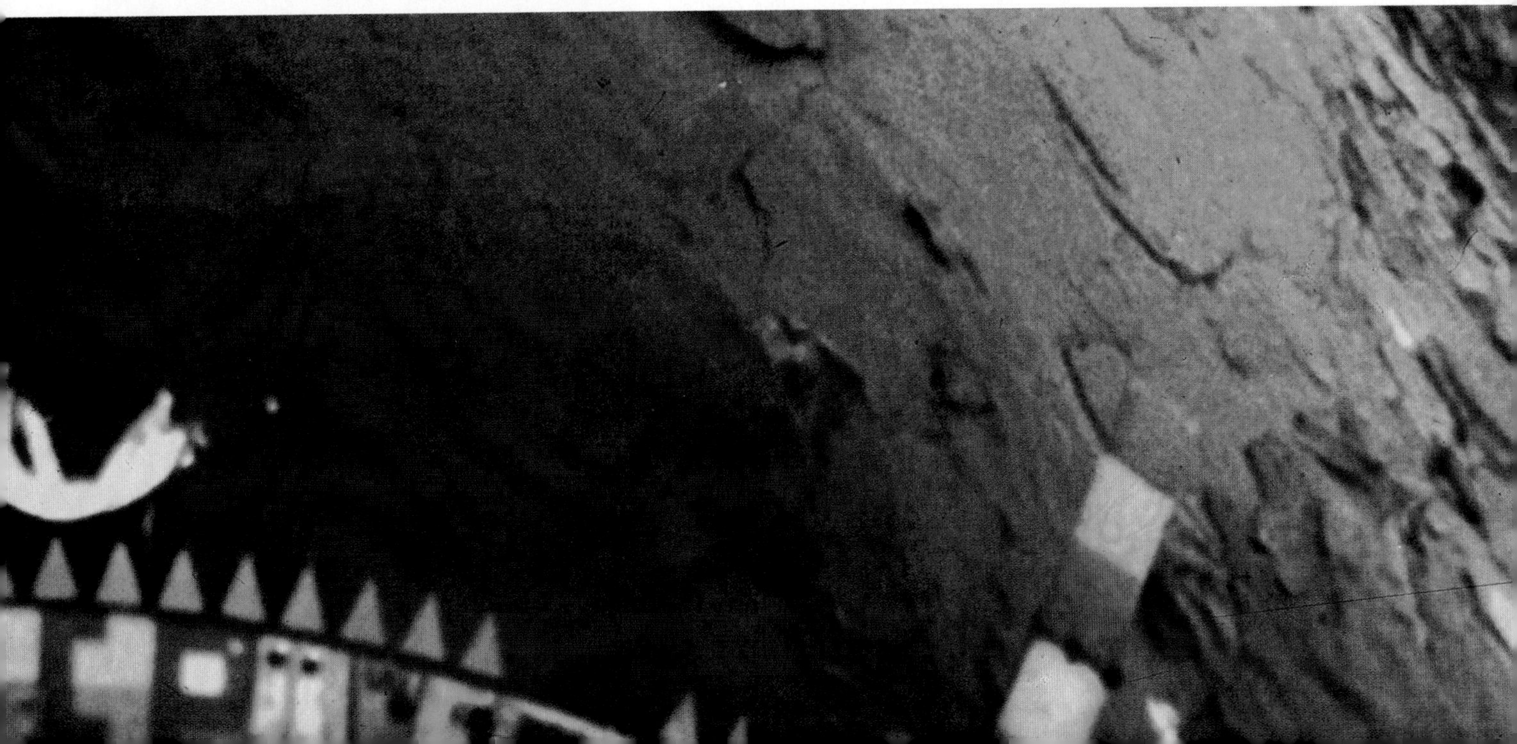

cumbed was remarkably sharp, showing a plain of flat, sharp-edged rocks under a sky as bright as a cloudy day on Earth. Three days later Venera 10 touched down 1,400 miles away; its camera recorded rounded rocks, interspersed with soil-like debris, apparently the result of chemical and wind erosion. Neither view showed signs of water in Venus' past.

A variety of Soviet and American probes visited Venus in the next decade. Four more Soviet craft landed, the last two not only taking color pictures that showed a glowering orange sky, but also scooping up and analyzing samples of what proved to be volcanic soil. In 1985, two spacecraft on their way to look at Halley's Comet released descent modules as they passed Venus. Each contained a small lander and a snow-white balloon with a gondola full of instruments; while the landers analyzed rocks, the balloons floated in the clouds, reporting for nearly two days on winds, temperatures and composition of the atmosphere. By this time, however, the Soviet space program was increasingly turning from Venus to Mars. What may be the last look at Venus for years began in September 1990, when the American Magellan probe began using advanced radar to map the surface from orbit. By bouncing radio waves off the planet and measuring the time it takes the waves to return as well as the intensity of the return signal, radar can provide such information as elevation, surface roughness and average slope. With resolution as fine as 400 feet across, Magellan's pictures showed unexpected geological change—mountains growing and collapsing, hardened rivers of lava 200 miles long, meteor craters deeper than the Grand Canyon. Like its toxic atmosphere, Venus' face was proving vastly different from that of its sister, Earth.

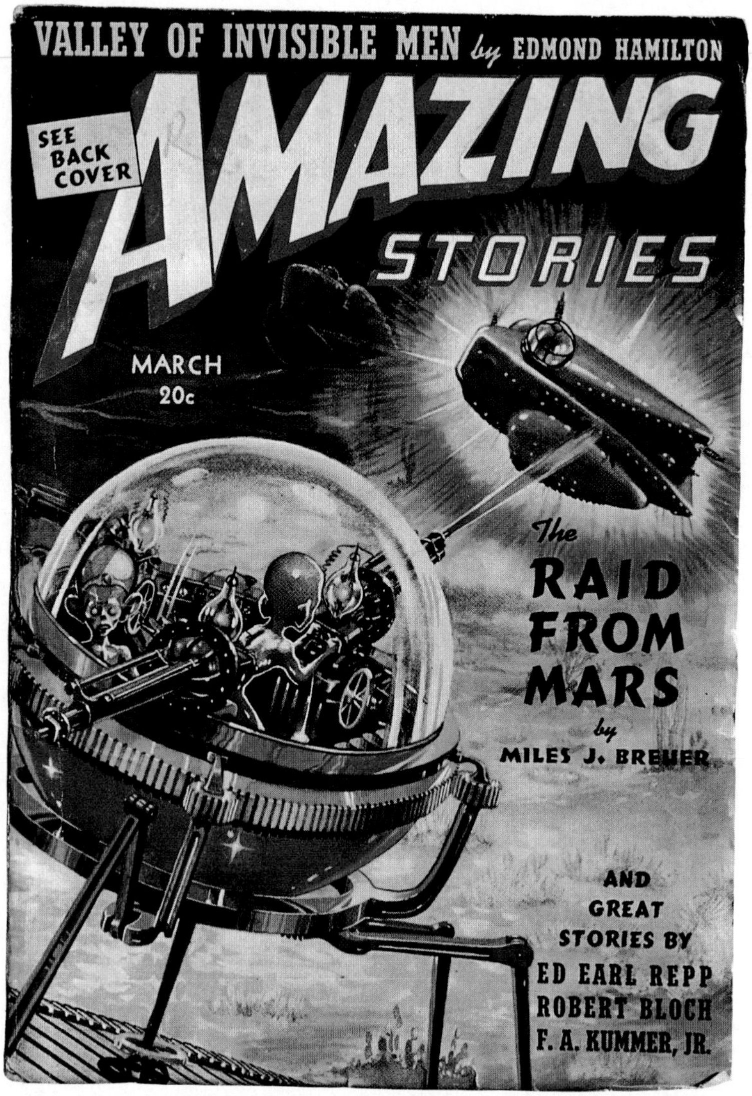
VALLEY OF INVISIBLE MEN by EDMOND HAMILTON
SEE BACK COVER
AMAZING STORIES
MARCH 20c
The RAID FROM MARS by MILES J. BREUER
AND GREAT STORIES BY
ED EARL REPP
ROBERT BLOCH
F. A. KUMMER, JR.

The possibility of life on Mars has long entranced science fiction writers. In Amazing Stories, *founded in 1926 as the world's first science-fiction magazine, sci-fi writers speculated that the Red Planet was populated by intelligent creatures possibly bent on ruling Earth.*

REVEALING THE RED PLANET

While the Venera probes were prospecting Venus, similar American spacecraft were venturing to Mars. The planet had long fascinated astronomers taken with the idea that Mars might support life. Using spectroscopy *(page 24)* they detected traces of elements that made up a tenuous atmosphere; some observers speculated that the bright and dark patches mottling the planet's surface indicated the presence of continents and oceans. In the late 19th Century, Italian astronomer Giovanni Schiaparelli mapped Mars with great precision, assigning place names still in use today. Schiaparelli also described a number of long, straight lines crisscrossing the surface, which he called *canali*, the Italian word for channels. These observations soon found a more fanciful translator, a wealthy American named Percival Lowell, who believed the canali were actually canals, built by a Martian civilization to transport water across an otherwise dry world. Lowell financed an observatory in Arizona where, despite his lack of formal training, he began an intensive study of Mars. He advanced his theories of Martian civilization in three popular books, which thrilled an eager public even while they annoyed skeptical astronomers, who believed that such canali as existed—many had never seen any—must be natural phenomena. But Lowell's Martians lived on in the science fiction of the 20th Century, and a number of modern astronomers conceded that some form of life, if only the most primitive, might indeed be found on Mars.

The dreams of Martian civilization were shattered in 1965 by pictures from the American Mariner 4, the first space probe to reach Mars. The images showed a pocked surface like the Moon; readings indicated an atmosphere so thin that it would be unbreathable even if it were pure oxygen—which it was not. Furthermore, spectroscopic observation of well-defined CO_2 absorption lines showed that the planet had little atmospheric pressure. (Gas under high pressure creates blurred lines in the spectrum.) In short, the planet proved to be a lifeless desert.

Nevertheless, much remained to be learned about Mars, and subsequent missions uncovered astonishing facts about the planet's past. Mariner 9, watching from Martian orbit in 1971 as a planet-wide dust storm subsided, discovered unmistakable signs of geological activity—huge volcanoes and a rift valley 100 miles wide and 3,000 miles long that split the surface to a depth of 2 miles. Even more provocative was the discovery of water-carved gorges lacing the Martian plains. If arid Mars had no canals, it once had had plenty of water.

In 1975 the United States launched a two-pronged mission that would give scientists a better understanding of Mars than of any other planet. Controlled by

FROM ORBIT TO TOUCHDOWN ON MARS

With Viking 1 riding in orbit around Mars (1) the orbiter releases the lander, nestled inside a saucer-shaped protective aeroshell (2). The lander flips over and engines fire aligning it into a landing trajectory (3). As the aeroshell dives into the Martian atmosphere (4) an ablative heat shield is seared by temperatures up to 2,800°F. The aeroshell is later jettisoned after a parachute has slowed it down (5). The lander's terminal-descent engines then fire at 4,600 feet (6) and slow the craft down to a 5-feet-per-second landing on the Martian soil (7). The orbiter, meanwhile, remains in orbit around Mars (8), mapping the planet with high-resolution photographs and relaying information from the lander back to Earth.

1
2
3
4
5
6
7
8

an 800-man flight team, the Viking probes were the most elaborate remote explorers ever launched. Each spacecraft had two parts: an orbiter to reconnoiter the planet from space and relay communications from the surface, and a lander that carried cameras, instruments to study weather and atmospheric makeup, and a special, $60-million package of chemical equipment to test the Martian soil for signs of life. Viking 1, the first to arrive at Mars, spent a month in orbit searching for a safe landing site before dispatching its lander in July 1976. After a descent of more than three hours, slowed by retrorockets, a huge parachute and, finally, three small rocket engines, the spidery vehicle settled its footpads on Chryse Planitia, the Plains of Gold. Within seconds it began taking its first pictures and sending them, as radio signals, on their 19-minute journey back to Earth.

These photos, the first of thousands from the two Viking probes over the next six years, showed sandy, rock-strewn terrain that was foreign but strangely familiar, remarkably similar to a terrestrial desert. The sky above had a salmon hue resulting from fine dust suspended in the air. The weather instruments registered light winds and bitter cold, ranging from -122° F. at dawn to -22° at noon. Other sensors measured the carbon dioxide content of the atmosphere at 95 percent, and detected nitrogen for the first time. But the key soil-analysis experiments would take more time to complete. A week after touchdown, guided by the lander's two cameras, a robot arm extended nine feet from the lander and scratched up a handful of soil with a scoop. The boom was then retracted and rotated 180 degrees until the scoop lay directly above a receptacle that led to three biological experiments. The receptacle's chute was covered with a screen to prevent particles larger than 1/25 of an inch from entering. The collector head was rotated and an electrically powered actuator/vibrator dislodged its precious sample into the chute.

In one test, the soil entered an incubation station and was subjected to an atmosphere of radioactive carbon dioxide and carbon monoxide, then exposed to the artificial light of a xenon lamp to simulate Martian sunlight. After five days, the soil was tested to see whether any organisms had turned the radioactive carbon gases into the carbon-based molecules of which all living things are made. In other experiments, soil was incubated with a broth of nutrients and then monitored to see if they gave off gases that would indicate biological activity. All produced equivocal results; later tests with heat-sterilized soil also produced the oxygen release, indicating that it was due to chemical reactions, not biological activity.

Because space was at a premium on the Viking craft, engineers were forced into new feats of miniaturization. As one scientist noted at the time, each of Viking's experiments would normally have required a 10-by-10-foot lab, with a 6-foot rack of electronics. Engineers, however, managed to reduce it all to a box the size of a typewriter. The result was an instrument so complex that engineers were never capable of getting all three experiments to work in one prototype on Earth. Some project scientists quietly opined that they would be pleased if just one experiment fulfilled its function on Mars. But despite snags including a jammed robot arm, each of the mini-labs performed its tasks flawlessly.

Most scientists concluded that the soil examined by the Viking landers was in fact devoid of life. But some continued to harbor the hope that exotic organisms might be found elsewhere on Mars. After all, they point out, the surface area of Mars is as extensive as all the dry land on Earth, and the Vikings may have had

Eerily reminiscent of desert scenes on Earth, the rocks and sand of the Plain of Chryse were captured by a camera aboard Viking 1, which landed on Mars in July 1976 after a near-half billion mile trip (inset). *The robotic arm on the Viking 1 lander consisted of two long, narrow pieces of steel spot-welded together. Capable of operating in a 120-degree radius, the arm could cover a surface area of about 95 square feet.*

the bad luck to land in the wrong places: A spacecraft landing on the desolate Bonneville Salt Flats of Utah might draw similar conclusions about life on Earth. At any event, these scientists say, Martian life is likely to be sparse and well-hidden from its harsh environment. The only conclusive proof that Mars is utterly dead will come when humans can rove its surface, in person or by remote control, testing samples gathered by turning over rocks and digging where they will.

THE GRAND VOYAGER

If the Vikings marked the pinnacle of remote-control surface exploration, their counterpart in long-distance discovery is the marathon mission of Voyager 2, now on its way out of the solar system. Launched in 1977, Voyager 2 took advantage of an unusual alignment of planets to conduct a grand tour of the outer Solar System. Jupiter, Saturn, Uranus and Neptune had all reached positions in their orbits that would allow a spacecraft from Earth to visit them in succession; the gravity of each planet would accelerate the probe like a slingshot and bend its course toward the next planet. This would make possible journeys otherwise beyond existing technology, reducing the flight time to Neptune from 30 years to 12. The enormous gravity field of Jupiter, for example, promised to provide Voyager 2 with

Hello, Out There!

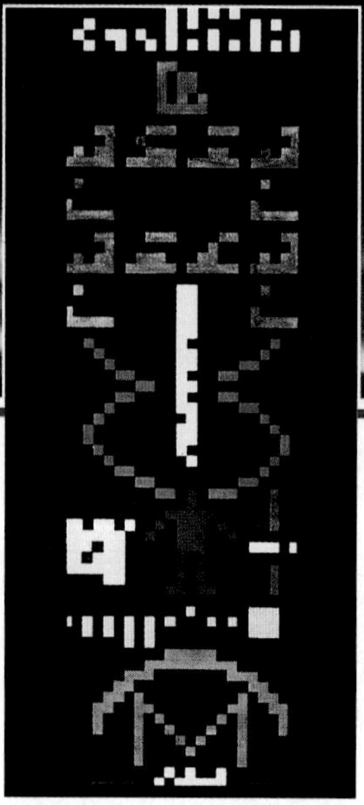

A 1974 radio message composed of 1,679 pulses (0s or 1s) was beamed toward the M13 globular cluster of stars from Puerto Rico. Astronomer Frank Drake, who devised the interstellar message, assumes that beings who receive it will be able to decode it by arranging the characters in 73 lines of 23 columns and then darkening the boxes corresponding to the 1 pulses to produce the image above, which includes the double helix of DNA, a human being and the telescope dish that sent the message.

"This is a present from a small distant world. . . We are attempting to survive our time so we may live into yours." These words, written in 1977 by then U.S. President Jimmy Carter, form part of an elaborate message accompanying Voyagers 1 and 2 on their journeys through the universe. Both crafts carry a 12-inch copper disk that includes greetings from Earth people in 55 languages, samples of music ranging from Chuck Berry's *Johnny B. Goode* to a Mozart aria and 115 electronically encoded photographs and diagrams. The hope is that a distant spacefaring civilization might one day intercept the Voyagers and learn something of the world where their odysseys began.

Other emissaries have been sent to the stars. In 1972 NASA launched Pioneer 10, followed a year later by Pioneer 11. Both spacecraft bear visual greeting cards engraved on small plaques. And in 1974 a radio message was beamed from a 1,000-foot radio telescope in Puerto Rico toward a cluster of stars 25,000 light-years away.

Scientists admit it is extremely unlikely that anyone will ever know whether Earth's cosmic messages have been received. In the case of Voyagers 1 and 2—now traveling at 38,000 miles per hour beyond the edge of the solar system—it will take at least 40,000 years before either craft passes within one light-year of another star.

The disks could well outlast the world where they were created. Encased in a protective cover, each record will carry its message intact for a billion years.

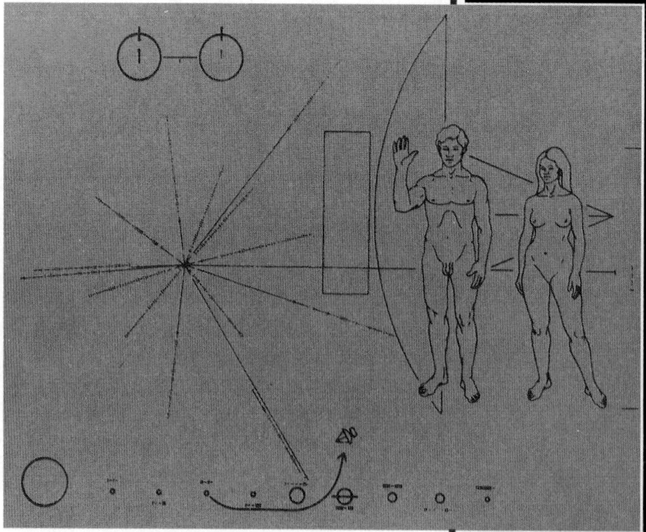

The plaques affixed to Pioneers 10 and 11 display figures of a man and woman with the spacecraft behind them. The 14 radiating lines represent pulsars—pulsating neutron stars—with the Sun as the home star.

This photo—one of the 115 electrically encoded on the Voyager disks—is meant to show the beauty of planet Earth, information about the atmosphere and avian flight.

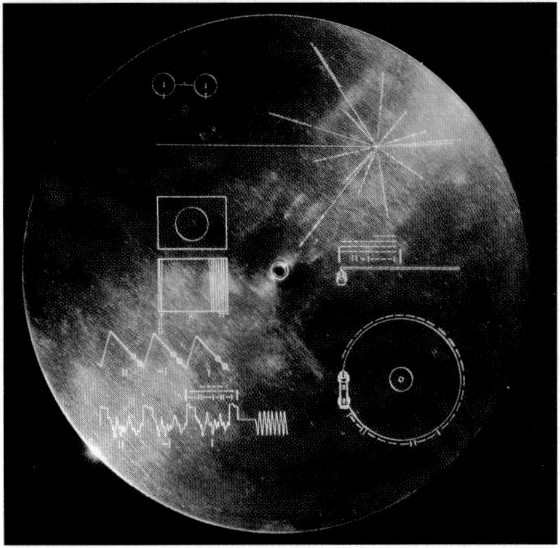

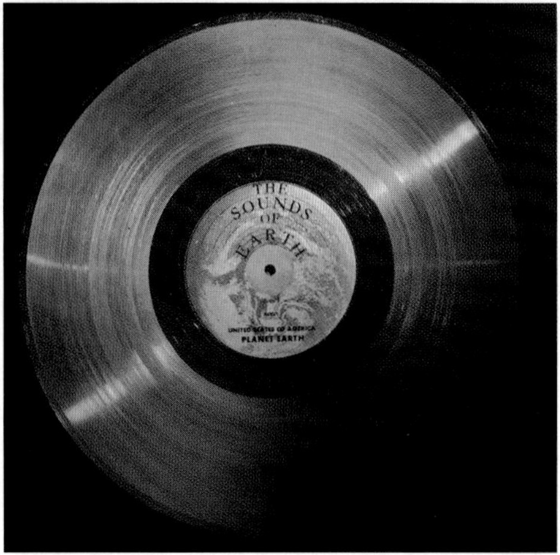
THE SOUNDS OF EARTH
UNITED STATES OF AMERICA
PLANET EARTH

A gold-colored aluminum cover protects the Voyager records; it also displays, in scientific language, instructions for playing the records. A cartridge and stylus are tucked away nearby on each spacecraft.

A wild dog baying, the first cries of an infant and a kiss are among the sounds recorded on the double-sided disks. The brainchild of astronomers Frank Drake and Carl Sagan, the 16 2/3-rpm records run nearly two hours.

a speed boost—relative to the Sun—of roughly 35,700 miles per hour. The launch window, however, would be open only from 1976 to 1978, not reopening for nearly two centuries. Scientists within NASA drew up blueprints for visits to all four planets, but were only able to secure funding for the first part of the proposed odyssey. The final mission description involved two probes—Voyagers 1 and 2—traveling to Jupiter and Saturn only, with Voyager 2 taking a course that would preserve the option of going on to Uranus and Neptune, if it held up long enough, and if NASA could convince Congress years later to supply the needed funds. (Both spacecraft were designed to last only five years.) Meanwhile, Voyager 1, propelled by a gravity-assist from Saturn, would travel 30° above the ecliptic—the plane in which all the planets, except Pluto, lie.

The two spacecraft were launched in late 1977, Voyager 1 departing two weeks after its sibling on a faster trajectory that brought it to Jupiter in March 1979 and to Saturn in November 1980. Voyager 2 reached Jupiter in July 1979, Saturn in August 1981, and then,with fresh funding from Congress, went on to Uranus in 1986 and Neptune in 1989 before journeying into interstellar space, where—like its sister craft—it will report on its environs well into the 21st Century.

Keeping a Voyager to the proper trajectory as its distance increases (Jupiter is about 500 million miles from Earth, Neptune 2.8 billion) requires enormous precision in determining the probe's course and speed. The necessary information comes from terrestrial tracking stations, which measure the spacecraft's angular position in Earth's sky and its distance from Earth. The tracking stations employ huge radio antennas (also used for communications) to follow the Voyagers. The dish-shaped antennas are focused on the faint signals from the spacecraft to produce angular measurements, and a technique based on the Doppler effect *(page 25)* produces the velocity changes. The so-called Doppler shift is the apparent change in frequency of a signal reflected from or emitted by a moving object as the object moves toward or away from the observer. In the case of Voyager, a precise signal is sent from the Earth station to the spacecraft, which retransmits it at a new frequency. Thus frequency changes are measured in both directions, providing the tracking team with very accurate velocity data, which in turn allows them to compute the distance traveled with extraordinary precision. As the spacecraft nears its target, it takes pictures of natural satellites against a star background—a technique known as optical navigation—to further refine its course. Voyager's rendezvous with Neptune was barely 60 miles off target—the equivalent feat, NASA engineers point out, of sinking a 2,260-mile golf putt.

During routine flight, a Voyager probe is stabilized with its radio antenna pointed toward Earth. Special narrow-field sensors keep the Sun and the bright star Canopus in view; if these spacemarks begin to drift, Voyager's computer knows that its orientation is shifting. Attitude control thrusters are activated and the tiny hydrazine-powered rocket motors jog the spacecraft back onto an even keel. Sometimes, however, the spacecraft must be pointed in a different direction to perform course correction maneuvers or to aim instruments during planetary approaches and flybys. At such times, another stabilization system takes over. Gyroscopes tell the computer exactly how much the thrusters turn the craft around each of three right-angle axes with an accuracy of one ten-thousandth of a degree; when the maneuver is completed, the computer reverses the movements, returning the sensors to positions where they can again lock onto the Sun and Canopus. Similar thrusters also are used to make the tiny changes of direction and speed needed to bring the spacecraft exactly on course; a difference of just a few miles per hour can throw the aim off by millions of miles at the target planet—much too far for high-quality images and measurements.

In fact, Voyager 2 approached the outer planets and their moons at such high velocities—accelerating to 60,000 miles per hour at Neptune—that its cameras had to track their subjects to prevent blurring of the images. The technique is similar to that used by experienced photographers—moving the camera while the shutter is open to hold the subject of the photograph in a fixed position. The problem was compounded by the fact that the light from the Sun at Neptune is 900 times fainter than on Earth, requiring "pans" that lasted for up to five minutes. The camera platform proved too jerky for the job, so the attitude-control thrusters had to be called into play. Ground controllers achieved the motion by sending Voyager 2 a message telling it to compensate for a fictitious attitude drift and causing the entire craft to pan while the photos were taken. Adjustments even had to be made to offset the jiggling caused every time Voyager's tape recorder stopped and then restarted to record digitized data. The resulting pictures were clear, and new communications techniques were employed to relay them to Earth without degradation. The Voyager vidicon cameras, similar to television cameras, built up each black-and-white picture from 800 horizontal lines, with every line made up of 800 dots, or pixels. The camera recorded a brightness value for each pixel on a scale ranging

GALILEO'S TOUR DE FORCE

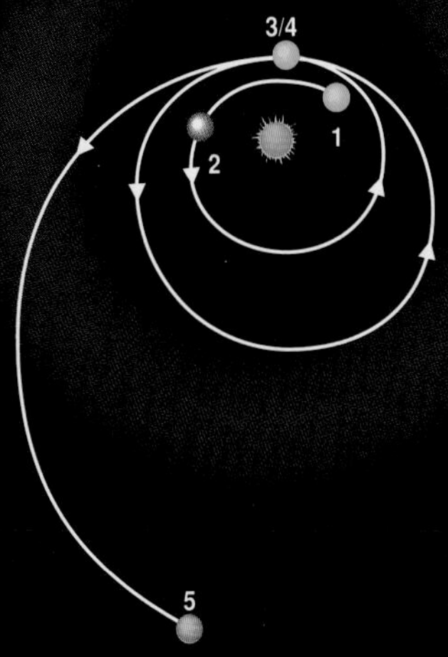
3/4
1
2
5

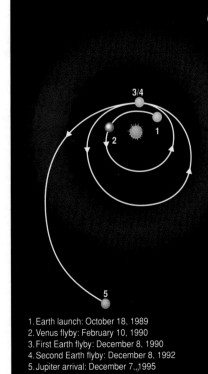

1. Earth launch: October 18, 1989
2. Venus flyby: February 10, 1990
3. First Earth flyby: December 8, 1990
4. Second Earth flyby: December 8, 1992
5. Jupiter arrival: December 7, 1995

A straight line is not necessarily the obvious route between two points—especially in space. Witness the flight of Galileo, a 2.8-ton spacecraft launched October 18, 1989. Its target: the giant planet Jupiter, which it plans to probe—along with the four largest Jovian moons.

Like Voyager 2, Galileo will use a gravity-assist trajectory to boost it along to its target. The technique involves being pulled toward a planet at an ever-increasing speed up to the point of closest approach, then breaking free after swinging around the planet and slingshotting out into space on a new course and with a faster speed relative to the Sun. Experts say that gravity-assist is now essential for interplanetary exploration, allowing probes to reach distant planets without the need for mammoth launch rockets.

In its circuitous voyage Galileo is targeted to fly by Venus once and the Earth twice, picking up speed each time, before heading for Jupiter, 580 million miles from Earth. During its second Earth flyby, more than three years after its launch, Galileo will pass within 200 miles of its home planet. The spacecraft's speed will increase from 78,900 to 87,200 miles per hour.

If Galileo had to rely on its 2,039 pounds of propellant, the total change in velocity it could generate would be roughly 1 mile per second. But the combined boost from all its planetary encounters, engineers say, will increase its speed by almost 7 times that amount.

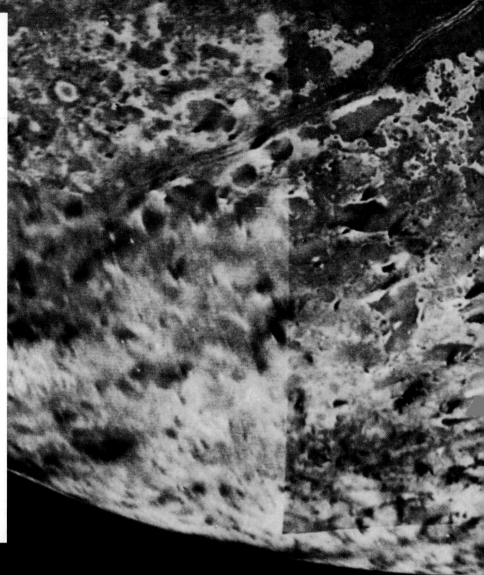

The 230-foot dish at Goldstone, California, is part of the worldwide Deep Space Network that tracked Voyagers 1 and 2 on their voyages through the solar system. The dish's large size allows it to pick up infinitesimally weak signals and then enlarge them using sophisticated amplifiers.

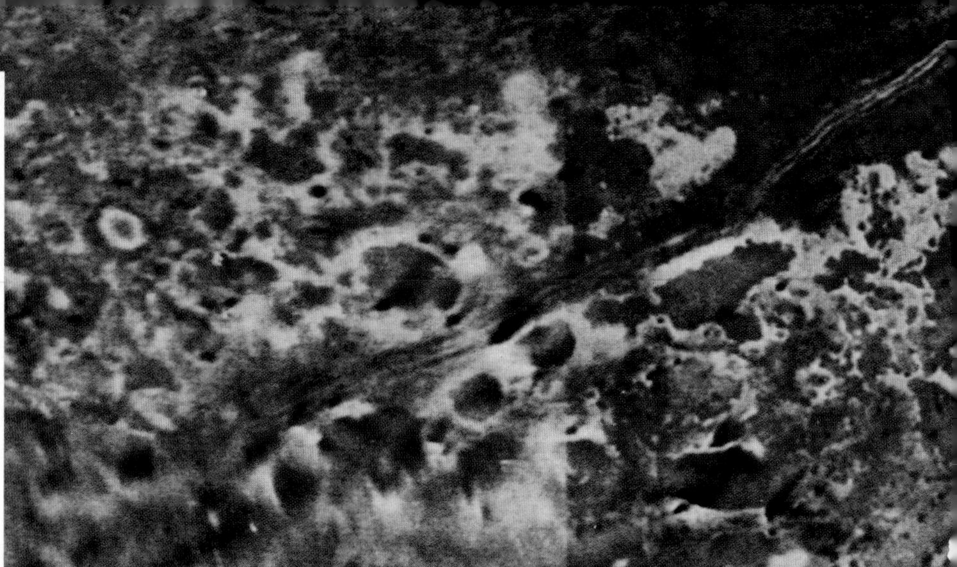

Near the end of its planetary odyssey, almost three billion miles from Earth, Voyager 2 skimmed by Neptune's largest moon, Triton, in August 1989. The coldest body in the solar system, with a surface temperature of -391° F., Triton may have once been a planet, captured by Neptune's gravity.

from 0 for black to 255 for white, a number that requires eight bits (a bit is a single digit of binary code) to transmit. Thus each image required more than five million bits to transmit—nearly a four-minute job for Voyager 2's system, its capacity diminished by the vast distance to Earth. Inventive engineers developed a technique that compressed the image data by comparing the brightness of adjacent pixels rather than assigning each an absolute value. Thus the average pixel could be described with just three bits, and Voyager 2 was able to send home far more pictures—6,000 from Uranus and its moons, 6,700 from the Neptunian system.

While Voyager skimmed by Neptune, the spacecraft's radio transmitter broadcast the momentous event at a power of 30 watts, about the same as a dim light bulb. By the time its signal reached Earth—a four-hour trip at the speed of light—it had weakened to just one-billionth of the power required to run a digital watch. A world-spanning system of antennas, NASA's Deep Space Network (DSN) plucked the feeble signal from the ether and relayed it, by communications satellite and land lines, to the California processing center where the digitized data was translated into images and scientific readings. Amplification of the signal was performed by a maser—an acronym that stands for Microwave Amplification by the Stimulated Emission of Radiation—which functions much like a laser. Instead of

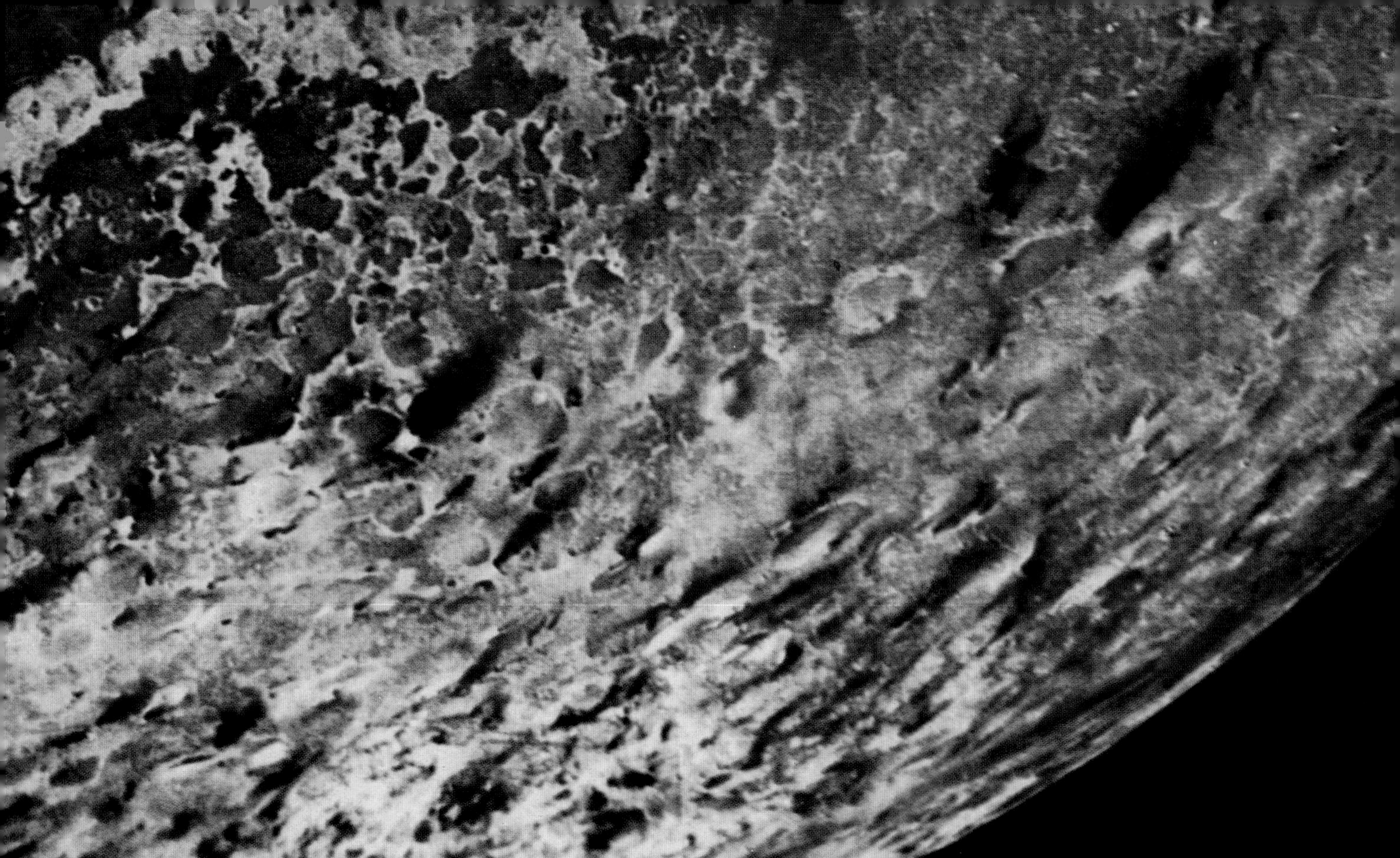

light amplication, however, a maser amplifies microwave energy. The DSN consists of three stations: Goldstone, California; Madrid, Spain; and Canberra, Australia, locations that allowed almost constant contact with the Voyagers regardless of the Earth's rotation. Each station boasts one mammoth 230-foot dish and several smaller dishes. To ensure reception of the faint transmissions from Neptune, however, the Goldstone array was augmented with the 27 antennas of the Very Large Array in New Mexico. Electronically linked to the DSN antennas, the VLA improved the signal-gathering capacity by a factor of three.

On their way to eternity after their final planetary encounters, the Voyagers will keep sending back information about their surroundings for decades. Astronomers estimate that in about 2012 Voyager 2 will leave the heliosphere, the part of space defined by the solar wind and its magnetic field. From that time on, the probe will explore interstellar space for several years, until its radioactive power generator finally becomes too weak to run its instruments and radio transmitter. The hydrazine fuel on Voyager 2—only 420 pounds' worth at takeoff—is expected to last until about 2030. The spacecraft's monumental journey of exploration will continue unreported, but by then another generation of incredible machines will be probing the solar system, to bolster the archive of celestial discovery.

THE HUMAN ADVENTURE

Gurgling and hissing like a sleeping dragon, the white and orange rocket assembly gleams in the predawn light, gently exhaling wisps of steam. Preflight checks are complete. Commander, pilot and crew lie back, strapped into their seats, staring straight up, waiting.

Suddenly, the rocket wakes with a roar, main engines straining to lift 4.5 million pounds. Seconds later, twin boosters breathe fire and the bolts leashing the rocket explode. Snorting twin flames 600 feet behind it, the world's first true aerospace vehicle, America's space shuttle, rises into the sky. One minute later, acceleration peaks and treble gravity presses the crew into their seats. Two minutes into the flight, when the pressure and noise seem never ending, the crackling crescendo decreases slightly, vibration abates, and the ride smoothes out. The burned-out boosters have separated to parachute back to the Atlantic, leaving the three main engines to carry the shuttle into orbit.

Now the shuddering, flame-breathing rocket is metamorphosing rapidly into a spaceship. Approaching 11,000 miles per hour and 80 miles high, the shuttle leaves the atmosphere behind; bright blue sky fades to black. As the main engines sip the last fuel and cut off, the orbiter discards the empty external tank, which disintegrates in the atmosphere. With the abrupt drop in acceleration, crew members lurch forward in their seats. Pencils and clipboards float free. Eight minutes away from the launchpad at Florida's Kennedy Space Center, the orbiter is already riding in an elliptical orbit 130 miles high. Two quick nudges from orbital engines will soon provide the final push into a stable, circular orbit.

Despite its breathtaking acceleration and 17,500-mile-per-hour cruising speed, the space shuttle is more like a truck than a sports car. Its tacked-together look—a stubby-winged, reusable orbiter riding an external tank and two boosters—and its 60-foot-long payload bay announce the vehicle's utilitarian nature.

The shuttle differs from early rockets much as a modern 18-wheeler—with all the comforts of home—differs from a spine-jarring, 1920s flatbed. Going into space for shuttle crew members of the 1980s and '90s means riding in a roomy cockpit

Streaming 600-foot-long flames from its two reusable solid rocket motors, space shuttle Atlantis *streaks into the Florida sky shortly after takeoff from Cape Canaveral.*

USA

instead of a cramped capsule. They orbit in shirt sleeves rather than spacesuits. And they come to the space program from laboratories and universities, not just from the cockpits of fighter planes.

FROM CAPSULE TO COCKPIT

America nearly sent its first official astronaut aloft in a fighter plane descendant. In the 1950s and 1960s, experimental X-15 rocket planes carried some pilots higher than 50 miles, earning them unofficial astronaut status. The Boeing X-20 Dyna-Soar—a shuttle-like, rocket-launched, reusable space plane destined for orbit—reached the mock-up stage. But the October 4, 1957 launch of Earth's first artificial satellite, the Soviet Sputnik, rang an alarm of national pride and turned the sedate space program into a space race. Three-and-a-half years later, President John F. Kennedy abandoned long-term value for immediate results in an all-out effort to put an American on the Moon. With the powerful X-20 launch rockets still on the drawing boards, the Dyna-Soar became extinct before it could fly, although the X-20 would later resurface in modified forms as Titan military and commercial rockets.

The Soviets had adopted an alternative approach—sending a cosmonaut aloft in a one-shot capsule—and NASA followed suit, shoehorning astronauts into spaces barely larger than their contour couches. Early capsules replaced warheads atop ready-to-fly, modified military missiles. After a single flight, the discarded capsule was useful only to decorate a museum. But despite discomfort and high cost, disposable capsules put the first man in space—Soviet Air Force Major Yuri Gagarin in his spherical Vostok 1 on April 12, 1961. Only weeks later, a similar rocket launched the first American into space.

On May 5, 1961, American astronaut Alan B. Shepard briefly entered space on a suborbital flight, launching the manned phase of the Mercury program. (Previous Mercuries had sent primates into space.) Shepard's bell-shaped Freedom 7 capsule, though more sophisticated than Vostok, was still a far cry from today's space shuttle. Shepard peered through a periscope instead of a window. Worse, he had no toilet. The flight was scheduled to last only 15 minutes, but planners had not planned on four hours of pre-launch delays. A discomfited Shepard finally had to urinate in his pressure suit. Minutes later, America's manned space program began as Shepard radioed "I have lift off, the clock is started." Two months later another suborbital flight was ridden by Virgil "Gus" Grissom. And within a year of Shepard's soggy hop, John H. Glenn whirled three times around the world in less than five hours, the first of four American astronauts to orbit.

Although the Mercury program proved that humans could survive space and control their capsules to some extent, it was time for the United States to take another step toward the Moon. That trip would require hefting a huge payload. Furthermore, moonbound astronauts must maneuver their capsules, find and dock with other spacecraft, stay in space for weeks at a time and leave the craft to walk on the Moon. NASA's Gemini program began to attack each of these goals with a two-man craft. Still lacking a toilet—after Shepard's uncomfortable incident, all the pre-shuttle astronauts used condom-like urine collectors and plastic bags—the all-new Gemini came complete with windows, ejection seats, reentry control and a computer guidance system. Each advance added weight, however, and Gemini

A SHOW OF CRAFT

Four spacecraft have dominated the U.S. manned space program during its first 30 years. On May 5, 1961, the Mercury-Redstone rocket (opposite left) *launched Alan Shepard, the first American in space, on his 15-minute flight. In the ensuing two years, Project Mercury took five more men into space, concluding with a 22-orbit, 34-hour mission by Gordon Cooper in May 1963. Next came Gemini, a two-man craft that rocketed 10 crews into orbit before the end of 1965. Gemini missions included orbital docking and rendezvous, spacewalks and long-duration flights that paved the way for the Apollo program, which took 12 men to the Moon's surface between 1969 and 1972. They rode the most powerful rocket of its time—the 36-story-tall Saturn V rocket, with five massive F-1 engines that generated the power of 85 Hoover Dams. Before Apollo drew to a close, America had committed itself to the next stage of its manned space program—the space shuttle. When it took to the skies for the first time in April 1981, the shuttle ushered in a new era. For the first time, a reusable rocket carried people into space.*

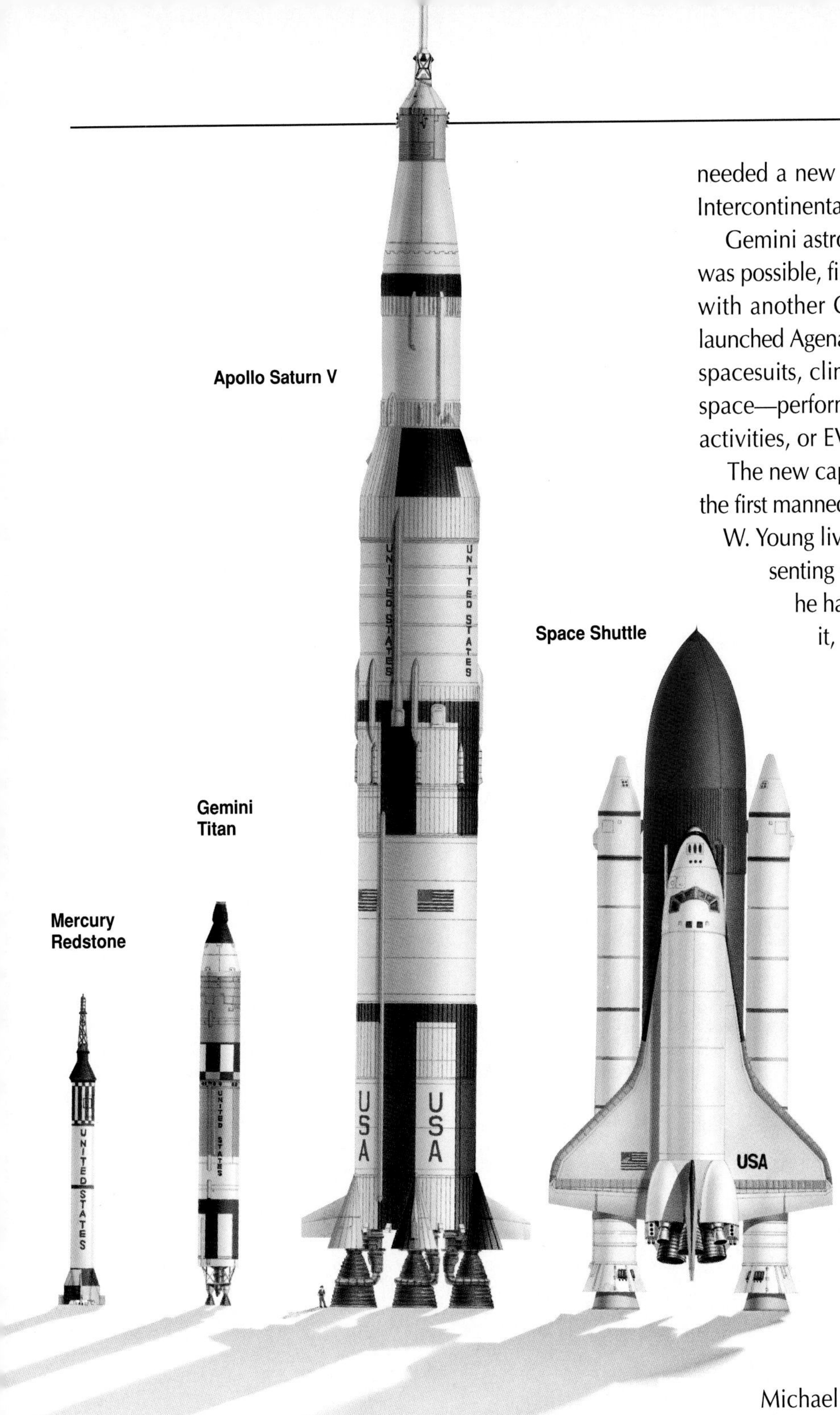
Apollo Saturn V
Space Shuttle
Gemini
Titan
Mercury
Redstone

needed a new launcher, the Titan II second-generation Intercontinental Ballistic Missile (ICBM).

Gemini astronauts proved that a rendezvous in space was possible, first with a small battery-powered pod, later with another Gemini, and still later with a separately launched Agena docking target. Furthermore, they donned spacesuits, climbed out of their capsules and floated in space—performing, in NASA's parlance, extravehicular activities, or EVAs.

The new capsules also afforded room for whimsy. On the first manned mission, Gemini 3, novice astronaut John W. Young livened up the nearly five-hour flight by presenting Gus Grissom with a corned-beef sandwich he had smuggled aboard. Space watchers loved it, but NASA was not amused.

Nine more Gemini flights followed, each mission taking one more step toward Apollo and the Moon. Gemini finished with a flourish—Edwin "Buzz" Aldrin's five-and-a-half hours of EVAs during a four-day mission ending on November 15, 1966. With weeks in space, EVAs and docking all realities, NASA had leapfrogged the Soviet space effort. The Apollo program came next, carrying more men and more weight, and riding the largest rocket of its time, a Saturn V. One of the Apollo flights would carry the first men to the surface of the Moon and back *(page 100)*.

Apollo 11's Neil A. Armstrong and Buzz Aldrin—chosen only because their turn on the rotation schedule happened to coincide with the historic flight—would walk the lunar surface first after descending from orbit around the Moon in *Eagle*, their lunar module. Michael Collins drew the assignment to remain in orbit aboard the command module, *Columbia. Eagle* could leave the surface of the Moon, but could never return to Earth, so Collins sweated out the Moon walk hours, terrified of having to return to Earth without his companions. Only when he saw the golden *Eagle* approaching his orbiting craft did he believe the three would pull it off. Eight years after Alan Shepard's 15-minute hop into space, two Americans had hopped on the Moon, dramatically besting the Soviets.

One of the most lasting results of Apollo transcended national pride. The magnificent photographs of the vibrant blue-and-white globe rising over the edge of the desolate Moon and in-flight photos of the "whole Earth" floating alone in black space almost instantly became international icons of global unity. But as magnificent as the Moon landing was, the ensuing five Apollo lunar missions—including Apollo 16, the fourth space flight of future shuttle commander John Young—generated diminishing public excitement. And the $25-billion ticket to the Moon suddenly seemed exorbitant. A gleaming white, 6-million-pound, 363-foot-tall rocket left Earth and a gray, charred, useless 12-foot command module returned. America could no longer afford throw-away spacecraft.

A new presidential exhortation—this time to save money—forced NASA back to the reusable space plane concept it had abandoned 20 years before. President Richard M. Nixon called for "a program to take the astronomical costs out of astronautics." NASA responded ambitiously. They envisioned a two-part vehicle that would take off like a rocket, orbit like a space capsule and land like a fighter plane. Both the launcher and the orbiter would fly again and again. Ground crews would make an orbiter flight-ready within two weeks of landing. In orbit, the vehicle would provide an experimental space platform for physicians, scientists and senators. And most important, the Space Transportation System, or STS, would deliver cargo to space at a tiny fraction of the previous cost per pound; the shuttle would pay for itself.

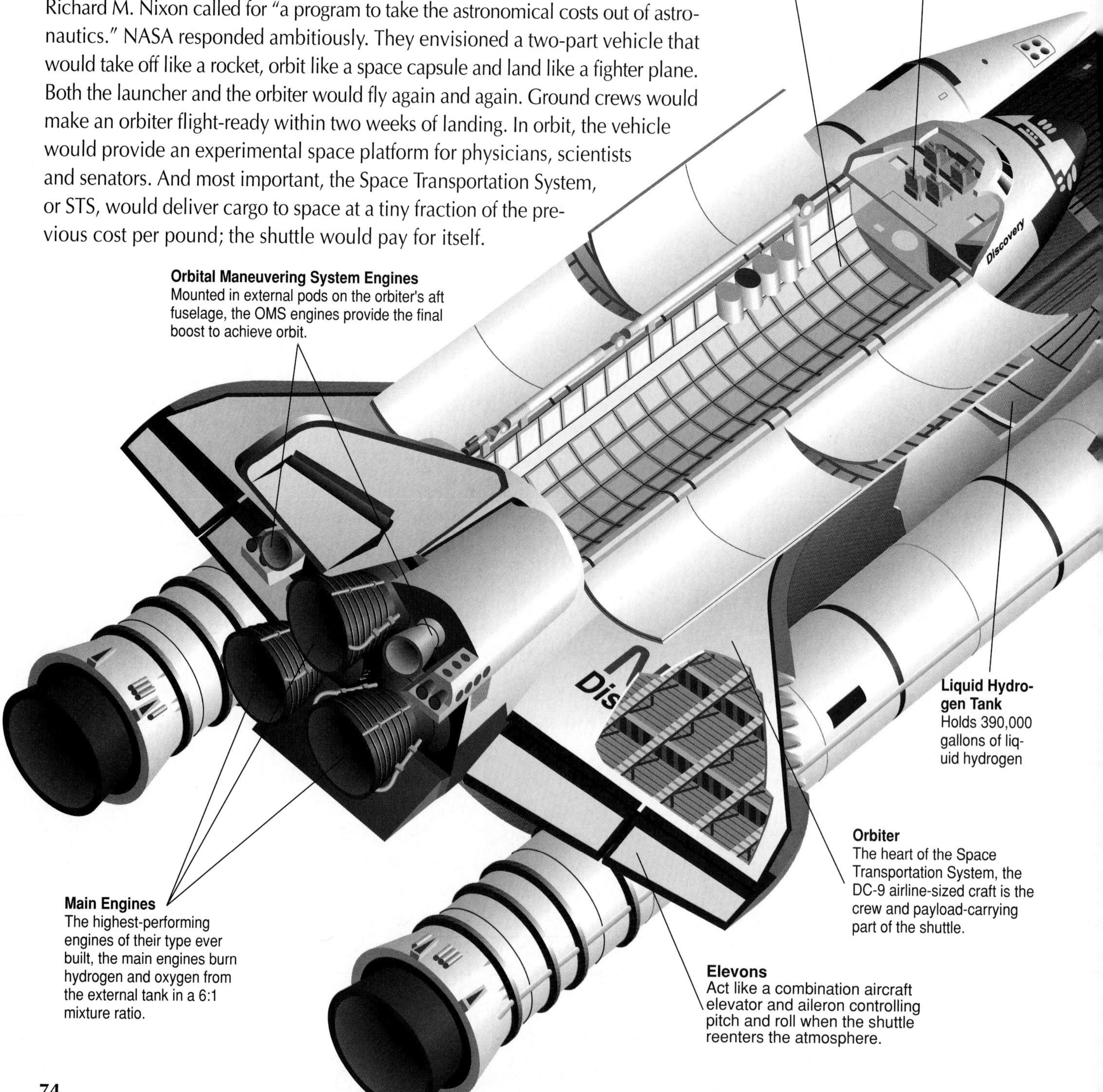

Flight Deck
Contains the flight controls and crew stations for launch orbit and landing; a middeck level underneath provides sleeping and eating accommodation.
Cargo Bay
A 60-by-15-foot area that stores the payloads the shuttle launches into orbit.
Orbital Maneuvering System Engines
Mounted in external pods on the orbiter's aft fuselage, the OMS engines provide the final boost to achieve orbit.
Discovery
Liquid Hydrogen Tank
Holds 390,000 gallons of liquid hydrogen
Orbiter
The heart of the Space Transportation System, the DC-9 airline-sized craft is the crew and payload-carrying part of the shuttle.
Main Engines
The highest-performing engines of their type ever built, the main engines burn hydrogen and oxygen from the external tank in a 6:1 mixture ratio.
Elevons
Act like a combination aircraft elevator and aileron controlling pitch and roll when the shuttle reenters the atmosphere.

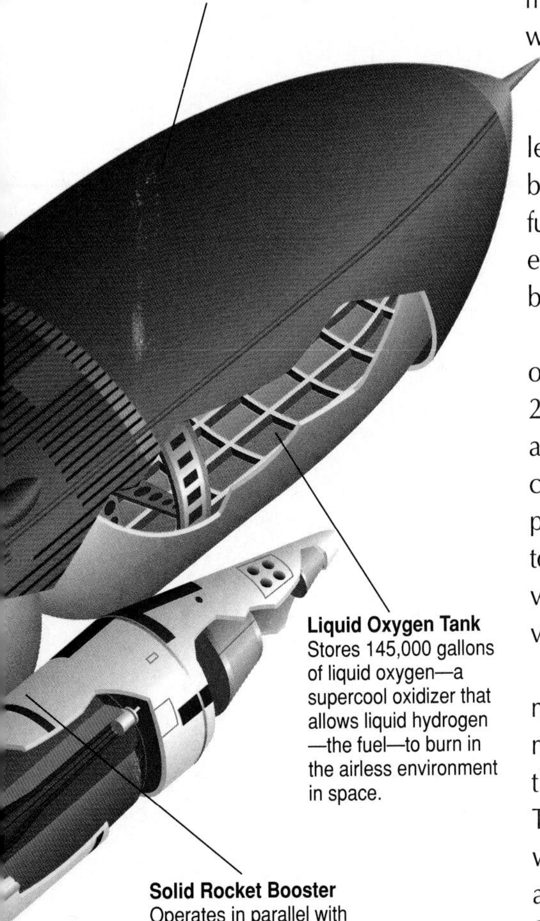
External Fuel Tank
The only major non-reusable part of the shuttle, the external tank provides the fuel and oxidizer for the orbiter's main engines.
Liquid Oxygen Tank
Stores 145,000 gallons of liquid oxygen—a supercool oxidizer that allows liquid hydrogen —the fuel—to burn in the airless environment in space.
Solid Rocket Booster
Operates in parallel with the main engines for the first two minutes after liftoff, providing the bulk of the initial thrust.

ANATOMY OF A SHUTTLE

The first reusable spacecraft—the American shuttle—consists of an orbiter with three main engines fueled by a giant external tank. Two solid rocket boosters provide additional power to help propel the shuttle into orbit.

A MACHINE'S MACHINE

The promise to become self-supporting notwithstanding, this $14-billion order loomed a little too tall for the American public. No longer in a space-spending mood, Congress cut the shuttle budget to one-fifth of Apollo's. The deluxe 18-wheeler became a cut-price work truck, its design compromised by having both to deliver satellites and to serve as a mini-space station.

Even in its stripped-down version, the shuttle presented engineers with challenges adding up to the world's most complex spacecraft. The orbiter would become the world's fastest winged craft and the boosters would be the first solid fuel rockets to lift humans, aided by three super-efficient main engines. To cut costs, engineers first discarded total reusability. The delta-winged orbiter is reusable, the boosters partly so. The external liquid fuel tank remains disposable *(page 76)*.

A complete shuttle weighs in at 2,250 tons ready to launch. The 122-foot orbiter—including its 49 engines, 23 antennas, 5 computers, up to 5 satellites and 2 to 7 people—accounts for more than 100 tons. To provide a safe haven for orbiter astronauts, it was necessary to construct a spaceship within a spaceship. The crew cabin, with its breathing mixture similar to earthly air (80 percent nitrogen, 20 percent oxygen), regulated temperature and sea level pressure, allows astronauts to orbit in socks, slacks and shirt sleeves. This welded-aluminum, pressure-tight vessel is attached inside the orbiter at only four points, isolating the crew from vacuum and temperatures ranging from -250° F. in the dark to +250° in the sun.

The flight deck fills the top floor of the three-story crew cabin. Mission commander—in charge of the flight—and pilot sit in a forward flight-deck cockpit, much more complicated than a jetliner's. Unlike the crews in early capsules, shuttle astronauts watch the Earth rotate beneath them through eight large windows. These triple pane, aluminosilicate and fused silica windows, the thickest viewing windows ever made for a spacecraft, withstand pressure and heat shock while affording crystal clear views, and reflect infrared (heat) rays with high efficiency. Six face forward, two are fitted into the ceiling and two more allow views of the payload bay from a crescent-shaped crew station behind the cockpit.

A quick float through the flight-deck floor—bypassing the ladder, which is rendered superfluous in zero gravity—brings an astronaut to the middeck. Sleeping arrangements, personal lockers, a space toilet, storage, electronics bays and a compact galley all fit into the 13-by-10-foot middeck. With the six quick-disconnect seats folded and stored, and with walls and ceiling made useful, the 130-square-foot room becomes a 995-cubic-foot living space. An airlock leads from the back of the middeck to the payload bay, the orbiter's truck bed, where several satellites or single cargoes as large as Spacelab fill the 60-by-15-foot area. This space truck can carry 65,000 pounds outbound, but only 32,000 pounds on the return trip.

In orbit, with the empty external tank long gone and the three main engines quiescent, the smaller Orbital Maneuvering System (OMS) and tiny Reaction Control System (RCS) engines take over. Both burn hydrazine and nitrogen tetroxide liquid propellants, and can share fuel in emergencies. Two large pods, lying above the main engines on each side of the tail, house one OMS engine each and the aft RCS engines.

OMS engines, "the most smoothly running pieces of machinery I've ever been around," according to astronaut Joseph P. Allen, ease the orbiter forward. By gim-

Power to Burn

Propelling a 4.5-million-pound spacecraft from liftoff to a velocity of more than 17,000 miles per hour in less than 10 minutes demands an awesome powerplant. The shuttle orbiter itself boasts three main engines, which are mounted in a triangular pattern on the aft end of the fuselage. Generating more than 37 million horsepower, they are the most efficient liquid-fueled engines ever built. The propellants are burned partially at high pressure and low temperature in a preburner, then burned completely at high temperature and high pressure in the main engine's combustion chamber. The result is a burn that is 99 percent pure—and a phenomenally weight-efficient design. The pumps that supply the combustion chamber with fuel weigh little more than a truck engine, yet they are capable of developing 75,000 horsepower.

Fed by two 17-inch-diameter feedlines, the shuttle main engines gulp 1,035 gallons of fuel every second from the gargantuan external tank. The 154-foot-long reservoir is actually two storage tanks in one. The larger tank contains the fuel—liquid hydrogen; the smaller one, at the forward end of the external tank, holds liquid oxygen, an oxidant that allows the propellant to burn in the airless environment of space. The two are connected by a 22.5-foot-long intertank.

To help keep the fuels properly chilled (liquid hydrogen is stored at -423° F.) the external tank is coated with inch-thick spray-on insulation. The polyurethane-like foam also protects the tank from the 2,000° heat experienced during the launch. In addition to feeding the shuttle's main engines, the external tank serves as the structural backbone for the shuttle during liftoff, holding the orbiter and two separate rockets in position. It

Each shuttle main engine (above) *can be throttled to provide anywhere from 320,000 to 512,000 pounds of thrust. The engines can also be gimballed—or deflected—up to 10.5° to help steer the shuttle during liftoff. A digital controller automatically monitors engine conditions and makes necessary corrections 50 times every second.*

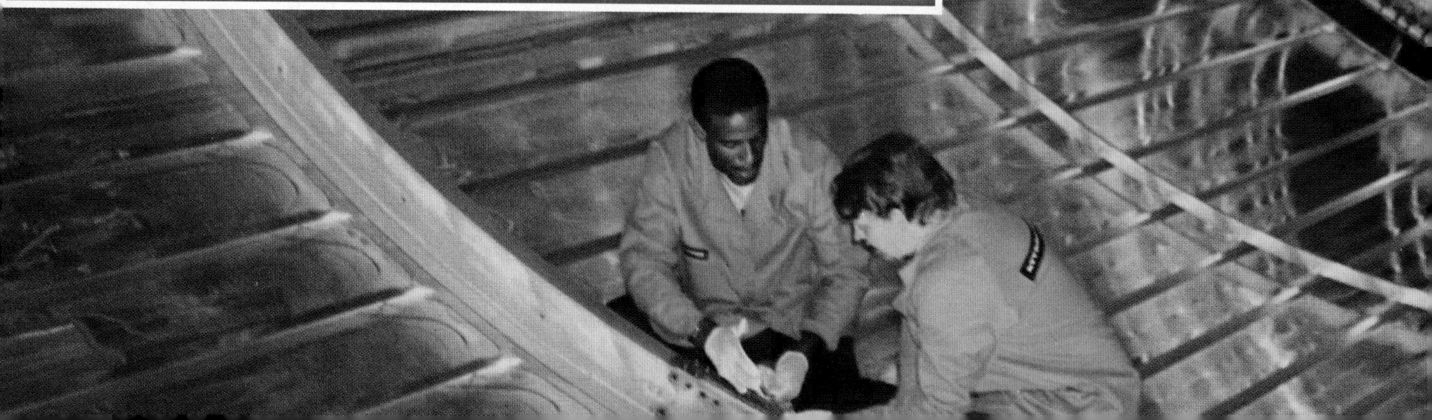

Crouching inside the external tank's hydrogen fuel tank, two workers are dwarfed by its cavernous size.

An empty external tank emerges from the giant assembly plant in New Orleans where it is constructed. Built of aluminum and steel alloys, the tank holds 145,000 gallons of liquid oxygen and 390,000 gallons of liquid hydrogen. The spike-like nose cap serves as a lightning rod.

is also the only major part of the shuttle that cannot be reused. Jettisoned eight minutes into the flight, the tank tumbles back toward Earth from an altitude of 69 nautical miles and burns up in the atmosphere over either the Indian or Pacific Ocean, depending on the trajectory of the launch.

Only a third of the power at liftoff comes from the three main engines. The rest is supplied by two strap-on solid rocket boosters, the most powerful of their type ever built. The boosters consist of four sections each, called casting segments, filled with aluminum, ammonium perchlorate and a polymer that binds the substance together. The viscous mix is poured around a removable core or mandrel. Cured by heat, the mixture forms a rubber-like mass called a grain. The core is then removed, leaving behind a geometrical pattern that controls the burn rate of the fuel. The 11-point star pattern used in the uppermost of the four segments, for example, yields the bulk of its thrust when the shuttle needs it the most—during the first few second after liftoff—by exposing more surface area at ignition. The segments are shipped by rail to Cape Kennedy, where they are stacked and attached to the external tank.

Two minutes after liftoff, each booster (often called the solid rocket motor) has consumed its 1.1 million pounds of propellant, and a series of eight separation motors disengages it from the external tank. A 54-foot-diameter drogue parachute pops out to stabilize the booster and begin its deceleration; two 136-foot main chutes then complete the job. The booster lands at 55 miles per hour in the Atlantic Ocean five minutes after separation. Divers attach towlines and the spent booster is dragged back to land, where it is disassembled, flushed out with high-pressure water hoses, tested and readied for another launch. Each booster is designed to be reused 19 times.

A 149-foot-long solid rocket booster undergoes testing in the desert at Promontory, Utah. Test firings are conducted at a bay that is capable of simulating the stresses that occur during a shuttle launch.

ORTON THIOKOL INC

Workers attach a fin to the 11-point mandrel that will be inserted into the forward segment of the solid rocket booster. A viscous fuel mixture then is poured around the removable core; later, after the mixture cures, the mandrel is removed, leaving behind an 11-pointed pattern that creates maximum power during the first few seconds after ignition.

After boosting the shuttle for the first two minutes of its flight, the solid rocket motors descend by parachute and fall into the Atlantic Ocean. Divers plug the nozzles, pump the empty motors full of air and then attach towlines to drag them back to shore, where they will be overhauled and prepared for another flight.

balling—or swiveling—the engines, a commander can steer the orbiter precisely. OMS burns slide the ship into orbit, then come into play for changes in orbit and for rendezvous maneuvers. With the ship flipped tail forward to prepare for reentering the atmosphere, these thrusters also act as brakes, initiating the start of the orbiter's return to Earth.

The prospect of a fiery dive through Earth's atmosphere created unprecedented design challenges. At 17,500 miles per hour, air friction heats parts of the orbiter's skin to nearly 3,000° F.—enough to melt steel, much less the aluminum that covers the orbiter. Past spacecraft designers had solved the problem with heavy heat shields that ablated during reentry to carry heat away. Shuttle engineers created several lightweight, reusable insulating materials to protect the orbiter. Nearly 2,300 light, flexible quilts of silica felt and glass cloth insulate less critical upper parts. Almost 25,000 rigid insulation tiles protect the orbiter's underside. Especially critical areas bear caps and panels made of reinforced carbon fiber.

Each of the orbiter's tiles begins life as a handful of common sand. Refined into pure silica fibers and pressed into a mold, they go into the world's largest microwave oven to dry before being baked. The 6-inch-square, 5-inch-thick tiles come out of the 2,300° oven cool enough on the edges to hold with bare hands while their centers still glow red. After baking, each tile is ground to fit its unique position on the orbiter's curved skin. A final borosilicate glass coating colors most of the tiles black. A few tiles, used in less critical areas, receive a white coating. Then dozens of technicians spend thousands of hours hand-gluing tiles to the orbiter using a silicone adhesive and nylon felt pads. But this handwork does not come cheaply. A single installed tile can cost $2,000.

Parts of the orbiter that meet the atmosphere head on—the nose and leading edges of wings—require even more protection. A material called reinforced carbon-carbon survives even higher temperatures than the tiles do. Engineers soak carbon-fiber cloth in resin and layer it in a process similar to that used in building a fiberglass boat. Then the hardened composite nose cap and wing panels are baked, reducing the resin itself to carbon. A coating designed to resist oxidation completes carbon-carbon.

Though the shuttle rarely loses tiles, 100 or so are damaged during takeoff and landing. Replacements are made by the orbiter's builder, Rockwell of California, by inserting plastic foam into a cast of the removed tiles or by cutting them, using a computer-controlled machine. All tiles are glued in place, but some are glued to panels that are then bolted to the orbiter. These removable panels provide access to internal components. A special laser tool measures the minute gap between the tiles. In addition to these replaced tiles, a further 500 to 1,000 may require repairs. Dents and dings are drilled out, filled with paste and sanded smooth.

During reentry the Orbital Maneuvering System engines are aided by the smaller RCS rockets, 44 in all, which accelerate and rotate the orbiter—a function they also perform in orbit. The six tiny vernier jets—two at the nose and four in the

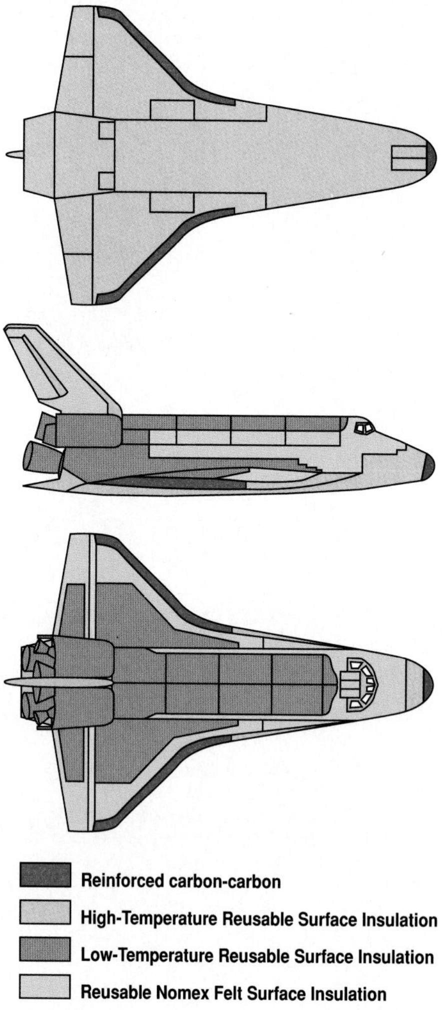
Reinforced carbon-carbon
High-Temperature Reusable Surface Insulation
Low-Temperature Reusable Surface Insulation
Reusable Nomex Felt Surface Insulation

HEAT RELIEF

To protect the shuttle from the searing heat of reentry, engineers designed a special system of tiles and blankets.

A worker at the Rockwell plant in Palmdale, California, attaches one of the heat-resistant tiles to the lower mid-fuselage of the shuttle's orbiter. Most of the gaps between the tiles are left open, though some—around the nosecap and in areas where the heat buildup is most intense during reentry—are filled with ceramic fabric gap fillers.

OMS pods—fine-tune attitude, the position in space. Like the OMS engines, verniers seem smooth and silent. Not so the fore and aft primary RCS thrusters, which sound and feel, says Allen, "like cannons and mortars firing." With a twist and turn of a hand controller, the commander can fire RCS thrusters to rotate the ship around any of its three axes, or accelerate in any direction.

The shuttle hand controller resembles a traditional airplane joystick. But on the orbiter, more than 17,000 pounds of wiring and electronics, called avionics, replace traditional mechanical links. This nervous system, housed in six bays in the middeck and aft fuselage, relays decisions made by the orbiter's computer.

Computer avionics automatically control launch, orbital insertion, deorbit maneuvers and the vehicle's fiery plunge through the atmosphere. Furthermore, the computers interpret hand controller movements, firing rockets in combination or actuating flaps and rudder during pilot-guided maneuvers such as docking and landing. The computer keeps track of the ship's position in space by combining data from an inertial measurement sensor—gyroscopes installed at right angles to each other that measure attitude changes around three axes—and a star tracker that locks onto certain key stars in daylight as well as darkness.

With computers in control most of the time and serving as a link to relay signals from flight-deck control the rest of the time, shuttle designers took the old saying "two heads are better than one" and multiplied it. Four IBM AP-101 computers—the latest of a family of machines flight-tested in combat aircraft—run the orbiter's systems during critical flight phases, all using the same custom-designed program. Though this may seem redundant, the four computers constantly compare decisions in order to avoid computer error. If one computer's results are out in left field, the other three cut it out of the loop. In the unlikely

CCCP

SHUTTLE, TOO?

The U.S.S.R.'s version of the shuttle, known as Buran, made its debut in November 1988, more than eight years after its U.S. cousin. Buran—Russian for snowstorm—rode into orbit on the back of an Energiya booster, with four strap-on boosters. After circling the world twice, the Soviet shuttle executed a flawless landing—on autopilot. Unlike the U.S. shuttle, the Russian counterpart can fly crewless. Still, it has hardly become a regular space express. By the end of 1990, Buran had but one complete flight under its belt.

Although Buran eventually may fulfill its function of returning cargo from Mir or helping build the still tentative Mir 2, some Western observers describe its future as questionable. Its expensive design has been compared to the extravagant projects of the Czars. Other design concepts in aerospace planes are being investigated, including a small air-launched shuttle.

USA

The giant crawler that transports the shuttle to the launchpad demands an 8-foot-thick roadbed to support the 17-million-pound weight of shuttle, crawler and launchpad. Shells fill the bottom of the bed to a depth of three feet; then comes two-and-a-half feet of limestone and a foot of asphalt. Eight inches of river rock tops it all off.

event that two, or even three, computers crash, one of these quadruplets can run the orbiter alone. And if all four break down, if they vote in a tie or if the primary flight software fails, yet another computer, running different software, takes over.

TO THE PAD

The first leg of the orbiter's trip into space begins on the back of a modified Boeing 747. Purchased used in 1970, then souped up and refitted to bear the extra loads of a piggyback orbiter, the plane carries the orbiter from its landing field—the dry lake bed of Edwards Air Force Base in California—to Kennedy Space Center to be reoutfitted and overhauled for its next flight. A special hoist lifts the orbiter horizontally so the carrier aircraft can roll under it. The orbiter is carried using the same three support points that attach it to the external tank.

An orbiter newly returned to Kennedy Space Center spends time in two gigantic service buildings before it travels to the launchpad again. In the 195-foot-high

Orbiter Processing Facility, an army of technicians, engineers and inspectors makes minor repairs, gives the orbiter a brake job, and reconfigures the payload bay for the next mission. Some large payloads, such as Spacelab *(page 115)*, may be installed at this time. While the orbiter gets spruced up for its next flight, the other shuttle components await final assembly in the Vehicle Assembly Building.

Built for the Apollo program, this gargantuan building towers 525 feet high and covers 8 acres. The VAB is so large, in fact, that when it was first used, the hot, humid air inside the building used to condense and form rain clouds when it came in contact with incoming cool air. (NASA engineers solved the problem by providing additional ceiling insulation and better venting.) Technicians can assemble two shuttles piece by piece in their normal vertical position—with room for the shuttle's mobile launch platform underneath and a hoist above. First, the recycled solid rocket boosters take shape, section by section, until they tower 149 feet high. Bolted to the mobile launch platform, they support the shuttle like legs. Next, the new external tank is fitted on to the boosters, forming the shuttle's backbone. And last, technicians flip the orbiter upright, hoist it high in the air, and lower it gently to its mounting struts on the external tank. Tolerances are stringent; the VAB's designers never imagined when they were creating a building for the Apollo V moon rocket that it would one day play home to a winged spacecraft. The crane operator has only an inch or two to play with on either side of the shuttle's 78-foot wingspan. Lining up the orbiter to the external tank and boosters demands a hair breadth's accuracy of less than 1/100 of an inch. At the end of the 25-hour mating process, during which two crane operators are assisted by an emergency stop operator and various observers, a complete shuttle stands ready in the VAB. But it takes months—not the two weeks NASA once predicted.

Another week of tests follows before the shuttle begins its four-mile trip to the launchpad. Then, a machine resembling a cross between a brontosaurus and a Caterpillar tractor backs under the mobile launch platform. Shrugging its four shoulders, it jacks eleven million pounds of platform and shuttle six feet up, and sets off—at a stately one mile per hour—toward the launchpad, grinding along a gravel road as wide as an eight-lane freeway and snorting exhaust through mufflers the size of Volkswagens.

If the huge buildings dotting the Kennedy Space Center landscape seem fantastic, NASA's two crawlers, the world's largest and slowest vehicles, at least fit the scenery. The design was originally inspired by strip-mining power shovels and features four double-tracked trucks supporting an adjustable platform the size of a baseball diamond. The crawler, weighing in empty at 6 million pounds, has 456 tractor cleats—each one tipping the scales at a ton. Twenty-inch hydraulic jacks at each corner lift and level the platform. Powered by four diesel engines, totalling 7,630 horsepower, this gigantic gas guzzler gets only about 30 feet per gallon.

Under the crushing weight of the loaded crawler, the roadbed's top layer of river rock is reduced to sand, which provides extra traction and stability.

As it nears the launchpad, the crawler suddenly proves how delicate it can be with its laser docking system making pinpoint parking possible. Then, after depositing the shuttle, the monster heads flat out for the garage—at two miles per hour. (Despite its snail's pace, the crawler comes equipped with seatbelts.) Two Crawler-Transporters have shared the chore of delivering the shuttle to its launchpad for every launch since the Apollo program's inauguration. The odometer on one of the crawler's recently passed the 1,000-mile marker.

Once installed on its pedestals in the center of the launchpad, the six-inch-thick steel launch platform comes into its own as an integral part of the pad. Together the two components must withstand the full force of five rocket motors gushing metal-melting flames and roaring loud enough to shake the shuttle apart. Openings for each of the two solid rocket boosters and one for the main engines allow flames to escape. Underneath the platform, the launchpad channels flames into a horizontal trench nearly 500 feet long, so they cannot bounce back and destroy the shuttle. To cut the dangerous sonic vibrations and pressure blowback, a sound-dampening system dumps up to 900,000 gallons of water per minute into the trench during the few seconds surrounding liftoff.

4

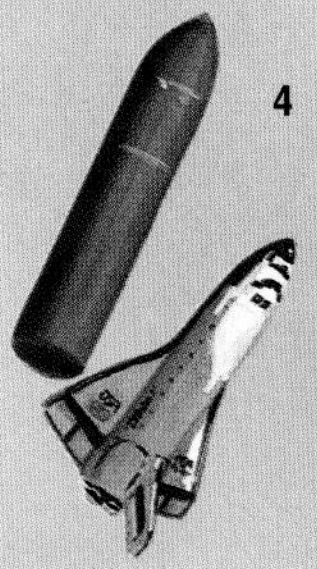

5

6

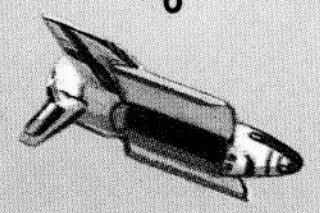

3

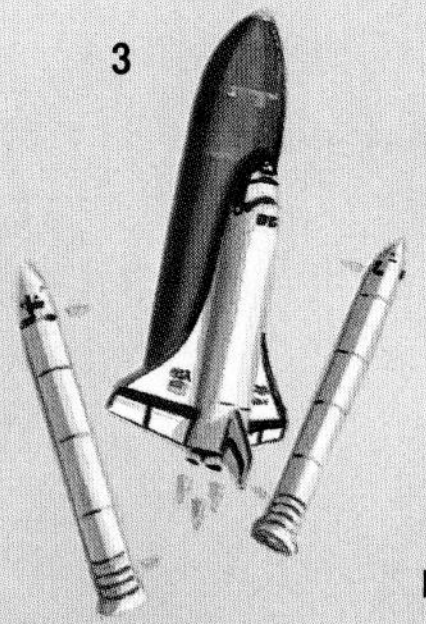

To one side of the pad, a 265-foot-tall fixed service tower provides access to the orbiter without obstructing its launch. Three hinged access arms bridge the gap between the tower elevator and the shuttle. A huge hinged, environmentally controlled room can swing a payload up to the orbiter, allowing clean installation. Driven by a pair of rail-riding trucks on the pad surface, this 130-foot-tall structure provides access to the orbiter's payload bay at 5 levels. Should a fast exit be required just before launch, an escape system provides 7 slide wires, each 1,200 feet long and each guiding a dangling gondola from the fixed tower to ground-level safety bunkers. Each basket can carry 4 technicians or astronauts to safety in a mere 35 seconds.

2

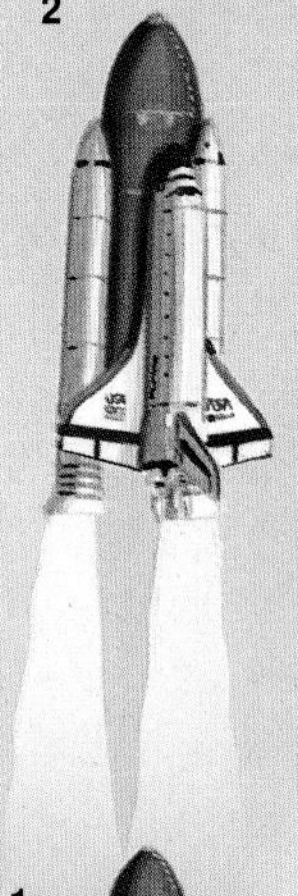

Barring launchpad emergencies, the technicians close the hatch and head for safety three miles away, leaving the astronauts utterly alone to face the start of a voyage fewer than 300 humans have ever undertaken.

1

LEAVING EARTH

By the time the launch countdown reaches T -8 seconds—just a breath-hold before liftoff—the astronauts have been sitting in the cabin in their fire-resistant flight suits for three hours. Commander, pilot and mission specialists have completed a long series of preflight checks, stowed their pencils and procedure manuals and lowered their helmet visors. The service bridges have swung back. A rocket ship stands poised to launch humans into orbit.

LIFTOFF TO TOUCHDOWN

1. With three main engines firing and two solid rocket motors ignited, the shuttle takes off.

2. One minute after liftoff, the shuttle passes through a brief period of maximum aerodynamic stress knows as Max-Q.

3. Two minutes into the flight, the solid rocket boosters are jettisoned.

4. Sixty-nine miles above the Earth, the external tank, drained of its fuel, is released.

5. The Orbital Maneuvering System engines are fired to put the shuttle into a stable circular orbit.

6. The shuttle orbits the Earth at 17,500 miles per hour.

7. The OMS engines fire, slowing the orbiter down by 200 miles per hour.

8. The shuttle enters the atmosphere with its nose pointed up at an angle of 28° to 38°.

9. Sixteen minutes to touchdown, the orbiter makes its first S-turn to reduce lift.

10. S-turns completed, the orbiter still approaches the runway at an angle six times as steep as a commercial jet.

11. The shuttle commander pulls the orbiter's nose up. Landing gear is released 14 seconds before touchdown.

12. Orbiter touches down at 215 miles per hour.

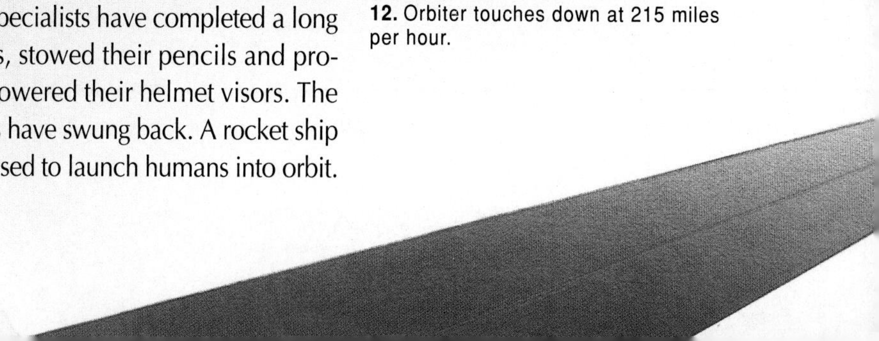

At T -6 seconds, the first of 526,000 gallons of liquid hydrogen and oxygen flow toward the main engines, sounding the first sizzling strains of a head-rattling crescendo of noise. A second later, the three main engines ignite in sequence, urging the shuttle upward with a million pounds of thrust. The sudden thrust associated with main engine ignition cants the whole shuttle two feet, and may have stressed the solid rocket booster joint that failed, destroying *Challenger (page 86).* The orbiter's main computers stand ready to shut down the engines and scrub the mission if all three main engines do not reach 90 percent thrust in the next four seconds. As the shuttle springs back, its tremendous weight compensating for the off-center thrust, igniters near the nose of the solid rocket boosters send a flame into the heart of the rubber-like propellant. As the flame spreads throughout the 1.1 million pounds of fuel in each booster, searing-hot gases are expelled from the exit cones of the engine nozzles. The awesome power unleashed by the two boosters triggers the blast that blows the eight 17-inch bolts holding the boosters to the launch platform. This is the irreversible step that unleashes the full fury of 7.725 million pounds of thrust, enough power to light the whole Atlantic coast.

7

The shuttle rockets upward, riding rough and loud. "Your whole soul knows when the solids light," comments physicist-astronaut Joe Allen. John Young, the fighter pilot voice of experience, called the ride into orbit "smooth, like a fast elevator." But commenting on the 200-foot-wide, white flame blasting from the solid rocket boosters and the huge cloud of steam, Young said, "I'm sure glad we didn't have rearview mirrors."

8

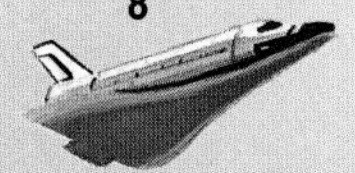

Immediately after clearing the tower, computers guide the shuttle into a gentle eastward arc, belly up, to add the Earth's rotational speed to its own—a gain of 1,000 miles per hour. The rapid acceleration presses the crew hard against their seats. Even a hand is difficult to move under the force of three times Earth's gravity—or 3 Gs. A payload specialist who weighs 160 pounds on Earth now suddenly weighs 480 pounds.

9

Sixty seconds after liftoff, all three main engines throttle back to 65 percent thrust. Here, where aerodynamic loads on the orbiter peak at a point known as Max-Q, or maximum vibration, the shuttle must slow its explosive acceleration to reduce stress on the orbiter's wings, windshield and large tail. But it soon streaks into thinner air, where the engines throttle up again.

10

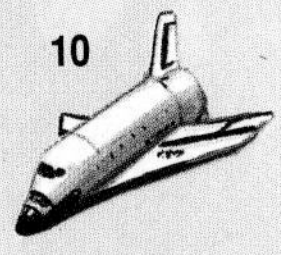

By T +2 minutes the shuttle has reached 3,000 miles per hour and an altitude of 30 miles. As the solid rockets burn their last bit of fuel, the noise level aboard the orbiter abates. Explosive bolts, fired by a computer command, free the boosters, and with a brilliant orange flash, tiny jets on each booster's nose and tail send it up and away from the orbiter. At 41 miles altitude they begin a descent softened by the world's strongest parachute system. Once in the water, special vessels retrieve the boosters and parachutes for reprocessing, saving $20 million per booster.

11

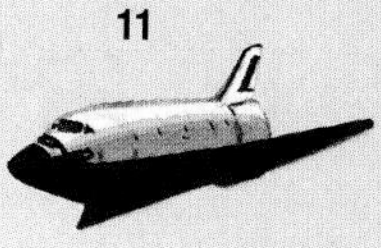

12

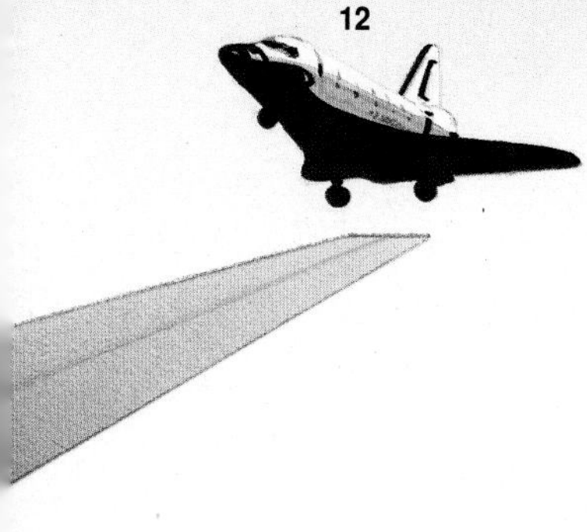

The thin upper atmosphere where the shuttle now travels no longer contains enough particles to scatter light, and the sky becomes black and transparent. Six minutes after liftoff, the orbiter's acceleration once again reaches 3 Gs—half of

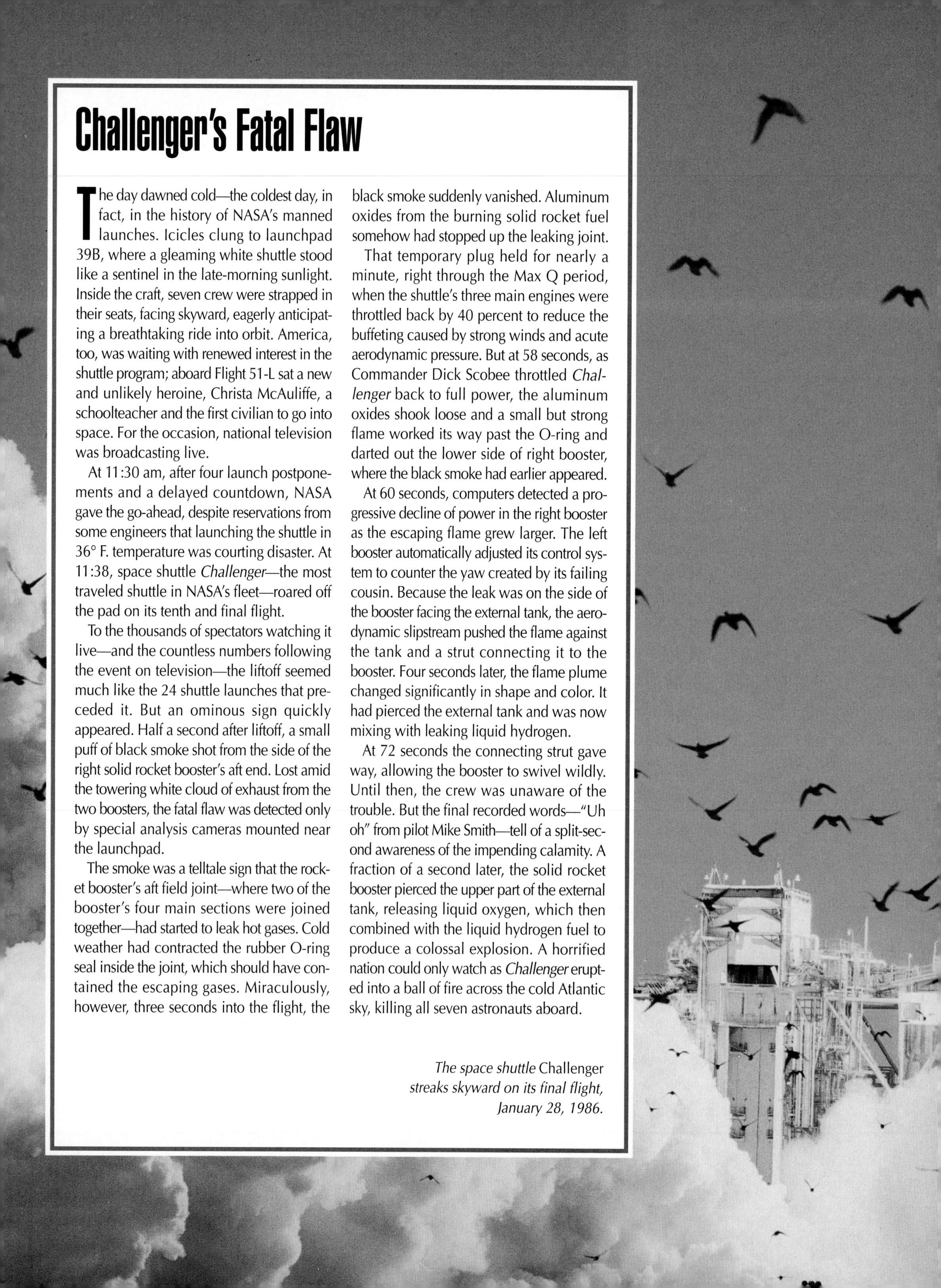

Challenger's Fatal Flaw

The day dawned cold—the coldest day, in fact, in the history of NASA's manned launches. Icicles clung to launchpad 39B, where a gleaming white shuttle stood like a sentinel in the late-morning sunlight. Inside the craft, seven crew were strapped in their seats, facing skyward, eagerly anticipating a breathtaking ride into orbit. America, too, was waiting with renewed interest in the shuttle program; aboard Flight 51-L sat a new and unlikely heroine, Christa McAuliffe, a schoolteacher and the first civilian to go into space. For the occasion, national television was broadcasting live.

At 11:30 am, after four launch postponements and a delayed countdown, NASA gave the go-ahead, despite reservations from some engineers that launching the shuttle in 36° F. temperature was courting disaster. At 11:38, space shuttle *Challenger*—the most traveled shuttle in NASA's fleet—roared off the pad on its tenth and final flight.

To the thousands of spectators watching it live—and the countless numbers following the event on television—the liftoff seemed much like the 24 shuttle launches that preceded it. But an ominous sign quickly appeared. Half a second after liftoff, a small puff of black smoke shot from the side of the right solid rocket booster's aft end. Lost amid the towering white cloud of exhaust from the two boosters, the fatal flaw was detected only by special analysis cameras mounted near the launchpad.

The smoke was a telltale sign that the rocket booster's aft field joint—where two of the booster's four main sections were joined together—had started to leak hot gases. Cold weather had contracted the rubber O-ring seal inside the joint, which should have contained the escaping gases. Miraculously, however, three seconds into the flight, the black smoke suddenly vanished. Aluminum oxides from the burning solid rocket fuel somehow had stopped up the leaking joint.

That temporary plug held for nearly a minute, right through the Max Q period, when the shuttle's three main engines were throttled back by 40 percent to reduce the buffeting caused by strong winds and acute aerodynamic pressure. But at 58 seconds, as Commander Dick Scobee throttled *Challenger* back to full power, the aluminum oxides shook loose and a small but strong flame worked its way past the O-ring and darted out the lower side of right booster, where the black smoke had earlier appeared.

At 60 seconds, computers detected a progressive decline of power in the right booster as the escaping flame grew larger. The left booster automatically adjusted its control system to counter the yaw created by its failing cousin. Because the leak was on the side of the booster facing the external tank, the aerodynamic slipstream pushed the flame against the tank and a strut connecting it to the booster. Four seconds later, the flame plume changed significantly in shape and color. It had pierced the external tank and was now mixing with leaking liquid hydrogen.

At 72 seconds the connecting strut gave way, allowing the booster to swivel wildly. Until then, the crew was unaware of the trouble. But the final recorded words—"Uh oh" from pilot Mike Smith—tell of a split-second awareness of the impending calamity. A fraction of a second later, the solid rocket booster pierced the upper part of the external tank, releasing liquid oxygen, which then combined with the liquid hydrogen fuel to produce a colossal explosion. A horrified nation could only watch as *Challenger* erupted into a ball of fire across the cold Atlantic sky, killing all seven astronauts aboard.

The space shuttle Challenger *streaks skyward on its final flight, January 28, 1986.*

United States

The white plume of a free-flying solid rocket booster traces its aimless arc against the Florida sky shortly after the Challenger *explosion, killing all seven astronauts aboard.*

United States
NASA
O-Rings
Two rubber seals failed at launch.
Escaping hot gases
Eventually pierce external tank

The first sign of impending disaster: A puff of black smoke (right) *betrays a leak in a joint in the right solid rocket booster. A failure in the O-ring seal* (inset illustration) *in the solid rocket booster allowed burning gases to escape, which eventually burned a hole through the external fuel tank and led to the destruction of* Challenger. *Boosters for all subsequent shuttle missions were redesigned; an improved sealing system featuring a third O-ring was one of 145 design changes implemented.*

what Alan Shepard had to endure, but still strong enough to make any movement difficult. Though astronauts' T-38 trainer jets sometimes reach more than 3 Gs for brief periods, the orbiter experience, says America's first woman in space, Sally Ride, "seems to go on forever."

Another half minute slips by, and the orbiter has all but escaped the atmosphere. Though astronauts are busy with their checklists when the main engines cease firing, they may have trouble hanging on to them. On the first shuttle orbit, pilot Robert Crippen even reported seeing washers and screws floating through the cockpit. The rocket has become a gravity-free spaceship.

Still attached to its empty external fuel tank, the orbiter dives slightly, aiming the doomed tank back toward the atmosphere. Sixteen seconds after a computer command shuts down the main engines and the commander confirms "MECO" (Main Engine Cutoff), yet another set of explosive bolts silently separates the orbiter from its empty tank, and the two briefly fly in formation. Because the orbiter arcs over belly up during its ascent, it flies between the tank and Earth. To clear the tank, which the astronauts cannot see, computers fire reaction control jets to step the orbiter sideways in a crabwalk away from the tank. Once safely clear of the orbiter, extra fuel is vented from the tank to set it tumbling toward the atmosphere where it breaks apart. The pieces disperse, falling in a "footprint" 600 miles long into the Indian Ocean or—when the shuttle is heading into higher orbits—into the Pacific Ocean.

Despite its 17,500-mile-per-hour speed—almost 10 times faster than a .308-caliber bullet fired from a rifle—the shuttle still lacks sufficient momentum to avoid the tank's fate. To achieve the necessary velocity and altitude, the Orbital Maneuvering System engines come to the fore. Depending on the mission, the orbiter needs either one or two OMS burns to achieve a stable orbit. On most flights, the first OMS burn boosts the orbiter another 100 miles away from Earth into an elliptical orbit that peaks at about 170 miles high. The second burn, necessary on every flight, occurs 45 minutes after liftoff as the spacecraft reaches the apogee of its orbit. This second, shorter burst of the OMS engines converts the shuttle's elliptical orbit to a stable circular one, 115 to 250 miles above the surface of the Earth.

Less than an hour after it stood trembling on the pad, a rocket ship has turned into a spaceship, then a satellite, sailing silently through space in a steady circular orbit around the Earth.

Cocooned in a sleep restraint bag, astronaut Sally Ride demonstrates one way of sleeping aboard a shuttle. Some astronauts choose to anchor their feet or upper bodies; others simply float untethered.

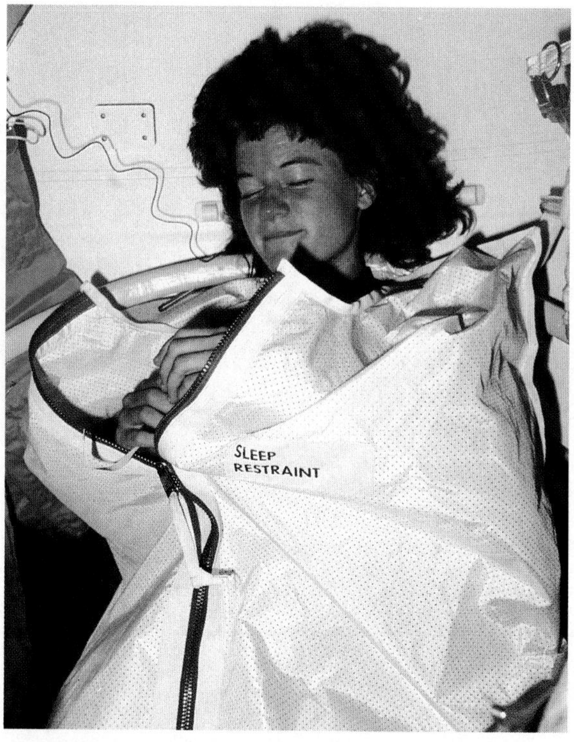
SLEEP
RESTRAINT

LIFE IN SPACE

This fall nullifies gravity, just as a plunge in a plane or a fast elevator does. But in orbit the fall continues, and the resulting weightlessness sets living in space apart from any other environment. Gravity's pull 150 or 200 miles from Earth is actually only marginally less than on the surface of the planet. But the centrifugal force aboard a spacecraft counterbalances the force of gravity and creates the weightless condition experienced by astronauts. At the dawn of the Space Age some scientists faced weightlessness with trepidation; the experiences of hundreds of astronauts and cosmonauts since then have demonstrated that it is an immensely pleasurable sensation. Shuttle astronauts such as Sally Ride have relished the experience. "The best part of being in space is being weightless," she says.

Moving through a room in space takes only a gentle push, but pushing a little too hard can turn an astronaut into a human projectile aimed at the opposite wall. At first, says Joe Allen, "you think you need to move around like Superman, with your arms held out in front of you." Soon, though, even novices float through the ship with the greatest of ease, sometimes finding that the orbiter has maneuvered around them, silently substituting a blank wall for the locker or hatch they were about to open.

The fun and ease of weightlessness—physicists call it microgravity to acknowledge that gravity still exists—affects every aspect of life in space. Nothing stays where it is put unless it sticks; there is nowhere to set an object down because, in the floating environment, up and down no longer exist. For an object to stay in position it has to be held there. During Apollo days, the problem was solved

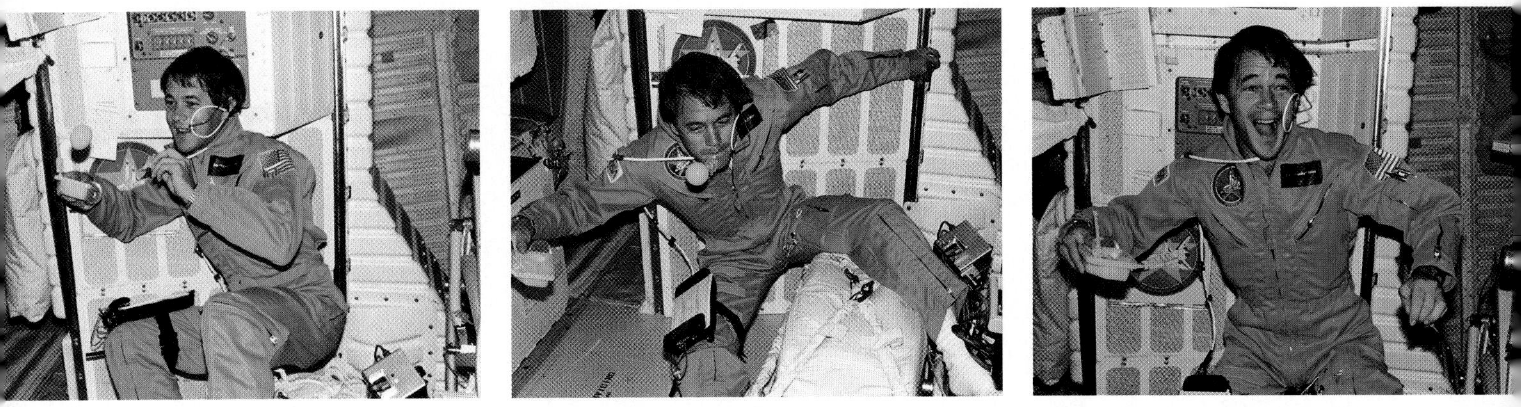

Weightlessness affects all aspects of living in space—including drinking. Here, astronaut Joseph Allen pursues a floating blob of orange juice before sucking it up with a straw. Liquids in space refuse to slide down the edge of a tilted glass and, once released from a container, tend to congeal into a sphere, kept in shape by the surface tension of the liquid.

with a device that is used even more ubiquitously on the orbiter: Velcro. This fuzzy hook and loop material, used on children's running shoes, shows up on pencils, cameras, food containers—nearly every loose object in the orbiter. Handholds and foot loops also abound. Even eating takes special equipment.

The age of nutritious paste squeezed from tubes has passed, replaced by the era of salmon, fresh bread, diced pears, butter cookies and lemonade. To save weight and space, many foods fly into orbit in a dehydrated form. Others store better if they are canned or irradiated. A few, like nuts and bread, need no special treatment. Many dishes come with a sticky sauce or syrup, making a spoon—which can be used in any position—the universal eating implement. Scissors are also handy for opening food packets. Shaking salt or pepper would only disperse the tiny grains in the air; liquid salt and pepper sauce replace them.

The shuttle carries no water into space; the life-sustaining liquid is produced by double-duty power generators. By chemically combining hydrogen with oxygen, the three duplicate devices produce both electricity and a perfectly potable byproduct, H_2O. The plentiful water won't pour while weightless, so drinking and getting water into food or beverage containers poses a new problem. Straws with clip closures solve the first problem—astronauts can suck the fluid through the straw and stem the flow with the plastic clip; a rehydrator that injects measured amounts of water through special food pack fittings solves the second. Astronauts can heat rehydrated packets in the galley's convection oven, or on a food warmer built into a large aluminum briefcase.

With rehydrated food and a tub of hot coffee, an astronaut is ready to sit down—or rather float over—and eat. Shuttle serving trays bristle with attachment points. Velcro, rubber-lined cutouts, binder clips, magnetic strips and leg attachment strips all make eating feasible. Astronauts gather in the middeck to share meals and clean up in space much like they would at an earthly picnic. They toss food containers into high-tech trash bags and wipe fingers, spoons, scissors and surfaces with disinfectant-drenched wet wipes. Germicidal cleaning spray and a small vacuum cleaner complete the cleaning equipment.

At the rear corner of the middeck, the toilet—perhaps the target of more public curiosity than any other shuttle system—seems a bit anticlimactic. It handles solid wastes much like a one-hole outhouse. A fan under the seat provides an air flow that replaces gravity and throws waste and paper against the sides of a lower container to avoid clogging the air filter. Astronauts of both sexes urinate into personal funnel-like devices attached to tubes. Again, airflow draws the urine into the lower container. Of course, the toilet includes the ubiquitous foot loops to keep an astronaut from drifting away. Turning off the airflow opens the waste container to the vacuum of space, quickly drying its contents, which are returned to Earth for disposal.

Because food, left to float, can lodge in hard-to-reach nooks and crannies, sanitation assumes astronomical importance. Airflow again comes to the rescue in the hand-washing station, located on the side of the galley. A clear plastic hemisphere with two wrist tubes contains the water spray, and an air stream sucks it down into a waste water tank. Body cleaning requires a washcloth moistened with a hand sprayer. Shaving, using conventional safety razors and cream causes no problems; whiskers stick to the cream. And astronauts carry a supply of disposable, paste-impregnated toothbrushes. The only problem is that there is nowhere to spit, so astronauts must swallow the edible toothpaste.

Perhaps the easiest part of life aboard the orbiter is sleeping. Some astronauts hit the sack in middeck bunks or in sleeping bags. Others don "Lone Ranger" sleeping masks and ear plugs and either tether themselves to a surface or slip on a loose seat belt. Those who prefer simply floating in the middle of the cabin often cushion their heads in case they drift against a wall or ceiling—or another sleeping astronaut. The autopilot can take over while the whole crew sleeps, but at least one astronaut sleeps wearing a communication headset in case of emergencies. On waking, the astronauts change clothes, stowing the used ones in plastic bags.

If they glance out the window, a sudden spectacular sunrise—one of 16 in every 24 hours—reveals the Earth in three dimensions, clearly curving from horizon to horizon. Too close for the "whole Earth" effect seen from Apollo, the 1,000-mile breadth of view still proves sublime. The whole big island of Hawaii, for example, sits like a blue-gray jewel in a bed of dark blue velvet. Even this close, the Earth seems to consist of nothing but clouds, water and vacant land. Most views give no hint of humans on Earth. Only the straight lines, seen when the orbiter overflies a large city, announce a human presence. Forty-five minutes after its abrupt rise,

NASA

Should a shuttle experience an emergency such as sudden depressurization, astronauts can seek refuge in a personal rescue enclosure (PRE)—a 34-inch-diameter ball made from urethane, Kevlar and a thermal protective cover. An astronaut climbs into the ball (above) *and is zipped shut by a fellow astronaut who wears a spacesuit. (Only two spacesuits are included on shuttles.) Sitting hunched over in a transparent mock-up of the ball* (right)*, an astronaut breathes using a portable oxygen system. A small viewing port is provided in the PRE to reduce claustrophobia.*

the Sun just as suddenly sets, and the Earth becomes a black blot on a field of stars. This velvety blackness is broken only occasionally by a flickering forest fire or lightning dancing from cloud to cloud or the twinkling lights of a large city.

RETURNING TO EARTH

While the shuttle wheels around the Earth, with its crew dispensing satellites from the cargo bay and occasionally venturing outside to make repairs, the payload doors remain open to expose their 1,800 square feet of heat-dissipating radiators. But as the shuttle crew prepares to reenter the Earth's atmosphere those doors become a liability. If astronauts fail to close them securely, the orbiter cannot land. And closing them has not always proved easy. During a shuttle flight in 1982, astronauts Jack Lousma and Gordon Fullerton aimed the orbiter's belly at the Sun. The scorching rays warped the whole craft into a banana shape, cramping the doors. They were only closed after the crew carried out a "barbecue roll," exposing all the shuttle's surfaces to the Sun and evening out the thermal expansion.

Once the hatches are battened down, the crew has to make sure everything inside the crew cabin is secure. Velcro works wonders in weightlessness, but deceleration and increasing gravity still could smash everything to the floor. Cameras, food trays, books, pencils, all must be stowed for landing. Mission specialists unfold and snap their seats to the middeck floor. With everything in place, the astronauts are ready to leave for home. They drink a quart of water and swallow salt tablets to replace fluids they have lost in space. To help avoid blood pooling in their legs—a potentially dangerous result of their return to gravity—they have donned pressure suits with built-in inflatable g-pants (the "g" standing for gravity). Helmets, boots and emergency packs complete the flight suit ensemble.

Coasting above Africa, half a world away from their California landing strip, the orbiter commander and its pilot flip the ship tail first. Facing away from their direction of travel, they fire the Orbital Maneuvering System engines for the third time. This final OMS burn lasts roughly three minutes, varying by a few seconds depending on the weight of the orbiter and its payloads. The burn empties the fuel tanks and slows the vehicle by only 200 miles per hour—less than 2 percent of its orbital speed. But this two-minute braking maneuver sends the orbiter skimming the upper reaches of the atmosphere with no power to reenter orbit.

Traveling at 17,500 miles per hour, the orbiter crashes into the first scarce air molecules, absorbing heat with each collision. To bring the orbiter's thermal protection into play, the pilot and commander have turned about face again, aiming the well-protected nose forward and the tiled belly down. A 40° angle of attack—the angle between the direction the orbiter is flying and the direction its nose is pointing—orients the orbiter for its role as an aerodynamic vehicle.

Now, accelerometers spring to life, quivering in response to the combination of deceleration and gravity. Astronauts begin to feel the pressure, gradually regaining the weight they lost in space and then some. Thirty minutes after the final, fateful OMS burn, the orbiter has reentered the atmosphere. Air molecules battered

The Right Stuff?

Applying to become a shuttle astronaut has at least one similarity with most other job hunts: the application form. Actually, there are five forms to complete, and NASA receives thousands of applications every year from aspiring astronauts. "We really don't have to advertise," says Duane Ross, NASA's manager of astronaut selection. The ideal candidate, according to Ross, is a "team player," with first-rate academic credentials and a diverse background that bespeaks an ability to adapt.

To be considered for a position aboard the world's most exclusive flying machine, pilots must be between 5'4" and 6'4" and have a minimum of 1,000 hours of pilot-in-command experience in jets. Mission specialists must have at least a bachelor's degree in engineering, biological science, physical science or mathematics and three years' relevant experience. Both must be U.S. citizens.

Final selection is based on a one-hour interview with a review board, part of a week-long series of exhaustive physical examinations and other tests such as writing a 1,500-word essay.

Successful candidates spend two years in basic training at the Johnson Space Center in Houston, studying subjects ranging from mathematics and meteorology to astronomy and computers. Roughly 45 weeks before a flight, a crew's formal training begins. Astronauts choose lessons, from a list of 800, that are appropriate for their particular tasks. Time also is spent in simulators. Ray Dell'osso, NASA's flight training manager, describes them as "machines that provide the shakes, rattles and rolls" felt during a launch.

Applications are available from NASA-Lyndon B. Johnson Space Center, Astronaut Selection Office, Mail Code AHX, Houston, TX 77058.

Aspiring astronauts experience weightlessness in a KC-135 cargo plane. Diving down and then pulling up into a steep climb, the plane arcs over before starting another dive. While it flies "over the top," zero gravity exists for 30 seconds or so.

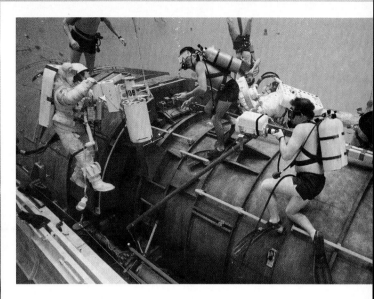

Astronauts rehearse tasks they will perform in space in a 1.4-million-gallon pool at Johnson Space Center known as the Weightless Environment Training Facility (WET-F), which contains a mock-up of the shuttle orbiter payload bay.

Standing in a mock-up of the aft end of the shuttle's flight deck, astronaut Sally Ride practices operating the craft's robotic arm.

into atomic particles stream past the orbiter's windows, emitting a growing ruddy glow. "I felt as if we were flying through a neon tube," said STS-1 commander John Young. The glowing particles eventually create an electromagnetic envelope around the orbiter, blocking all radio contact with Earth for 15 minutes. The increasing air friction slows the orbiter and sends temperatures on the nose, wing and tail edges soaring. As air density increases, the orbiter's reaction control rockets lose effectiveness, and its aerodynamic control surfaces begin to work. They include a rudder on the 26-foot-tall tail, a large body flap beneath the main engines and elevons—small flaps on the wing that can tilt up 40 degrees and down 25 degrees. The craft's broad delta wings and the round lifting body—a descendant of wingless designs dating back to the 1950s—keep the orbiter from dropping like a stone. The spaceship has become the world's fattest and fastest glider.

As the commander regains radio contact, about 12 minutes before touchdown, he is still streaking through the sky at more than 8,000 miles per hour. While the forward speed is impressive, the vertical speed is even more so—the orbiter plummets toward the ground at 140 miles per hour, faster than a free-falling skydiver.

To further reduce speed, the computer swings the orbiter through a series of wide, steep S-turns called roll reversals, sometimes rolling the craft up to 90° on its side. The maneuvers have a similar effect to the turns that a skier makes to slow his descent down a mountain. During the roll reversals, the computer can fine-tune the bank angle, and therefore the amount of braking, to ensure that the orbiter reaches its landing strip at the correct speed. The orbiter announces its imminent arrival with a double sonic boom as it returns across the sound barrier.

Landing the orbiter harks back to the days of the experimental X-15 rocket planes. The commander switches to manual control and takes her in "dead stick"—gliding in without power, without a second chance at the runway. "Fighter pilots are crazy enough to enjoy the idea," said former astronaut Michael Collins. And former fighter pilots still land the shuttle.

Even after the S-turns, the orbiter rushes toward the runway at an angle six times as steep as a commercial jet. A microwave landing system—similar to the one used by commercial jets—transmits data to the orbiter, pinpointing its location. A Plexiglas display screen on the window allows the commander to check airspeed and altitude without diverting his eyes from the landing site. Less than 20 seconds before touchdown, the commander finally pulls up the nose, flattening his precipitous plummet to a manageable 1.5 degrees—and slowing to a little more than 200 miles per hour, less than twice the landing speed of a commercial jet. Seconds later, at 400 feet above the ground, he lowers the landing gear, spreads the two-piece rudder into a V-shaped speed brake and takes a deep breath waiting for the main wheels to kiss the dry lake bed at Edwards Air Force Base. As he applies the brakes, the wheels spit smoke and dust. The commander eases down the nose wheel and the orbiter begins its final mile-and-a-half roll along the runway.

The shuttle began its voyage as a rocket, spent a week as a spaceship and satellite, and returned as a glider. Now, shortly after the wheels grind to a stop, a ramp is attached to the front of the orbiter. The hatch opens and the crew jauntily descends the steps of a portable ramp to the ground. Behind them, the orbiter stands nearly inert, hissing and ticking as it cools, waiting for a piggyback ride home to Kennedy Space Center to begin the cycle once again.

Atlantis
NASA
United States

Shuttle Atlantis *touches down on the dry lake bed at Edwards Air Force Base in California. Landing a near-100-ton craft at more than 200 miles an hour can test even the toughest tires* (inset). *After a flight in 1985,* Discovery *shredded one tire and blew another after the brakes locked on the right landing gear.*

The shuttle's return is a far cry from the experience of the first man who went into space. When Yuri Gagarin returned to Earth in a spherical Vostok capsule codenamed Cedar, he reentered the atmosphere not in a glider, but in a nearly inert, supersonic cannonball. Even though covered with heat shielding, Cedar soon glowed red hot. The Vostok's abrupt plunge crushed Gagarin with g forces nearly 10 times earthly gravity and more than 5 times what landing shuttle astronauts feel. More than four miles from Earth, Cedar's hatch was blown and Gagarin bailed out. Cedar descended under its own red-and-white parachute, landing less than two hours after takeoff. Gagarin landed nearby in a field where a woman and her young daughter were planting potatoes.

Unlike the Americans, whose missions landed in the ocean, the Russians always opted to bring their cosmonauts back to land, mainly because their capsules had to be designed to survive the possibility of an aborted launch (the early trajectory of Soviet craft takes them over land). They could also rely on their country's vast unpopulated steppe regions to serve as landing targets roomy enough for errors in reentry trajectories. Although there was no risk that cosmonauts might drown—as almost happened to Mercury pilot Gus Grissom when his capsule sank shortly after landing in the Atlantic Ocean—there were unexpected dangers. In March 1965, during the flight of Voskhod 2, Pavel Belyayev and Aleksei Leonov overshot their landing area by 2,000 miles and ended up in a snow-covered forest in Siberia. Soviet officials were hampered by the fact that the capsule's radio beacon had broken off during landing. The cosmonauts were located a few hours later and eventually skied to recovery helicopters, but not before being forced to retreat inside their capsule to fend off roving timber wolves.

LEARNING TO WORK ALOFT

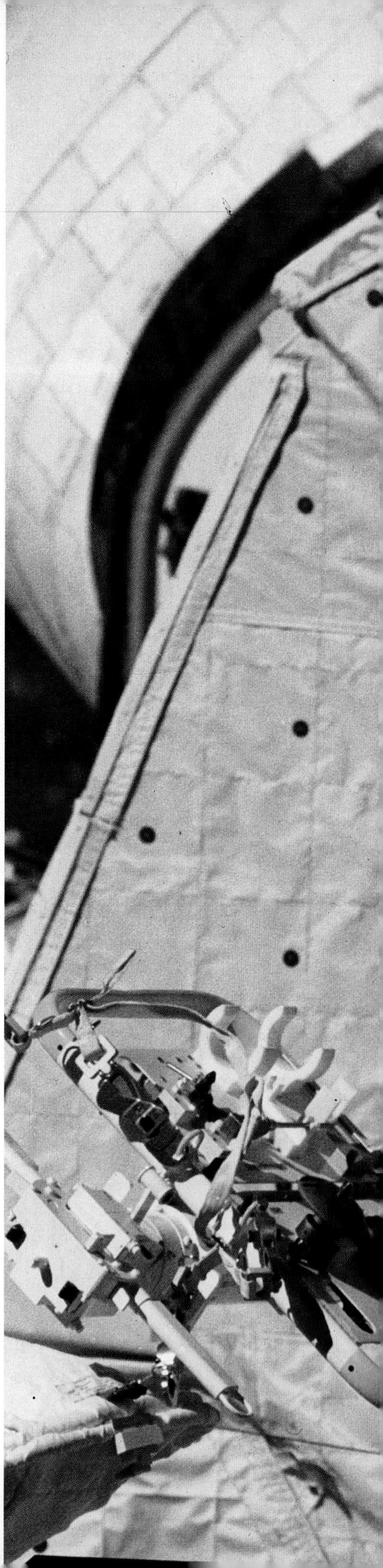

At the end of 1980, after eight months of scrutinizing the Sun, the $240-million Solar Maximum Observatory satellite went dead; fuses blew and cameras succumbed to bombarding radiation. Three-and-a-half years later, on a Sunday morning in April, a lone cosmic repairman, clad in a bulky white spacesuit and strapped into a cumbersome jetpack called a Manned Maneuvering Unit was trying to bring the balky equipment in to the shop.

U.S. astronaut George "Pinky" Nelson, flying his first mission ever, had ridden the shuttle *Challenger,* along with his four fellow crew members, to a record-high orbit 300 miles above the Earth to make this service call. Jokingly, the team had dubbed itself the "Ace Satellite Repair Company." Their plan was simple. While the mission's commander, veteran Robert Crippen, flew the shuttle alongside the ailing Solar Max, Nelson would fly over, latch onto the satellite with a pair of mechanical jaws attached to the front of his suit, and, with a burst from his backpack's gas-powered thrusters, stop it from spinning. Then the shuttle would pull closer and a robotic arm would tuck the satellite into the cargo bay, where the actual repairs would be carried out by Nelson and crewmate James van Hoften.

In theory, Nelson's part of the operation was to take only a few minutes. But now he was hanging over the brilliant curve of Earth with a major problem on his hands. He had zeroed in on the target, but his mechanical jaws had failed to close. Over the headphones, Nelson heard Crippen suggest another try. His heartbeat quickening, Nelson made a second approach. Once again, the jaws refused to engage. Frustrated, Nelson retreated a few feet, and examined them; finding nothing apparently wrong, he went back for a third run, which was again a failure. Nelson radioed, "The satellite's pitching into me." Crippen replied, "It looks like you may have bumped it a bit, Pinky." Indeed, Nelson's repeated charges had set the satellite rolling and tumbling end over end, turning it into a flailing peril. "Watch out for the solar array," Crippen warned, as a panel shaved past.

Held securely by foot restraints on a platform at the end of the remote manipulator arm, astronaut Bruce McCandless works inside the space shuttle orbiter's cargo bay with an electric wrench.

wester
WEST

Disconcerted ground engineers debated what to do, for if Nelson could not stabilize Solar Max, the capture attempt would have to be scrubbed. The Ace Satellite Repair Company's $50-million house call would have come to naught.

Once, astronauts had flown into space merely as pilots to guide their spacecraft. Now, armed with an array of equipment that looked like it traced its provenance to the imagination of science fiction writers, two repairmen stood poised to demonstrate just how sophisticated working in space had become.

LUNAR CHORES

Coming almost 15 years and several dozen spaceflights after the first trip to the Moon, the Solar Max salvage operation might have seemed a routine undertaking. But as Nelson and his colleagues discovered, even elementary tasks take on a formidable aspect in the hostile environment of space. Weightlessness, the lack of an atmosphere and ever-present radiation (streaming from the Sun and from throughout the universe) pose substantial obstacles to working in space and have yet to be overcome fully. In a sense, all human forays into this alien realm have been training runs, on which survival skills have been honed and equipment fine-tuned in the expectation of one day making still bolder voyages to nearby planets, and perhaps ultimately, the distant stars.

The tentative Mercury flights of the early 1960s—a half-dozen up-and-back sorties in cramped capsules—gave few hints of the technological advances to come. Although the fresh-faced crop of Mercury astronauts, all trained test pilots, possessed dexterity and quick wits in abundance, most of their time in space was spent toggling an occasional switch and pushing a few buttons. Later Mercury flights involved more piloting, but largely, astronauts just went along for the ride.

This inactivity was dictated mainly by ignorance, since space scientists had only minimal knowledge of how the rigors of liftoff, zero gravity, reentry and splashdown might affect the human body. Considering the possible hazards—not to mention the additional limitations imposed by the cramped quarters of the Mercury modules— astronauts could hardly be assigned a full roster of duties.

Even the Gemini crews, who made an astonishing 10 flights in barely two years, 1965 and 1966, were limited in the work they could perform by the close confines of their temporary abodes. But by then, physiologists had monitored enough bodily responses to satisfy themselves of the relative safety of spaceflight, and engineers had begun refining instrumentation and machinery with an eye to a more ambitious undertaking: a trip to the Moon. Thus, when Michael Collins and John Young took to the skies in 1966 on Gemini 10, ground handlers confidently assigned them jobs that kept the duo toiling overtime for close to four days.

The pair docked their Gemini spacecraft with an orbiting 26-foot-long Agena rocket, and pulled alongside another Agena, left in space by a previous Gemini mission, to retrieve an experimental packet stowed on its flank. Collins undertook two Extravehicular Activities, or EVAs, ducking out of the hatch for a few minutes to take pictures, and then later leaving the capsule altogether to fetch the Agena packet. This proved a Chaplinesque venture. A hand-held jet gun, which released pressurized nitrogen gas through three nozzles, was used by Collins to thrust himself forward, backward, up and down through space. Instead of aiding navigation though, the gun propelled Collins along an almost uncontrollable course. He float-

ed about haplessly, first sailing directly into the path of the capsule's attitude control thrusters, then coming perilously close to severing the 50-foot umbilical cord tying him to his ride home.

If Gemini 10 was supposed to be, as Collins said, a bridge between "the rudimentary Mercury capsule and the sophisticated Apollo system" that would land men on the Moon, NASA engineers clearly had their work cut out for them. Providing astronauts with the equipment needed for a safe and productive journey to the Earth's nearest celestial neighbor would demand every iota of technical know-how NASA experts could muster.

With each ensuing three-man Apollo mission in the late 1960s, the dedicated NASA personnel showed that they were equal to the challenge. By the time Apollo 11's Neil Armstrong made that giant leap for mankind in July 1969, setting his booted foot down in the lunar dust of the Sea of Tranquillity, astronauts had graduated from passive excursionists to all-purpose handymen, boasting well-stocked toolkits loaded with an assortment of gadgetry. On this and five following lunar expeditions, concluding with Apollo 17 in December 1972, a total of 12 astronauts bounded about the Moon's arid seas and pale highlands, wielding tailor-made rakes, shovels, hammers, clamps, tongs, tripods, scoops and drills with which to execute a host of scientific chores.

A primary charge of both Apollo 11 and subsequent teams was to bring back samples of lunar silt and rocks in order to satisfy the curiosity of planetary geologists, who were, one scientist said, like medieval monks awaiting "the arrival of a fragment of the True Cross." The primordial lunar material, subjected to 4.5 billion years' worth of volcanic upheavals and meteorite storms, held clues not only to the fundamental nature of the Moon itself, but also to the very formation of the Solar System.

Apollo 17 astronaut Harrison Schmitt scoops up a precious sample of lunar soil using a specially designed collector. Scientists were so worried that the Moon might carry harmful bacteria that the first astronauts returning from the Moon were required to spend two weeks in a germ-proof van. The suspicions proved unfounded, however, and later astronauts were spared the quarantine period.

Apollo 11 did differ, however, from ensuing missions in at least one detail. Since NASA officials were unsure how safe conditions on the Moon would prove to be for astronauts, they instructed Armstrong and fellow moonwalker Edwin "Buzz" Aldrin to stuff contingency samples of lunar soil into spacesuit pockets soon after leaving the Lunar Module, *Eagle*. The word "contingency" implied the possibility that some life-threatening dangers could be encountered on the Moon. Had Armstrong and Aldrin felt inclined to leave in a hurry—say, because the lunar surface would not support their weight—NASA wanted to ensure that they at least brought home a few souvenirs.

Because the early one-piece Apollo spacesuit would not permit astronauts to bend easily at the waist, scoops that resembled tiny square-jawed power shovels were used to pick up the collected material. Later missions would follow more elaborate procedures; fine-tined rakes helped lunar workmen harvest dime- and quarter-sized pieces of rock. Starting with Apollo 15, astronauts also managed to bring back samples from eight feet below the lunar surface. To do this, they used a battery-powered drill that drove carbide-tipped sectionalized bore and core stems into the soil. The resulting cylindrical cores of rock contained layers that charted

The Men on the Moon

When President John. F. Kennedy stood before Congress in May 1961 and asked the U.S. to commit itself to landing a man on the Moon before the end of the decade, many admired the audacity of his vision. Few were confident of its realization.

NASA's prodigious expertise was quickly channeled into the $25-billion challenge. Crucial to success was the right rocket. NASA found its answer in the gargantuan Saturn V, a 363-foot-tall behemoth capable of lifting 250,000 pounds off the pad. Next came the question of how to reach the Moon. The "direct ascent" approach, using a single booster to propel a spacecraft directly to the Moon, and the Earth Orbit Rendezvous, placing two rockets into Earth orbit, where a lunar spacecraft would then be constructed, were rejected in favor of a third, innovative approach—Lunar Orbit Rendezvous. At the heart of LOR was a three-man command module (CM), a service module (SM) with engine and fuel, and a Lunar Module (LM)—all launched by Saturn V, whose final stage would propel the three-part spacecraft out of Earth orbit toward the Moon. Once in lunar orbit, the LM lander would separate from its mother craft and descend with two astronauts to the surface. Following their exploration, the two would ascend back into lunar orbit aboard the LM's upper stage. After a rendezvous with the command module and service module (CSM), the entire crew would return to Earth.

The fulfillment of Kennedy's pledge came a mere five months before the deadline. On July 16, 1969, Neil Armstrong, Edwin "Buzz" Aldrin and Michael Collins blasted off from Cape Kennedy aboard Apollo 11, its awesome F-1 engines gulping 15 tons of fuel a second. Four days later, the LM *Eagle* separated and began a two-hour descent toward the Sea of Tranquillity. With less than 20 seconds of fuel left in their descent engine, Armstrong settled the craft onto the lunar surface, bringing a dream to life.

With neither atmosphere nor weather to disturb them, the lunar footprints of Apollo 11's Aldrin and Armstrong will display their crisp, clean impressions thousands of years hence.

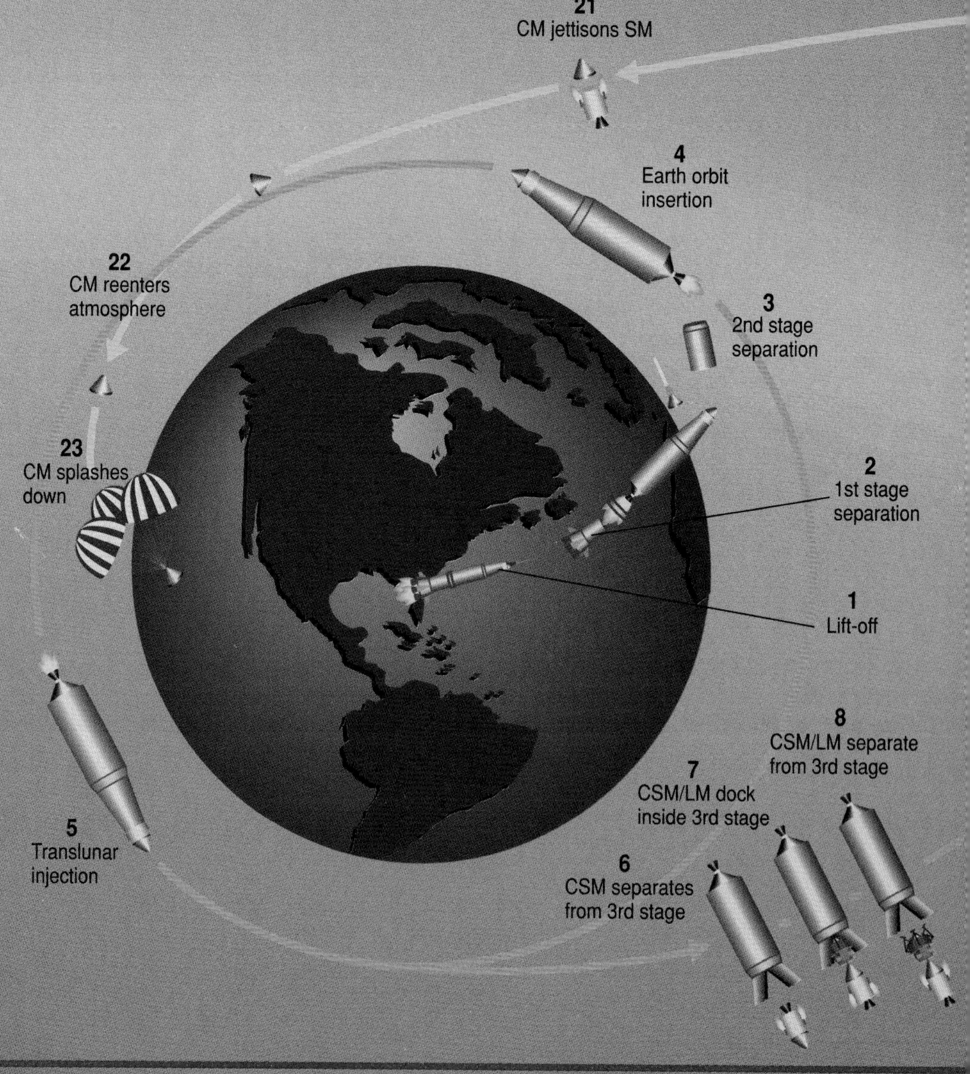

21
CM jettisons SM
4
Earth orbit insertion
22
CM reenters atmosphere
3
2nd stage separation
23
CM splashes down
2
1st stage separation
1
Lift-off
8
CSM/LM separate from 3rd stage
7
CSM/LM dock inside 3rd stage
5
Translunar injection
6
CSM separates from 3rd stage

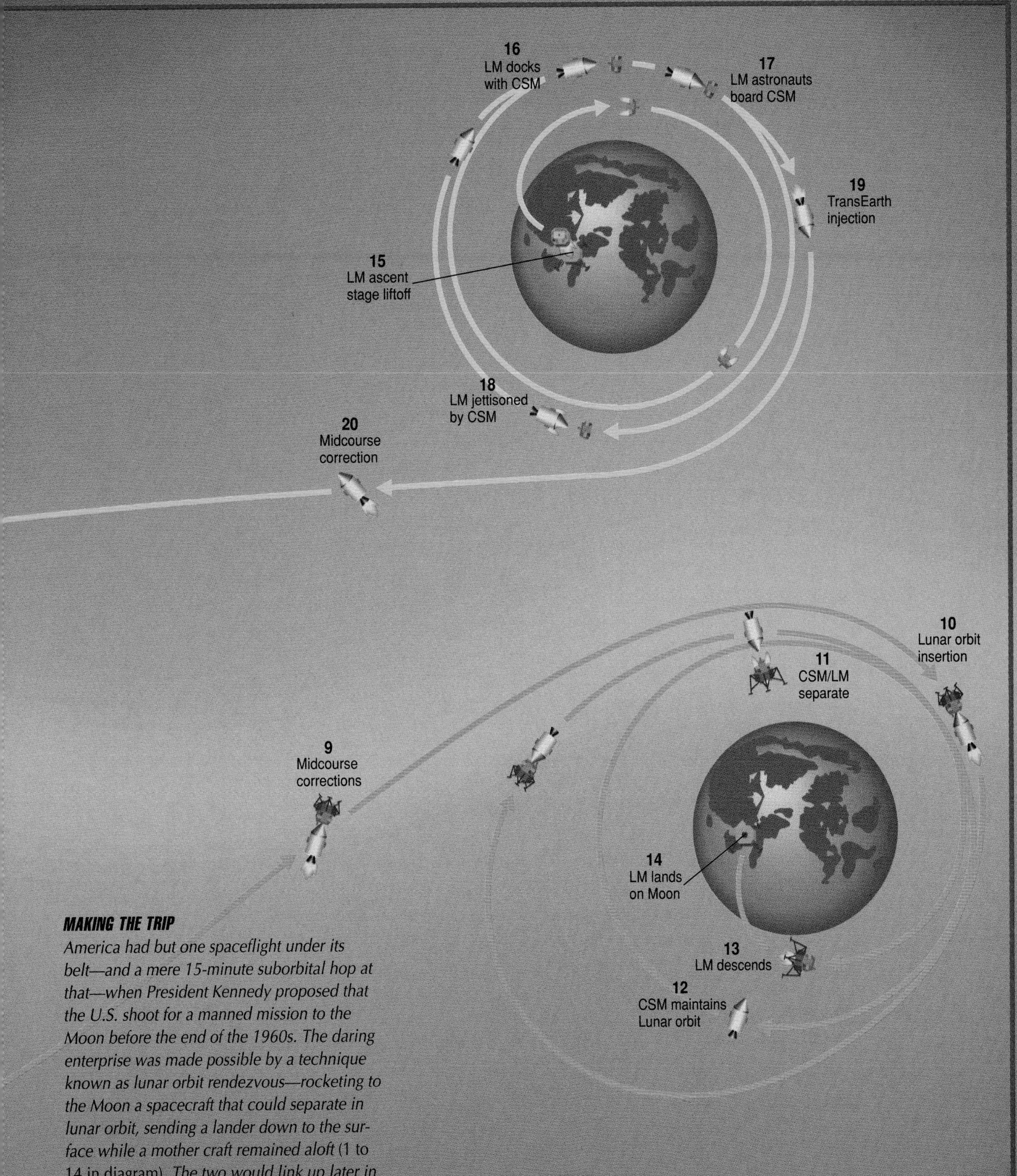
16
LM docks
with CSM
17
LM astronauts
board CSM
19
TransEarth
injection
15
LM ascent
stage liftoff
18
LM jettisoned
by CSM
20
Midcourse
correction
10
Lunar orbit
insertion
11
CSM/LM
separate
9
Midcourse
corrections
14
LM lands
on Moon
13
LM descends
12
CSM maintains
Lunar orbit

MAKING THE TRIP

America had but one spaceflight under its belt—and a mere 15-minute suborbital hop at that—when President Kennedy proposed that the U.S. shoot for a manned mission to the Moon before the end of the 1960s. The daring enterprise was made possible by a technique known as lunar orbit rendezvous—rocketing to the Moon a spacecraft that could separate in lunar orbit, sending a lander down to the surface while a mother craft remained aloft (1 to 14 in diagram). *The two would link up later in lunar orbit and the crew would return to Earth after jettisoning the lander* (15 to 23).

the story of millions of years of geological evolution. The much-sought-after rock and soil were placed into aluminum trunks, which NASA referred to as "sample-return containers." The astronauts, always opting for the casual over the formal, called them simply the "rock boxes," just as the "contingency samples" became the "grab samples."

Back on Earth, geologists gleefully combed over the valuable collection brought back from the six lunar landings—842 pounds of material that averaged out to $3 million per ounce—subjecting the rocks to every conceivable test. They ground them up, shaved them into razor-thin slices, scrutinized them under electron microscopes, and measured their radioactivity. From these analyses, scientists learned that the Moon, over its existence, has been inundated by huge lava flows and peppered by an incessant rain of meteorites.

The haul of rocks and dust was the material expression of humanity's newfound facility for labor in space. But the Apollo astronauts also executed assignments whose benefits, although less physically tangible, were manifold. In effect, they assembled at their landing spots the components of a full-fledged laboratory to provide earthbound scientists with a constant readout of the Moon's vital signs.

In terms of science, perhaps the most immediate yet long-lasting payback for these working Moon missions came from the laser retroreflectors that accompanied Apollo 11, 14 and 15, and which are still active today. Consisting of prismlike reflectors ranging in number from 100 to 300—each about the width of a silver dollar—the device serves as a target for laser beams fired from Earth-based observatories in North America, Hawaii, the Soviet Union, Australia, Japan and France. Shot from a telescope at the speed of light—186,000 miles per second—a concentrated beam hits the array and bounces back to a detector at the respective observatory. By measuring the time of the round trip to an accuracy of one billionth of a second, scientists are able to calculate the distance between Earth and the Moon to an error of just six inches. These exact lunar-distance measurements establish the longitudes of earthbound observatories on different continents with unprecedented precision. That information can then be used to keep track of the steady creep of the large, interlocking continental plates that form the Earth's crust. By recording the shifting distance between the Earth and the Moon, scientists can also measure librations, the irregular rotation of the Moon about its center, caused by the satellite's elliptical orbit and uneven distribution of mass.

Each of the Apollo teams set up a seismometer to keep tabs on lunar tremors, caused by both internal tectonic shiftings and the impacts of good-sized meteorites. The final two Apollo missions in 1972 also carried seismic mortar rounds; by exploding them and then recording the shock waves as they bounced off different subsurface regions, scientists were able to analyze the interior composition of Earth's airless companion. Beginning with the very first Moon landing, astronauts at their various lunar landing sites deployed instruments to capture ionized atoms speeding in from the edges of the Solar System and beyond. They also set up a squat-shaped device known as a spectrometer to follow surges in the stream of electrons, protons and other charged particles that escape from the Sun's outer atmosphere—a phenomenon known as the solar wind. Resembling an air conditioner, the device caught the particles and determined from whence they had flown and how fast they had traveled.

Along with this bevy of instruments, the last three Apollo parties left behind three Lunar Rovers, which lent to each landing site a quality of eerie abandon. The Rovers looked like stripped-down buggies with exposed chassis, orange fiberglass fenders, wire mesh wheels, tool carriers, and assorted, odd-looking antennas and cameras sprouting from the Rover frame. For all their makeshift appearance, these utilitarian vehicles performed better than their designers expected, giving astronauts the power to roam farther and faster—even at a staid top speed of about eight miles per hour—than they ever could have by foot. The first visitors to the Moon, for example, covered 0.4 miles of terrain by foot; using the Lunar Rover, the last Apollo crew logged 22.4 miles during their two-day stay.

When they were ready to roll, the astronauts simply pulled down the vehicle, like a Murphy bed, from a bay on the side of the Lunar Module, unfolding its three-tiered frame and spring-mounted wheels. The wheels were crafted from flexible zinc-coated piano wire and the lightweight supermetal, titanium. In all, the 10-foot-long, 6-foot-wide vehicle weighed in at under 462 pounds on Earth—a man-

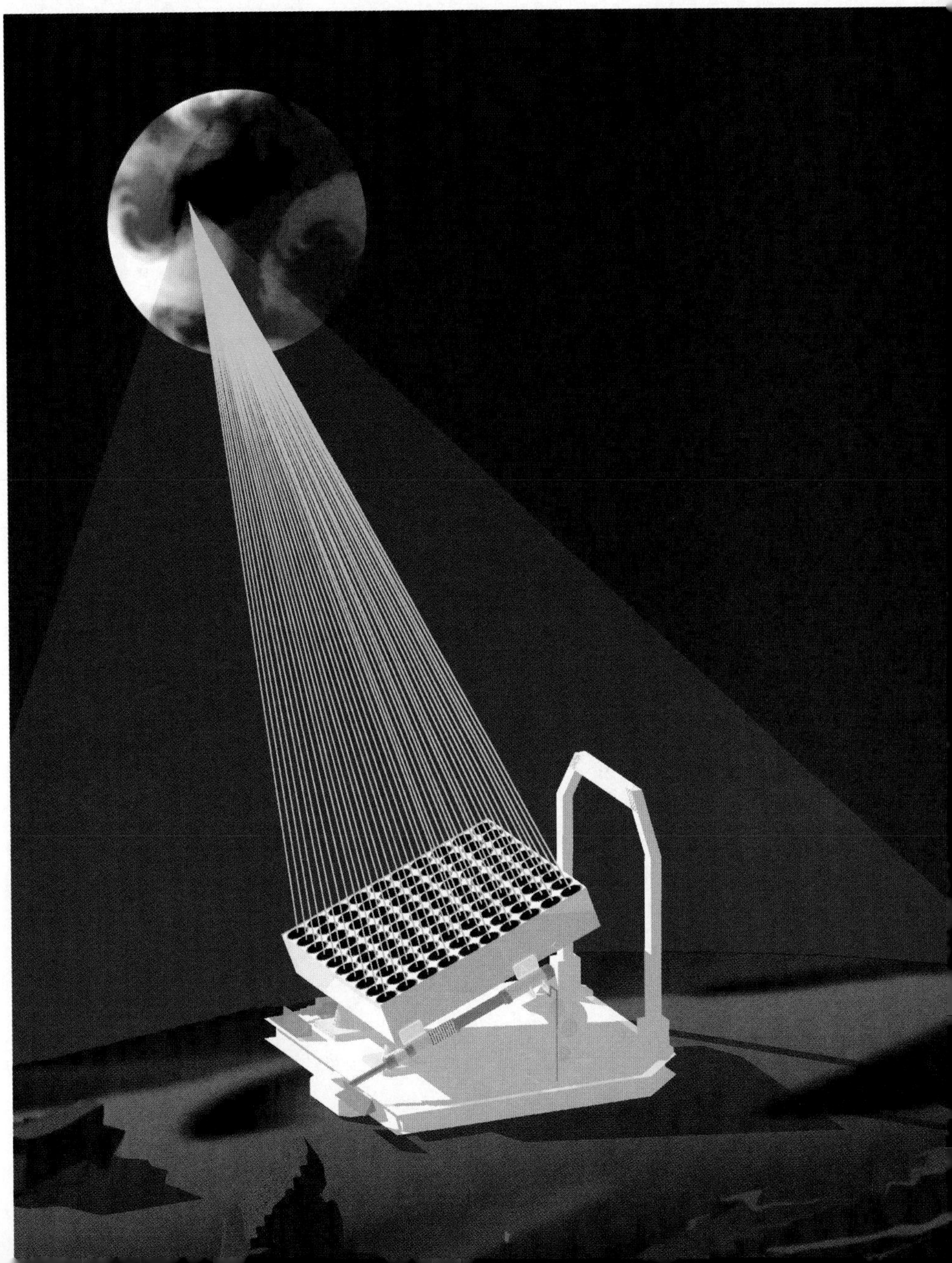

SHOOTING FOR THE MOON

During the late '60s and early '70s, five laser reflectors were set up on the Moon. Apollo astronauts took up three; two were sent on unmanned Soviet craft. The devices are used to measure the distance between Earth and the Moon with phenomenal accuracy. Hitting the record-album-sized reflectors from Earth and getting a return, however, is a tricky proposition, requiring up to 1,000 shots.

ageable 77 pounds under the one-sixth gravity of the Moon. And whereas the average car is designed to carry no more than half of its own weight, the Rover could carry almost three times its weight; two men and their life-support systems weighing 400 pounds each, and another 340 pounds of tools and collected materials.

With no reference points by which to judge distance, the astronauts on their seven-hour expeditions never knew how far away the craters, ridges, gorges and mountains within their view really were. To find their way back to the Lunar Module after their outings, the drivers retraced the Rover tracks across the lunar fields, bleached as snow in the glare of noon. Feeling bold on their last day, Apollo 15's David Scott and Jim Irwin abandoned their tracks on the final leg of their trip and attempted a shortcut, confident that the Rover's sophisticated navigation system, feeding data from three onboard gyroscopes into its computer, would guide them if their memories proved fallible. Although crater walls and ridges masked their view of the Lunar Module for minutes at a time, they emerged right on target.

Altogether, the three Rovers clocked nearly 55 miles of rugged travel, with only one repair required—not covered by warranty. In a mishap with a hammer, Eugene Cernan ripped the fender extension off Apollo 17's Rover. This required an instant fix, since without the extension, Cernan and his partner, Harrison Schmitt, would be showered with debris kicked up by the wheel. With panache, NASA engineers whipped up a plan for an ersatz replacement from duct tape and plastic navigational maps. The astronauts executed the repair, thus enshrining Cernan and Co. as the first automotive mechanics to do business on the Moon.

The Lunar Rover ran on two 36-volt batteries that fed power to four quarter-horsepower motors mounted on each wheel. Designed strictly for off-road jaunts over bumpy territory, the Moon buggy gave at least one jostled astronaut the feeling of being "in a small boat on a rough sea."

The first lunar car repair: After a fender was torn off on Apollo 17's Rover, astronauts Cernan and Schmitt cobbled together a makeshift one, held in place by a camera clamp.

$240-MILLION REPAIR

Less than a year after the Apollo 17 repair, a team of Skylab astronauts were called upon to perform a far more arduous and chancy job. Virtually from the moment of liftoff on May 14, 1973, Skylab had been plagued by mishaps. Just 63 seconds into the launch, as the mammoth Saturn V rocket shouldered its multi-ton payload past the 28,000-foot mark, the buffeting caused by aerodynamic forces ripped off the lab's 800-pound meteoroid shield. This lightweight shield was to have protected the orbiting research vessel from being roasted by the Sun's rays, and engineers calculated that without it, the temperature of the outer skin would reach a sizzling 325 degrees F.; inside temperatures would soar past 160 degrees. Not only would such high heat ruin the film and medical supplies—critical to the mission—stored in the lab, but it also might cause the workshop's blanketing foam insulation to break down chemically and release toxic gases. These would be difficult to vent and could prove hazardous to the crew, slated to arrive the next day via another rocket. In addition, one of the two wing-like solar panels that were to provide power for the lab's life-support systems and experiments was also gone, torn off by the errant meteoroid shield. And to top it off, one of the aluminum mounting straps from the disengaged heat shield had caught on the remaining solar wing and now bound it tight, preventing it from unfurling.

On the ground, a NASA engineer rapidly assembled a replacement Sun shield using five $12.50 telescoping fishing rods. Resembling an oversized folding umbrella, the new sunshade, covered with metallic fabric, could be extended through a science experiment airlock and opened almost flat atop the cylindrical Skylab cabin. As for the unwanted strap that was hobbling the solar array, engineers hoped a specially made tool that resembled a pair of long-handled tree-pruning shears would do the trick. With this extra baggage, the crew soared from the launch pad on May 25, 10 days behind schedule, but still confident of success.

The parasol worked just as planned. After their ship had docked with Skylab—which had indeed taken on the feel of an extraterrestrial sauna, although luckily without any trace of the feared toxic fumes—commander Charles Conrad and pilot Paul Weitz entered the lab, poked the umbrella out the scientific airlock and had it in place in no time. The astronauts then retreated to the relative comfort of their capsule to await a drop in Skylab's temperature. By the second night, the ambient temperature was a comfortable 80 degrees, and the lab greeted its first occupants. On June 7, Conrad and third crewmember Joseph Kerwin succeeded in freeing the solar panel with a few snips from their shears. Almost immediately, the array began producing enough electricity for the crew to carry out the full schedule of experiments with their flying science kit.

Notwithstanding their larger successes, the Skylab researchers had to deal with an assortment of bothersome snafus—clogged water pipes, jammed telescopes and fizzled fuses—all of which sent a clear message. The more complicated space machinery became, the more adept space travelers would have to be at working in space to fix things. NASA engineers always had planned for contingencies, but as they began to consider the requirements for such projects as permanent bases in orbit, or stations on the Moon or Mars, they encouraged contractors to opt for modular design, so that whole units or subunits of circuitry, piping or instrumentation could be removed in one fell swoop. This would ease the burden on zero-gravity repairmen, who, despite NASA's best efforts, still found extravehicular activity taxing work.

In crafting the Solar Maximum Mission satellite during the late 1970s for launch in February, 1980, designers at NASA's Goddard Space Flight Center in Maryland took this very approach, fitting separate systems together in compartments that could be popped out and replaced by identical self-contained assemblages. Naturally, everyone operated on the belief that these precautionary measures would be rendered unnecessary by the proper functioning of the satellite. But by the time the orbiting Solar Max satellite's attitude control system failed in November 1980, engineers—with a certain feeling of relief—realized that their foresight had paid off. The entire project would not have to be junked; it could be repaired.

The work that awaited George Nelson and his crewmate James van Hoften dwarfed any ever before required of astronauts. To capture and repair Solar Max they would have to execute several difficult maneuvers perfectly, using equipment—the Manned Maneuvering Unit, the jawlike Trunnion Pin Attachment Device (TPAD) and the robotic manipulator arm—with which they had practiced only on simulators. The astronauts knew, having learned from the experiences of their predecessors in space, that no matter how closely the testing of equipment in water-filled "buoyancy tanks" or with the aid of computers might approximate conditions in space, it never fully prepared one for the real thing.

Nelson and van Hoften would do everything as a team, except for roping in the satellite, which would fall to Nelson alone. The rescue began on the second day of Shuttle Mission 11, after the crew of *Challenger* had fulfilled another of their mission tasks—releasing the Long Duration Exposure Facility satellite *(page 132)*. Together, the two Solar Max repairmen began by slipping from the shuttle's middeck into the airlock, a seven-foot-long tube separating the pressurized crew quarters from the bus-sized cargo bay, which has its doors thrown open to space. On Gemini and Apollo EVAs, each exit from the capsule had meant depressurizing the entire cabin, and then, after the spacewalk was over, repressurizing it. On a ship the size of the shuttle, this was impractical, and so its designers provided an airlock with tightly sealing hatches at either end to serve as a transitional zone between areas.

Two unoccupied, pressurized spacesuits await their astronauts in the shuttle's airlock. Foot restraints for offsetting the zero-gravity environment are seen above the helmet visors.

Once in the airlock, Nelson and van Hoften undertook a series of standard procedures. They ran through numerous checks of their spacesuits, prepared the tools they would need to repair Solar Max and then donned the suits, bottom halves first. The tops, minus clear bubble helmets, hung in niches in the airlock wall, and to put them on, the astronauts first slid in from below, then released the latches holding the suits. A pressure-tight metal ring sealed the halves. Next came the Snoopy caps, with sewn-in microphones and earphones, and the gloves; then, the helmets, spritzed with a defogging agent and adorned with video cameras. After two leak checks to make certain that their suits were airtight, Nelson and van Hoften completed a 40-minute "prebreathe," inhaling pure oxygen from the life-support system, the part of the suit resembling a backpack, in order to purge the nitrogen from their bloodstreams. Had they entered the vacuous environment of space—even in the safety of their suits—without ridding their blood of nitrogen, the would-be repairmen might have fallen victims to a potentially fatal condition known as the bends. Familiar to scuba divers, the condition arises when nitrogen bubbles collect in the body's joints as the air pressure (or, for divers, water pressure) around the body is reduced after a stay in a compressed atmosphere.

Their prebreathe completed, and eager to work, the suited astronauts battened the middeck hatch and opened the airlock valves to vent the pressurized air out to space. During this time, the pressure inside the spacesuit was lowered from

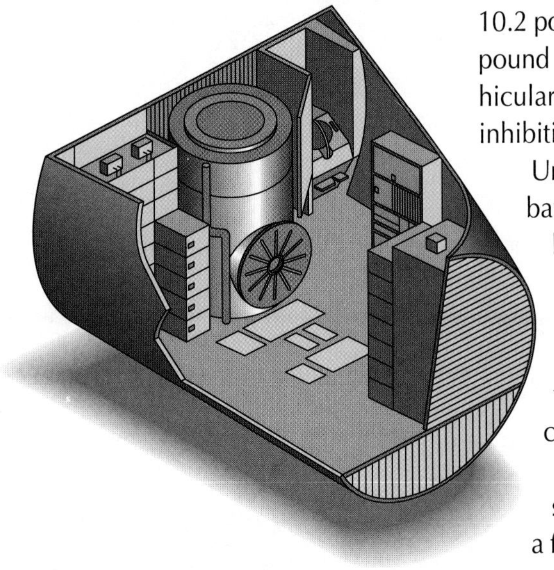

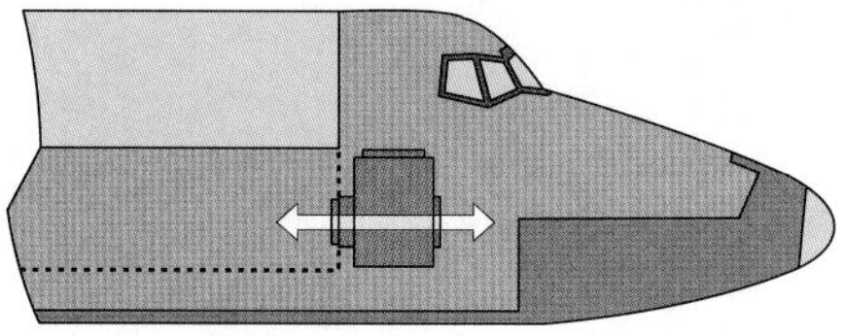

LEAVING THE SHUTTLE

Located at the aft end of the shuttle's mid-level deck, the airlock serves as a decompression/compression chamber. Before leaving the shuttle, astronauts inside the airlock breathe pure oxygen; the pressure in the airlock is then reduced from 12 pounds per square inch to 0—the same pressure outside the spacecraft. At the end of their Extravehicular Activity (EVA), the astronauts reenter the airlock through the cargo bay, the six-by-ten foot cylinder is repressurized and the astronauts return to the shuttle.

10.2 pounds per square inch to 4.3 pounds (normal atmospheric pressure is 14.7 pound p.s.i.), just enough pressure to keep an astronaut safe during an extravehicular activity, but not enough to make the suit inflate like a balloon, thereby inhibiting body movement.

Unfastening the outer hatch, the pair emerged into the airless, gravityless cargo bay. Taking advantage of the built-in railings that crisscross the walls of the bay, the duo moved along hand over hand, trailing tethers designed to prevent unwanted straying. Both astronauts felt a wave of cold break around them, the shocking iciness of a near-vacuum. On their way across the bay, Nelson and van Hoften passed over an aluminum canister fastened to the forward end of the bay, housing an experimental 360-degree wide-angle camera. Experiments like this have flown on most shuttle flights since June 1982. Depending on space and weight restrictions imposed by the main shuttle payloads, these so-called Getaway Specials can be placed aboard a flight for a mere $3,000, as long as NASA has to provide neither electricity nor manpower for them. The experiment containers range in size from 2.5 to 5 cubic feet; the larger size can accept up to 200 pounds. The program has been patronized by groups ranging from foreign governments to students. Two high schools from New Jersey, for example, raised the money to send an ant farm into space to see how the insects would respond to zero gravity. Unfortunately, the ants died from dehydration during their voyage aloft.

Nelson and van Hoften headed for the Flight Support Stations, one anchored to the forward port, the other to the starboard wall. Here, during a shuttle flight, the aluminum-framed Manned Maneuvering Units hang locked in place, their batteries charged and nitrogen tanks full. The Flight Support Station serves as a parking lot for the jetpack. To attach the maneuvering unit, an astronaut backs into the support station; two couplers near the shoulder and a lap belt lock the jetpack to the astronaut's spacesuit.

Developed after 10 years of design and $30 million worth of funding, the MMU looks, at first glance, like a reclining chair of the sort sold on late-night television advertisements. But, as astronauts Bruce McCandless and Robert Stewart had demonstrated during its first workout in February 1984, just two months before Nelson's and van Hoften's flight, these 338-pound wonders endowed wearers with phenomenal acrobatic skills, enabling them to control movement in six dimensions. A tilting joystick on the right arm controls pitching, yawing and rolling motions. Adjusting pitch tilts the MMU and its operator forward or backward at any angle; yaw turns the operator to the left or the right along the horizontal plane; roll rotates the operator head over heels in a sideways direction. A button located on the right-hand control, "inertial hold," also allows the operator to maintain a fixed attitude.

On the left arm, a push-pull joystick controls movement forward or back, left or right, up or down. Engineers at Martin Marietta Aerospace in Denver, Colorado, designed the system for a normal cruising speed of no more than four miles per hour, and preferably closer to one or one-and-one-half miles per hour, about the pace of a walker on Earth. Otherwise, a hapless astronaut might find himself lost in space, and—supposing the mother ship somehow was unable to track him by radio or by the signal lights on his backpack—stranded horribly in orbit.

Suitably Crafted

Spacecraft do not come any smaller; this one is barely the size of a human being. But like its previous incarnation—the Apollo moon suit worn by the 12 men who bounded about the lunar surface—the spacesuit worn by shuttle astronauts outside their craft can sustain a human life in the harsh, airless vacuum of space, offering oxygen, radio communication, a regulated temperature, drinking water and even a toilet.

Because it is composed of a complex network of layers, this craft takes time to board. A virtually naked astronaut begins suiting up by putting on the urine collection device, worn by men like a jockstrap and by women like a diaper. Next comes the liquid cooling and ventilation garment—a mesh layer made of spandex, resembling one-piece long underwear. It is embedded with 300 feet of plastic tubing that circulates cool water to prevent overheating. To communicate with the shuttle, the astronaut slips on a skintight "Snoopy Cap" containing a built-in headset.

Ready now for outerwear, the astronaut next steps into the pants—or lower torso assembly—which includes built-in boots. He then pushes head-first into the hard-shell upper torso. Both torso assemblies are made up of several layers including an outer layer woven of Kevlar, Teflon and Dacron, which protects the astronaut against radiation exposure, temperatures that range up to +250° F. and micrometeorites traveling faster than bullets. The innermost layer of polyurethane-coated nylon contains oxygen and is designed to exert pressure on the body that is similar to, though lighter than, the Earth's atmospheric pressure. The upper and lower torso assemblies are connected at the waist by an airtight sealing ring. The spacesuit gloves—the one part of the suit tailor-made for each astronaut—and helmet are then attached by the same sealing system.

Now snugly ensconced in the 107-pound suit, the astronaut must make one final adjustment before stepping into space: The switches on the chest-mounted control module are turned on to activate the life support system on the torso back. This pack-like device is the suit's power station, circulating oxygen and water, controlling temperature and pressure—providing the ingredients that turn spacesuits into spacecraft.

During NASA's free-spending Apollo days, each astronaut wore a custom-made spacesuit (above). *Unlike today's two-piece shuttle suit* (right)*—selected "off the rack" for each astronaut—the Apollo suit was a one-piece garment entered from behind and zippered all the way up the back. Later Apollo suits featured a zipper at the waist, where a flexible joint was added to facilitate sitting in the Lunar Rover.*

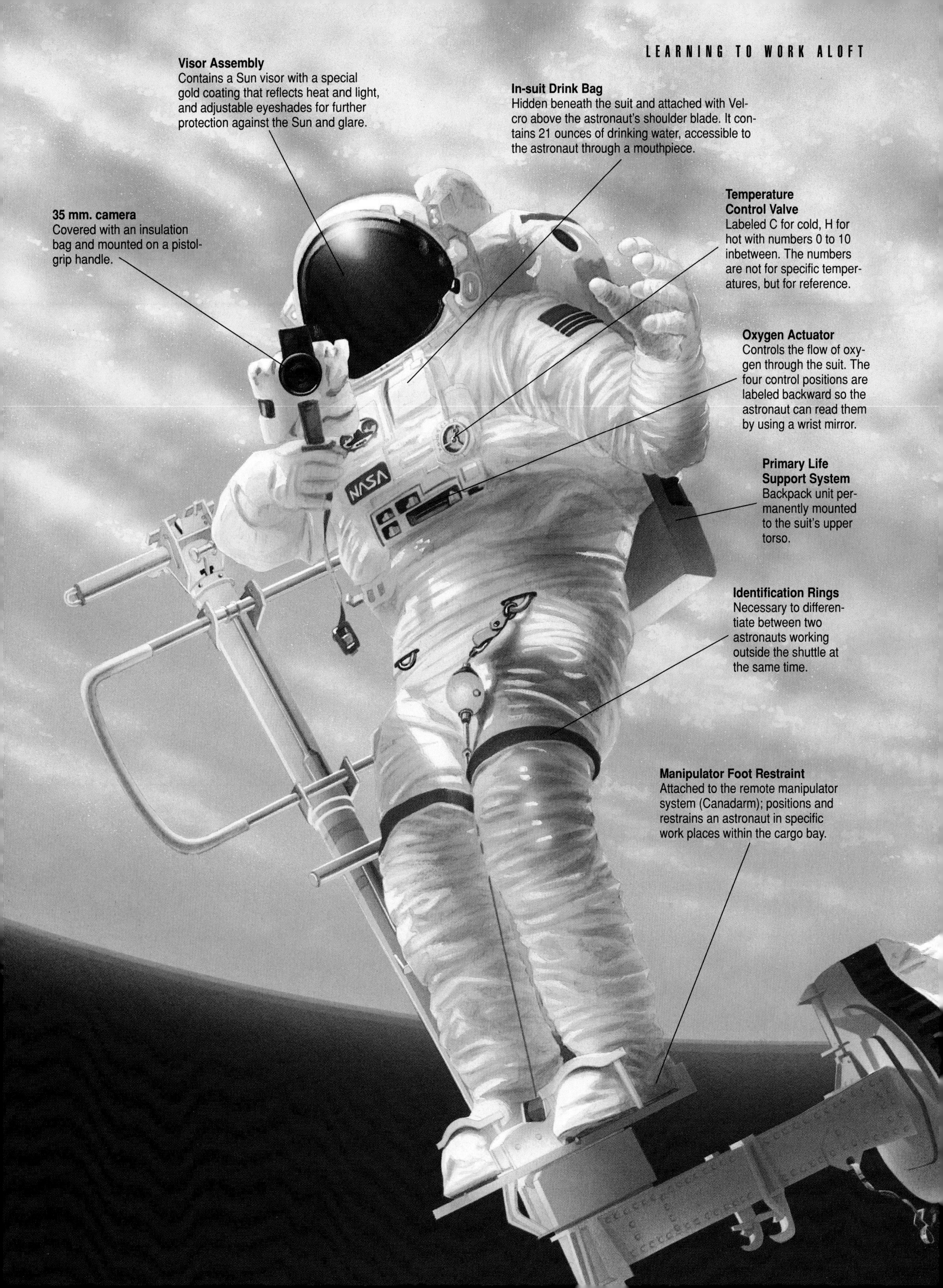
Visor Assembly
Contains a Sun visor with a special gold coating that reflects heat and light, and adjustable eyeshades for further protection against the Sun and glare.
In-suit Drink Bag
Hidden beneath the suit and attached with Velcro above the astronaut's shoulder blade. It contains 21 ounces of drinking water, accessible to the astronaut through a mouthpiece.
35 mm. camera
Covered with an insulation bag and mounted on a pistol-grip handle.
Temperature Control Valve
Labeled C for cold, H for hot with numbers 0 to 10 inbetween. The numbers are not for specific temperatures, but for reference.
Oxygen Actuator
Controls the flow of oxygen through the suit. The four control positions are labeled backward so the astronaut can read them by using a wrist mirror.
Primary Life Support System
Backpack unit permanently mounted to the suit's upper torso.
Identification Rings
Necessary to differentiate between two astronauts working outside the shuttle at the same time.
Manipulator Foot Restraint
Attached to the remote manipulator system (Canadarm); positions and restrains an astronaut in specific work places within the cargo bay.
NASA

It was NASA's dedication to preventing just this type of tragedy that had led it to settle on the MMU in the first place. Early attempts at providing astronauts with a way to motor about in the vicinity of their spacecraft received mixed reviews. Ed White, the first American to walk in space, had moved around the Gemini 4 capsule during his 1965 flight with a hand-held unit that fired compressed oxygen from three thrusters. They proved difficult to control. Denizens of Skylab were asked to test a Buck Rogers-like contraption with the exalted title of Foot Controlled Maneuvering Unit, known more simply as jet shoes. The supposed advantage of the jet shoes was that they were operated by the feet, leaving the arms free. But astronauts, who had to learn a set of foot movements to fire and steer the FCMU, quickly and loudly voiced their displeasure. The jet shoes went the way of the hand-held unit. The situation improved somewhat for the final Skylab crew, who spent several days testing out a precursor to the MMU called the Astronaut Maneuvering Unit. Powered by nitrogen thrusters and stabilized by onboard gyroscopes, the AMU allowed its wearers to jet around Skylab's large workshop area. Just in case anyone yearned to take it for a test spin outside, NASA engineers built the unit slightly larger than the orbiting lab's largest hatch.

Now, a decade later, as George Nelson readied himself for the attempt to rescue the Solar Max, he could be confident that he had the best machine for the job. He stepped into the support station's footclamps, which keep an astronaut stationary while backing into the MMU, and fastened himself into the MMU. Van Hoften waited in the aft end of the cargo bay, preparing tools for Solar Max's arrival. Nelson's MMU was furbished with an unusual attachment, the Trunnion Pin Attachment Device, which fastened across the arms and protruded from the front of the outfit, looking something like a fire plug. The TPAD featured a set of jaws designed to latch onto a large pin protruding from the side of Solar Max. Thus attired, Nelson stood poised on the threshold of the cargo bay. He fingered the MMU's controls, triggering the release of compressed nitrogen gas, which spurted out of the backpack's propulsion nozzles and thrust him out into space, over the bright limb of the Earth below with its gem-hued seas and lacelike clouds. But Nelson was not there to admire the view. He headed for the crippled, pickup-truck-sized satellite, which spun slowly, half a football field away from him.

Moving carefully, Nelson took 10 minutes to ford the gap. The shuttle's television cameras provided a live broadcast of the event, with Nelson standing out as a brilliant but humblingly small figure against the velvety black celestial backdrop. The 5,000-pound Solar Max flashed white and gold as sunlight caught its two windmill-like blades with their arrays of solar power cells. Calibrating his angle of attack perfectly, Nelson slipped carefully between the turning blades and gave a squirt of his jets to synchronize his motion with that of the satellite.

But here, Nelson suffered the frustration of those three fruitless docking attempts (investigations would later reveal that a solar blanket, added to the wall of Solar Max after the blueprints were made, had prevented the TPAD from latching on to its target). Then he had to face the fact that his time was running out. The MMU's fuel supply was reaching the level at which he would, by NASA rules, be forced to turn back. In the urgency of the moment, fellow astronaut Crippen hazarded the suggestion from inside the shuttle that he might try to arrest the satellite's rotation by hand. Game for anything at this point, Nelson positioned himself at the

With its fuel tank loaded with 26 pounds of nitrogen to feed its 24 propulsion nozzles, the Manned Maneuvering Unit (right) *can propel an astronaut miles away from the shuttle. All major MMU systems are duplicated, preventing a breakdown from stranding a human satellite in permanent orbit. The MMU is directed with hand controllers* (below). *The left-hand joystick propels an astronaut up or down, forward or backward, right or left; the right-hand controller governs pitch, roll and yaw, and has an inertial hold button on top of the handle that puts the MMU in neutral.*

LEFT-HAND CONTROLLER COMMANDS

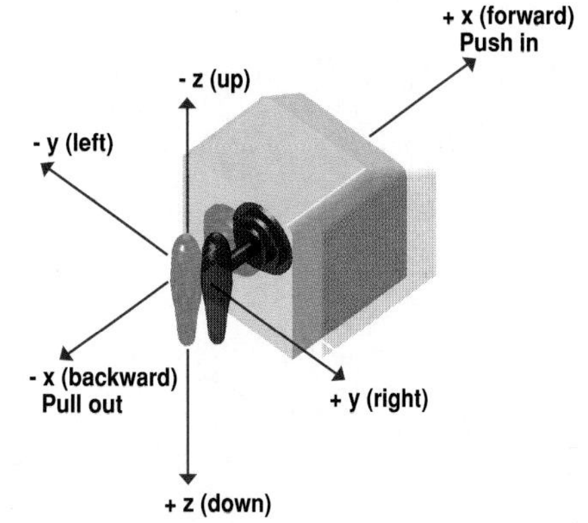

+ x (forward)
Push in
- z (up)
- y (left)
- x (backward)
Pull out
+ y (right)
+ z (down)

end of one of the solar panels. There, grasping the panel with both hands, the space repair man vainly attempted to wrestle the renegade Solar Max into submission.

Disconcerted, Nelson returned to the shuttle. Meanwhile, Crippen and ground controllers palavered, trying to figure out how to bring the flailing satellite to bay. Finally, a daring tactic was devised. With Nelson and van Hoften still suited up and waiting in the cargo bay, Crippen chased down his target and, exhibiting his superb maneuvering skills as a pilot, engineered a flyby that brought the 100-ton orbiter within close enough range for another member of the crew, Terry Hart, to make a grab at Solar Max with the extendable robotic arm, also known as the Canadarm because it had been built by Toronto's Spar Aerospace.

Seven years and $100 million in the making, the 50-foot-long, computer-guided arm is articulated by motor-driven joints at wrist, elbow and shoulder. The wrist features three joints, permitting pitch, roll and yaw; the shoulder can pitch and yaw; the elbow has a single joint allowing it to bend. To protect the internal mechanisms from extreme temperature shifts, engineers had shielded the lightweight graphite epoxy arm with layers of gold-covered insulation. Workers even wore white gloves when installing the protective sheathing to keep it free from the natural oils of their fingertips, which would hamper the gold's effectiveness.

RIGHT-HAND CONTROLLER COMMANDS

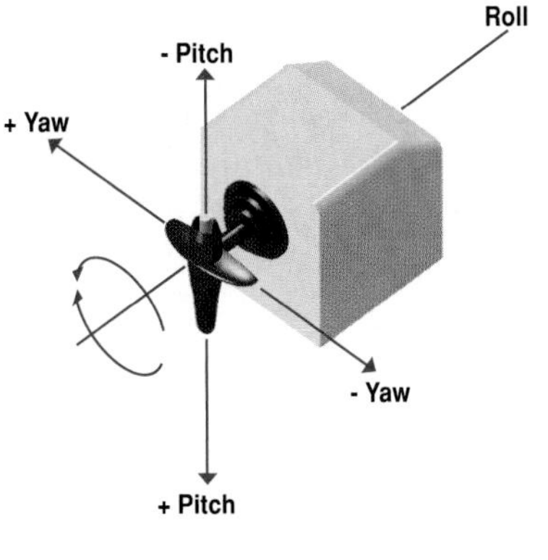
Roll
- Pitch
+ Yaw
- Yaw
+ Pitch

Although the arm weighs a scant 905 pounds on Earth, in space it can handle payloads weighing up to 65,000 pounds, the equivalent of a fully loaded bus. On this score, Solar Max posed no problem; Hart's real concern lay in not tangling the Canadarm's booms in the solar arrays, or otherwise further damaging the satellite. To complicate matters, Solar Max was rotating at 0.5 degrees per second—five times faster than the arm was designed to handle. From his post in the left rear window of the crew compartment, Hart watched the white arm extend toward the target. The shuttle was sailing over the Indian Ocean on the dark side of the Earth, and Solar Max was illuminated only by harsh floodlights from the cargo bay. Hart made four tries, all misses.

By this time, flight controllers had begun to worry that capture, if it came at all, might come too late. When the satellite had begun tumbling, its solar cells had stopped receiving enough sunlight to generate electricity; consequently, the onboard systems had switched to battery power, which was now running out. If the power went, Solar Max would freeze irreversibly and become just another piece of space flotsam. Engineers at Goddard Space Flight asked that the shuttle back off until Solar Max had been brought under control, and then engaged in a marathon, overnight session of computer signaling, finally succeeding in returning the satellite to its slow, axial rotation pattern in the wee hours of the morning.

Heartened by this victory, the Challenger crew moved in at midmorning—24 hours after the first attempt—to make a last stab. All over the world, NASA people awaited the outcome. The shuttle drew near, Hart grabbed, and Crippen radioed back the news. "Okay, we've got it," he said, with typical astronautic understatement. But in Mission Control restraint was not an issue. An ecstatic cheer went up.

It remained for van Hoften and Nelson to make the trip out of the airlock and into the cargo bay again to carry out the actual repairs. They labored steadily for seven-and-one-half hours to remove the faulty fuse panel and mend the sick coronagraph, a camera used to photograph the tenuous halo of gases surrounding the Sun. To ease his efforts, van Hoften stood with his feet clamped onto a plate on the end of the Canadarm. This freed both hands for work and gave him leverage, which ordinarily does not come easily to a person floating free in space. At times Nelson, who gained stability by holding onto the satellite with one hand, hovered beside his colleague in a tableau that lent the cargo bay the air of a hospital operating theater.

Commander Robert Crippen, standing at a set of displays and switches at the flight station at the rear of the shuttle's flightdeck, can maneuver the Canadarm to any position. Two closed-circuit television cameras mounted on the arm provide closeup views.

These were odd surgeons, though, for their tools dangled at all angles from hooks on their spacesuits. Wrenches, screwdrivers, sockets, shears and other tools that go into space may look like ordinary hardware, but each piece has undergone a rigorous design and testing process. Handholds for pliers, for instance, have to be expanded to accommodate the bulky fingers of spacegloves. Ratchet wrenches must have low resistance during the part of their operation cycle when the wrench is rotated backward to make a driving stroke. A low "backdrive" helps ensure that a bolt will only rotate in the required direction. Sockets for the wrenches have to be forged from materials that will not expand or shrink too much in the large temperature swings of space.

To keep gears and bearings from seizing up in the vacuum of space and under the wildly fluctuating temperatures, engineers had to concoct special dry lubricants. Baked by the Sun, liquid lubricants would become too thin, while at -150° F., the same lubricant would freeze rock hard. Finally, tools with separate components have to be fitted with attachments to prevent their coming apart, for in the almost-frictionless realms of space, small pieces, like a ratchet head, can be set sailing away at a brisk clip by only the slightest touch. All tools are tethered; when not in use they normally are stowed carefully in boxes and pocketed bags in the cargo bay and airlock.

Among the specialized instruments with which van Hoften and Nelson were armed were a torque wrench, or module servicing tool, a cable cutter and an electric screwdriver. As they clambered over the satellite, the pair followed step-by-

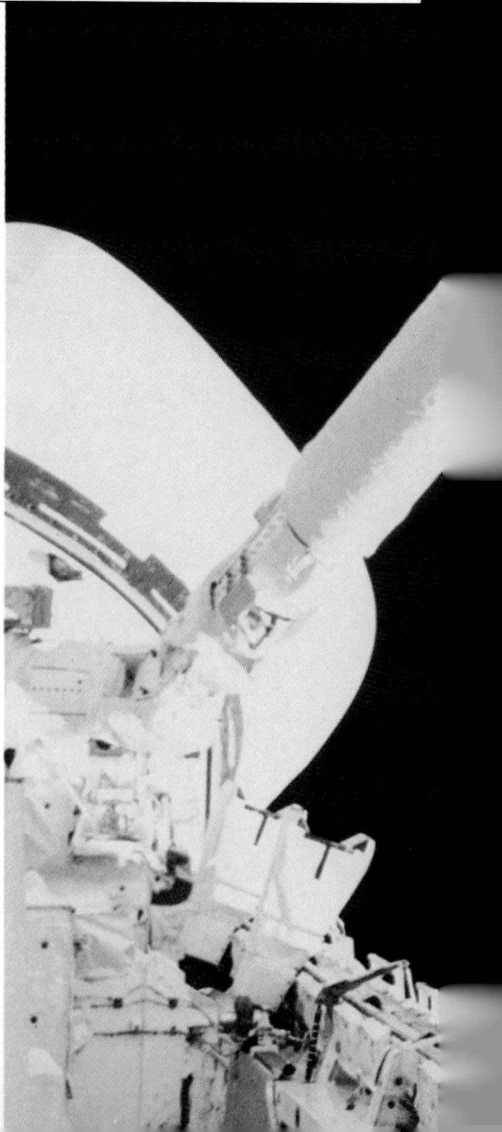

The remote manipulator system—also known as the Canadarm—works like a human arm, with an articulated shoulder, elbow and wrist. The six electrical motors that power the joints are each the size of an orange. Together, the six motors can move a 65,000-pound satellite using less than half the power of a portable hair dryer.

Known as the "end effector," the hand of the robotic Canadarm (shown here without its skin) houses three snare wires. When the hand grabs onto a payload, a ring rotates, closing the wires snugly around its target like a noose.

step repair instructions communicated to them from inside the shuttle by mission specialist Dick Scobee. (Occasionally, astronauts refer to snapshot-sized spiral-bound notebooks attached to their cuffs. These may contain repair and service instructions and illustrations as well as emergency procedures should a spacesuit system fail.) Their first line of attack was to unscrew the two bolts that fastened the attitude control module to the satellite's flank. This unit, which weighed 500 pounds on Earth, contained the defunct fuses. To remove the bolts, van Hoften wielded the specially designed torque wrench. Once he had latched the boxy, battery-driven device onto the module, it was simply a matter of flicking a switch to select the desired torque, then watching a counter to determine when the bolt had twirled all the way off. Slipping the hefty module—a featherweight in zero gravity—away from the satellite, the astronauts muscled into place a fresh unit, complete with hardier fuses, and reversed the procedures.

TOP
Like a spacebound surgeon, James van Hoften operates on the ailing Solar Max satellite at the aft end of the shuttle cargo bay, removing and replacing defective parts that had rendered the $240 million satellite useless.

The next job required more finesse, but by this time, the astronauts had regained their confidence after the failed capture attempts. Van Hoften sliced through Solar Max's insulation to expose the cover of the coronagraph and unfastened several screws on its face plate with a power screwdriver. Reaching back among the thick bundles of wires with cutters, he snipped one set. This allowed him to get at the electronics box, which he pulled out and exchanged for a new one. It remained only to reconnect the wires to the box by screwdriver, and mend the wound in the satellite's skin. Because they finished the repair ahead of schedule, van Hoften donned the other MMU, stationed on the cargo bay's starboard side, and the tired but happy twosome used the next hour to evaluate the MMU's maneuvering abilities. After another night sitting in the *Challenger's* cargo bay, Solar Max was sent on its way. Almost immediately, it began chattering at its ground controllers, who pronounced it back in good health.

The Solar Max repair bolstered NASA's faith, and within seven months, shuttle crews were dispatched to snare two other broken-down pieces of equipment, the Palapa B-2 and Westar VI communication satellites. Having learned their lesson, the space agency eschewed the TPAD, opting instead for an improved grappler called the Apogee Kick Motor Capture Device, which resembled a skeletal dish antenna, and possessed a long stinger for threading into the satellite's rocket nozzle. The satellites rode back to Earth in the cargo bay for retooling and relaunch.

An elated NASA foresaw an era of dynamic growth in space work, in which shuttle crews not only delivered, but also routinely salvaged and performed maintenance on a host of orbiting equipment. In a less sober appraisal of man's new status, one cartoonist drew a sketch of two antenna-headed aliens pulling up to a pair of tool-clutching shuttle astronauts on EVA and saying, "Excuse me, but we've got this ping in our $3 forward ionized radomic thruster lock fibulizer...;" blazoned on the shuttle's nose was MR. SPACE WRENCH FIX-IT SERVICE.

FLYING LAB

Much to the relief of researchers, who had long complained that shuttle missions placed more emphasis on derring-do than worthwhile scientific objectives, the 1980s also proved a rewarding time for work of a more refined nature. With the maiden launch of Spacelab in November 1983 aboard the shuttle Columbia, the technological might of a laboratory on Earth was brought to outer space.

Spacelab was developed over the course of a decade—and at a cost of close to $1 billion—by the European Space Agency. Originally known as the European Space Research Organization, the Paris-based consortium was formed in 1973 by Belgium, Denmark, Germany, France, Ireland, Italy, the Netherlands, Spain, Sweden, Switzerland and the United Kingdom. Researchers worldwide had decried the enormous expense of doing science in space.

Technically, Spacelab is referred to as an "attached" payload, meaning that it rides along with the shuttle both ways, without being dumped out. In fact, the lab is not a single entity, but a series of components that can be put together in different configurations, depending on the desires of the scientists in charge. There are two basic units, the pressurized, cylindrical crew modules of about 13 feet in diameter that feed on the shuttle's power and life support systems, and the U-shaped pallets that hook onto them like coal cars onto a locomotive, and sit exposed to the sky. The pallets are basically open cargo containers, with equipment such as telescopes and earth-sensing equipment bolted to them. Since the crew module comes in two sizes, 14 and 23 feet long, a given Spacelab mission can include anywhere from one to three pallets holding up to 6,000 pounds of instruments apiece. It is also possible to fly Spacelab with no crew module and as many as five pallets—each bolted together with 12 aluminum alloy joints—or with one long crew module and no pallets. Each pallet weighs 2,650 pounds and can support a ton of instruments for each yard of its three-yard length. Some pallet-mounted instruments are automated; others need to be controlled—from inside the core module, from the shuttle's flight deck or from the ground.

For safety reasons, Spacelab travels into orbit empty of astronauts. Only after launch do crew members float into Spacelab through a crooked aluminum tunnel attached to the shuttle airlock. With an internal diameter of 40 inches, the transfer tunnel allows the passage of crew in shirt sleeves or spacesuits, with or without packages. The tunnel is a modular structure; segments can be joined to bridge the gap with the Spacelab module, depending on its location in the payload bay.

Once inside the lab, the payload specialists, generally picked for their expertise in a given scientific field, stand at two floor-to-ceiling banks of movable racks to perform experiments, able to enter resulting data directly onto computers built into the wall for transmission to Earth. They also have a voice line to their own mission control facility in Huntsville, Alabama, (previously located in a building next to mission control in Houston, Texas) and the roster of scientists giving advice from the ground as the experiments unfold generally has an international flavor. On Spacelab's pioneer mission in 1983, for instance, there were 69 experiments from 14 countries.

Although occasional snafus have dogged it—astronauts on a flight in 1985 were pressed into service to vacuum monkey and rat droppings that had inadvertently floated free of specially designed cages—Spacelab still offers the best hope for breakthroughs in a number of disciplines, including several key areas of physics. Space plasma physicists expect to glean insights into interactions between the Earth's magnetic field and the barrage of particles and ionized gases, called plasmas, that flow from the Sun and stars and may influence weather patterns by interfering with the atmosphere. Similarly, atmospheric scientists have sent remote sensors aloft in Spacelab to measure and chart the distribution of chemical compounds and elements in the atmosphere at altitudes ranging from 5 to 150 miles above the Earth. Other cameras, pointed groundward, have mapped the terrain below with a degree of accuracy hard to achieve by conventional, earthbound techniques, and have produced surveys of such resources as vegetation, schools of fish and roads that surpass assessments carried out by airplane.

Astronomers savor Spacelab's berth far from the Earth's madding atmosphere, which mars the view of even the most powerful telescopes. Water vapor, dust —the very molecules of the air—all absorb and deflect incoming radiation. Instruments mounted upon the Spacelab's pallet suffer no such insults. Spacelab has flown numerous sensors, including a detector for spotting X-rays emanating from stars; a Very Wide-Field Camera, for scanning broad regions for emissions in the ultraviolet range, typically produced by either very young or very old stars; and a Far Ultraviolet telescope, which harkened to the faintest whispers of radiation in the same wavelength. All these were kept trained on their targets by the Spacelab's Instrument Pointing System. A device with hairbreadth aim, the system can keep a moving telescope focused on an object the size of a dime from a distance of more than two miles away.

One of the most far-reaching applications of Spacelab centers on another offshoot of physics, materials science, which studies the properties of both organic and inorganic substances, from proteins to metals to space-age composites. The Holy Grail of materials science is the perfect crystal—of any substance. A perfect crystal enables researchers to frame, with greatest precision, the atomic structure of the material, and, consequently, to understand how that material can be altered, made in bulk or otherwise manipulated. Such knowledge is critical to biologists and pharmaceutical researchers attempting, say, to elucidate the AIDS virus. By knowing a virus' structure, pharmacologists stand the best chance of tailor-making vaccines or drugs that will disable or destroy it. In the case of the AIDS virus, biologists are using Spacelab to try to create an enzyme inhibitor that will block the virus' natural life cycle.

Growing crystals in the lab on Earth is a daunting undertaking, because, as the crystals grow, gravity warps them. But, with their miniature furnaces, trays full of prismlike chambers containing bits of protein suspended in liquid, and other paraphernalia, the Spacelab crews engaged in modern-day alchemy, and opened the way for zero-gravity factories of the future.

Those who have acted as science's emissaries in orbit voice the view that their experiences have laid the

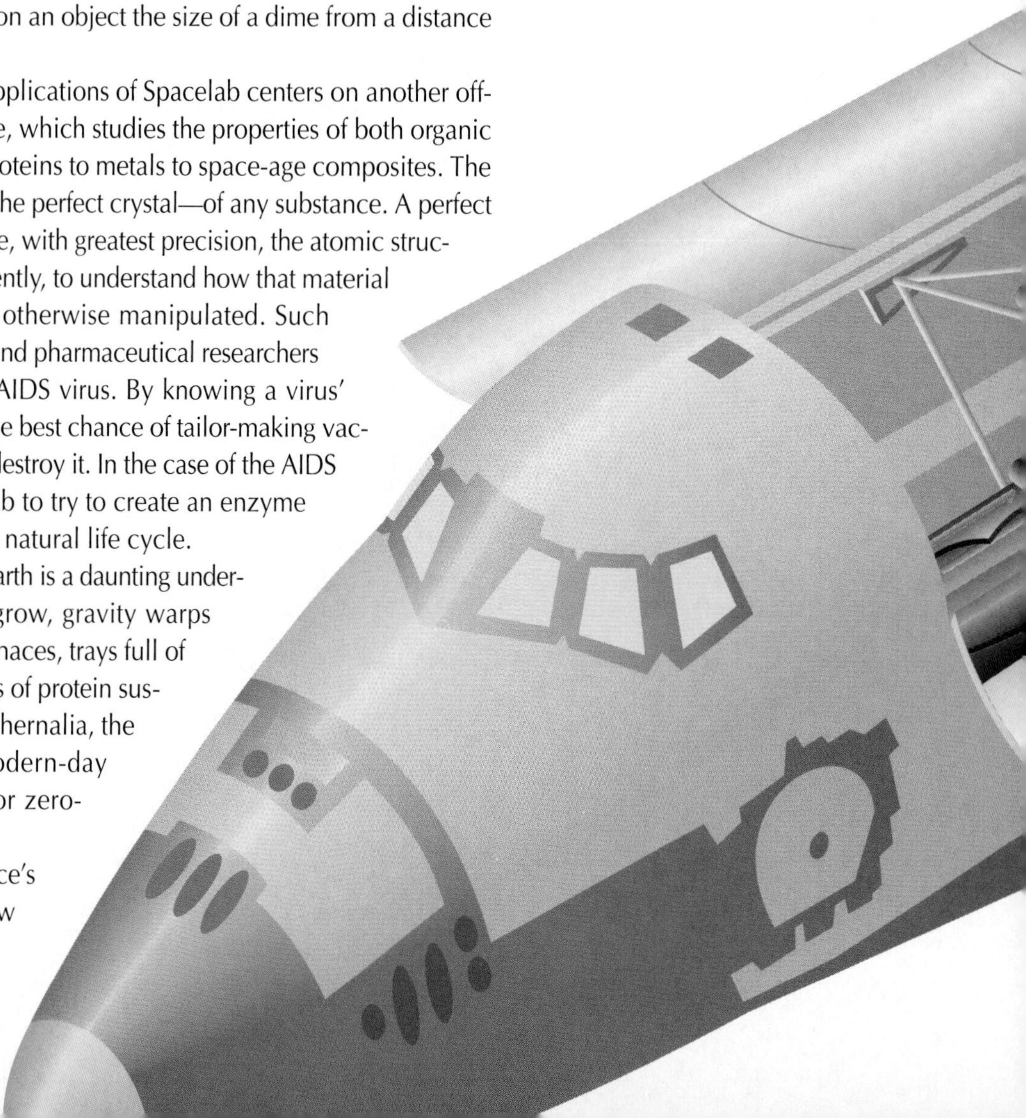

SCIENCE IN SPACE

Spacelab's long module—23 feet long and 13 feet in diameter—contains a main aisle lined with 19-inch laboratory racks that can hold up to 645 pounds of scientific instruments and equipment. The U-shaped pallet at the end of Spacelab can carry antennas, telescopes and other sensors. A shorter module allows up to three pallets to be attached.

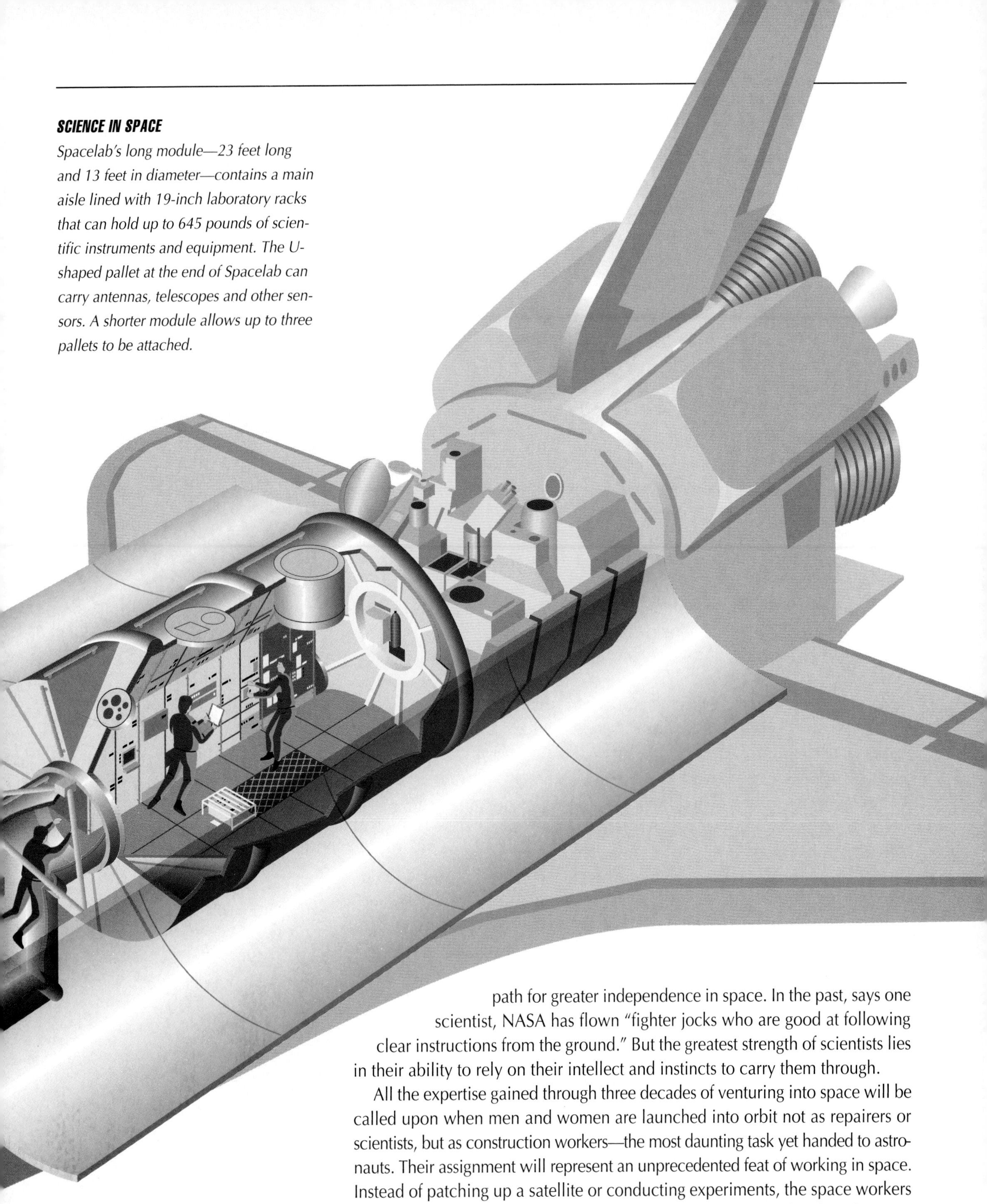

path for greater independence in space. In the past, says one scientist, NASA has flown "fighter jocks who are good at following clear instructions from the ground." But the greatest strength of scientists lies in their ability to rely on their intellect and instincts to carry them through.

All the expertise gained through three decades of venturing into space will be called upon when men and women are launched into orbit not as repairers or scientists, but as construction workers—the most daunting task yet handed to astronauts. Their assignment will represent an unprecedented feat of working in space. Instead of patching up a satellite or conducting experiments, the space workers of the 1990s will be building something new—an almost 500-foot-long home in the heavens called space station Freedom.

STATIONS IN THE SKY

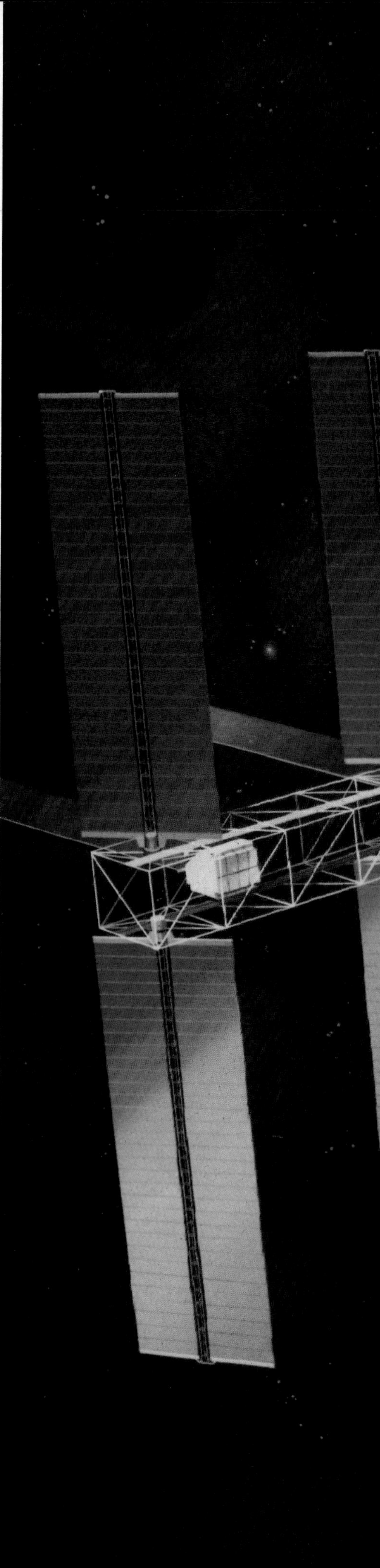

It will be an unusual place to call home—a cluster of metal cylinders huddled under a network of trusses, with solar panels, antennas and scientific bric-a-brac sticking out akimbo. But whatever it might lack in style will be more than made up in location. Circling 260 miles above the Earth, space station Freedom will provide a uniquely challenging and rewarding place to live and work by the turn of the 21st Century.

A joint venture involving the United States, Canada, the European Space Agency and Japan, Freedom carries a hefty $30-billion price tag. Still, it is unlikely to go wanting for tenants, and not just because of the sublime views it will offer of the Earth below and the stars above. Freedom will provide scientists and astronauts of Western nations with their first long-term habitat in space since a two-story orbital workshop called Skylab. As roomy as a three-bedroom house, Skylab served as a home away from home for three groups of American astronauts in 1973 and 1974. By that time, the Soviet Union already had launched the first of its Salyut workstations. They provided Soviet cosmonauts with a home in the sky, off and on, for 15 years, before a more spacious, versatile space station—Mir—was lofted into orbit in 1986.

Mir (the Russian word for peace) and Freedom are important symbols of the direction the international space program will take in the next century. Finally, men and women will actually live in space, instead of making relatively brief forays into that alien environment. And yet this is an objective fraught with unparalleled difficulty. Space contains not even the basics for human survival—no food, no water, no air. Temperatures vary from -250° to +250° F.; radiation presents risks not yet fully understood. Moreover, living in space means living unencumbered by gravity, offering advantages, yet also exacting its own physiological price.

Despite these complexities, or perhaps because of them, the lure of space has proved overwhelming, impossible to deny. Confronting a vast, dangerous and exotic world and creating a permanent niche within it seems to speak to some of the most basic of human needs. Like the men and women who journeyed from the

During the 1990s, NASA plans to construct the United States' first permanent space station, Freedom, using the shuttle to ferry up the parts.

FREEDOM
esa
USA
NASA

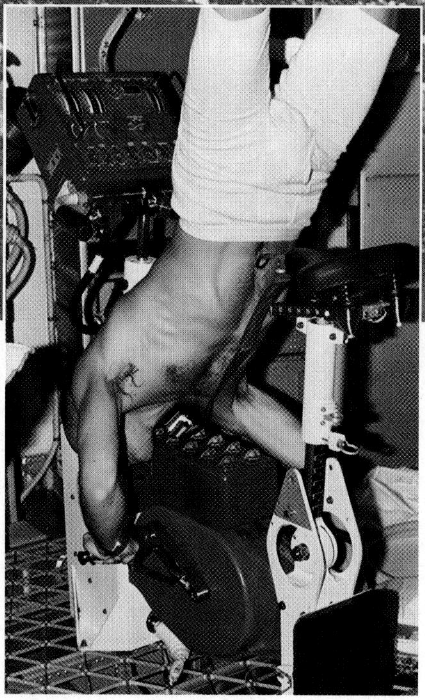

Skylab, America's first space station, floats over its home planet in 1973. Skylab 2 astronaut Alan Bean (inset) *pedals a stationary bicycle using his arms. On the previous Skylab mission, fellow spaceman Charles Conrad pedaled nonstop for 90 minutes and claimed—since that was the duration of a single orbit—that he had bicycled around the world.*

Old World to the New centuries ago, today's pioneers are prompted by the desire to meet a great challenge, the yearning to surmount the insurmountable, the irrepressible urge to forge on to new frontiers.

A HOME IN SPACE

By the time Apollo 17, the last Apollo Moon mission, returned from the parched lunar surface in December 1972, the future of America in space seemed rudderless. The dramatic appeal by President Kennedy in 1961 to land a man on the Moon by the end of the decade had galvanized the nation and provided a clear goal. That goal—seemingly fantastic and unattainable when it was first proclaimed—had been achieved, but now, with six Moon landings behind them, Americans had lost much of their enthusiasm for space exploration. What had once inspired and awed now seemed only to elicit ennui and indifference.

Faced with a nation apathetic to the lunar missions and reluctant to commit vast sums of money to any new project, NASA downscaled its immediate plans to put astronauts in orbit for extended stays in space. Instead of space stations built from scratch—what many had foreseen as the centerpiece of spaceflight in the 1970s and 1980s—NASA engineers opted for a single orbiting abode, cobbled together from components developed for Apollo and the earlier Gemini two-man missions. The station itself was actually the third stage of the Saturn V Moon rocket, with liquid oxygen and hydrogen fuel tanks removed. The result was Skylab, a 118-foot-tall workshop that would serve as home for three trios of astronauts on missions ranging from 28 to 84 days starting in the spring of 1973.

The station took to the skies on May 14, 1973, propelled 270 miles aloft on top of a modified Saturn V rocket. Two weeks later, the first of its crews, veteran astronaut Charles "Pete" Conrad and neophyte spacemen Joe Kerwin and Paul

The cross spider Arabella fared poorly during her early attempts to spin a proper web in the zero gravity of space. She later produced results akin to those of an earthbound spider.

Weitz blasted off in a Saturn 1B to dock with the lab. The first order of business was to make some badly needed repairs, installing a makeshift Sun shield to make up for insulation ripped off during the station's launch, and freeing a snagged solar panel *(page 104)*. Then the trio settled down to 28 days of living, sleeping and working aboard their commodious home. Actually, Skylab was more a "hotel" than a home: During the following year two other crews checked in. In July 1973 former moonwalker Alan Bean arrived with Owen Garriott and Jack Lousma for a 56-day sojourn; in mid-November the last Skylab trio—Gerald Carr, William Pogue and Edward Gibson—boarded Skylab with an extra 160 pounds of groceries for the longest mission, 84 days.

Compared with the Mercury, Gemini and Apollo spacecraft in which astronauts barely had been able to leave their seats, Skylab was a veritable palace. Whereas the 4-by-5-foot, bell-shaped interior of the single-passenger Mercury capsule offered less than 100 cubic feet of living space, Skylab boasted almost 12,000 cubic feet, allowing its inhabitants to move freely, vaulting off walls and performing other zero-gravity hijinks. ("We never went anywhere straight," proclaimed Skylab 1 commander Conrad. "We always did a somersault or a flip on the way.") They also had such welcome amenities as a wardroom, featuring a table with electronic heaters to warm the crew's meals; tiny private bedrooms with reading lamps; an air-suction toilet, equipped with a lap belt and foot straps to secure astronauts to the seat; and a collapsible shower. The latter proved something of a mixed blessing: Because water did not flow as it does on Earth, they had to rub soapy water over their bodies, then literally vacuum both themselves and the fabric shower stall to mop up the water, a process that could take up to an hour.

Skylab's name was an apt choice. During the 171 days astronauts spent aboard her, the sky-based laboratory played host to 270 experiments, including investigations of the Sun's activity, surveys of the Earth's resources and studies of the human body's adaptation to long-term living in space. A 12-ton solar observatory containing 8 telescopes captured 160,000 pictures of the Sun, including spectacular and unprecedented images of the violent eruptions of solar flares, high-energy particles that leap, flamelike, thousands of miles off the Sun's surface. Aimed in the other direction, Skylab's Earth Resources Experiment Package (EREP) probed natural phenomena and environmental and resource problems. Five clusters of cameras, scanners and radars observed erupting volcanoes, locust plagues, tropical storms, geological features of earthquake-prone regions, snow and ice cover, ocean currents, tree blight, drought, crop distribution, deforestation, strip mining and more. In addition, the astronauts performed 19 experiments selected from more than 3,400 submitted by high school students in a competition. One involved female cross spiders, which regularly spin webs with nearly concentric circles. In space, the spiders, Anita and Arabella, were at first disoriented by zero gravity. They had to be coaxed out of their containers, and they spun disorganized webs with the strands not even in the same plane. But after a few days, they found their "zero-g legs" and started producing normal-looking webs.

Not surprisingly, the organism of greatest interest was *Homo sapiens.* The astronauts performed a host of biomedical experiments in which they were their own guinea pigs. Probably no group of men has ever been so thoroughly examined for so long a period of time. Provided with a schedule that planned virtually every minute from the time they got up to the time they went to sleep, the astronauts kept track of every mouthful of food they ate and noted every urination and bowel movement. (Skylab 3 pilot William Pogue actually received a reprimand from Mission Control in Houston for not freeze-drying his vomitus for analysis back on Earth.) They measured the girth of their calves, thighs, waists, chests, biceps, and necks; they sat in chairs that were spun at 30 revolutions per minute to test for motion sickness. Electrocardiograms monitored their heartbeats; "bunny caps" with electrodes kept track of their brain waves while they slept.

Concerned that living in zero gravity would deprive astronauts of adequate exercise for muscles and the cardiovascular system, NASA engineers equipped Skylab with a stationary bicycle known as an ergometer. The first crew averaged only about half an hour a day and suffered the worst deconditioning of the three crews. About halfway through the mission, the first Skylab crew started to have difficulty completing cardiovascular tests; after returning to Earth, they had trouble walking. It took them 16 days to match preflight performances on the stationary bicycle and their heart rates shot up 10 beats per minute higher than normal. (In space, heart rates had dropped by 20 beats per minute.) Skylab's second and third crews, who exercised an hour to an hour and a half each day, returned in better physical condition, despite their longer stays in space.

After orbiting the Earth 1,214 times, and logging 34.8 million miles, the final Skylab crew reluctantly closed up its home in space and returned to Earth in February 1974. With NASA's budget reined in by a public grown blasé to space exploits, the days of a manned Skylab were over. "I hate to think we're the last guys to use it," lamented astronaut and solar physicist Edward Gibson, who later wrote a textbook, *The Quiet Sun*, based on data gleaned during his mission. "She's been a good bird," agreed Mission Control. Mothballed, Skylab floated empty—bereft of guests from the planet below. Day by day its orbit decayed, drawing it closer to Earth. On the night of July 11-12, 1979, more than six years after it was launched, the defunct laboratory reentered the atmosphere, cutting a fiery swath along a path thousands of miles long. Fortunately, of 16 possible reentry routes, Skylab followed the least damaging, mostly over open ocean and the barren central desert of Australia. In the end, the $2.6-billion program ended up as charred debris strung out over the Australian Outback—and the Aussies presented a U.S. Department of State representative with a $400 fine for littering.

DOCKING FLEXIBILITY

The outgrowth of two generations of workstations, Russia's Mir space station offers new flexibility and comfort, including individual sleeping stations. Launched in 1986, it features six docking ports, allowing different modules to dock at the same time, carrying supplies and scientific equipment. Five are at one end—four at 90-degree angles and one along the main axis—and one at the aft end.

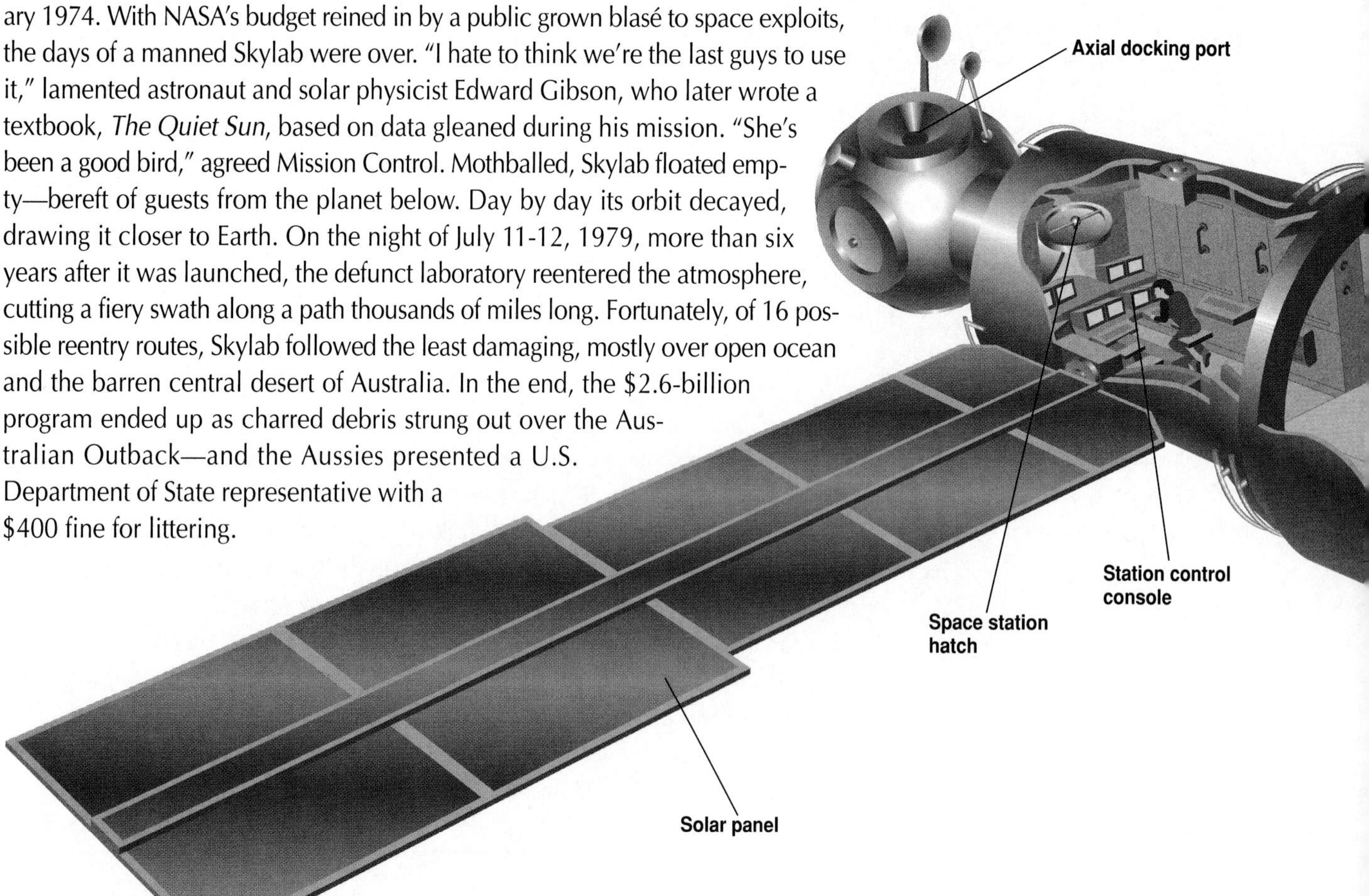
Axial docking port
Station control console
Space station hatch
Solar panel

PEACE IN SPACE

Skylab's endurance record of 84 days for a single mission did not stand for long. Having conceded the Moon race to the United States in 1969, the Russians turned their attention to building habitats for low-Earth orbit. They had launched the first of their Salyut workstations by 1971—named "Salute" in honor of the 10th anniversary of Yuri Gagarin's pioneering spaceflight. In 1978, Soviet cosmonauts beat Skylab's record with a 96-day mission. The next year, a Soviet crew completed a 175-day trip in space that exceeded the duration of all three Skylab missions combined—aboard the 44-foot-long, 22-ton Salyut 6. Other, even longer, missions followed throughout the '80s, and by early 1990, Soviet cosmonauts had accumulated nearly 16 man-years in orbit, far outstripping the Americans.

For all its successes, however, the Soviet program was not without setbacks. After a 23-day mission aboard Salyut 1 in 1971, three cosmonauts boarded their Soyuz 11 capsule, undocked from their workstation and prepared to leave space. Retrorockets were fired and the craft returned automatically to Earth. After a perfect touchdown, a rescue crew rushed to the capsule ready to help the cosmonauts, whom they expected to be weakened by three weeks in space. But when they opened the spacecraft's hatch, the recovery team found the three men dead in their seats. A valve on the Soyuz 11 capsule had failed just before reentry, resulting in the loss of the cabin's life-sustaining air while the craft was still 100 miles above the Earth. With no pressure suits to save them—the capsule was too small to include that luxury—the men had died after vainly trying to close the leak with a hand crank.

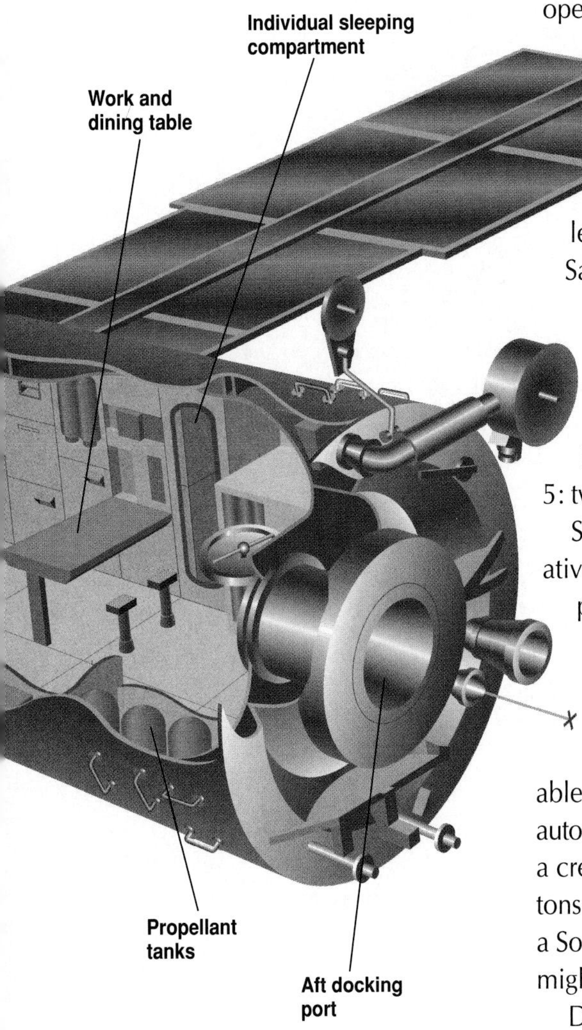
Individual sleeping compartment
Work and dining table
Propellant tanks
Aft docking port

Salyut 1 was never used again; in fact, Soviet manned flights did not resume for more than two years and the station was "de-orbited"—sent back into the atmosphere to burn up—in October 1971. In 1972 and 1973, two stations were orbited, but failed before crews could be launched. A third Salyut launch was attempted but its Proton booster failed before reaching orbit. But in the mid-'70s, successful missions took place aboard Salyuts 3, 4 and 5: two military spacecraft and a civilian version.

Salyuts 1 through 5 were first-generation vehicles and their missions were relatively short, lasting two months or less. To extend their staying power, Russian planners designed a second-generation Salyut with two docking ports (one at each end of the cylindrical-shaped station) and a new refuelable propulsion system. With these refinements in place, Salyut could be refuelled, allowing its orbit to be boosted periodically to prevent reentry into the atmosphere. It also could be restocked with food, water, air and other "consumables," which could be ferried up either in a manned Soyuz spacecraft or in an automated cargo ship called Progress. Russian engineers calculated that supporting a crew of three for a year required 1.5 tons of food, 3.3 tons of oxygen and 5.9 tons of water. But most important, the cargo flights could dock to one port while a Soyuz remained attached to the other port, reducing the risk that a cosmonaut might be stranded aboard the station if a balky supply ship failed to undock.

During the nearly nine years they were operational, Salyut 6 and 7 played host to 59 cosmonauts, including Svetlana Savitskaya, the first woman to do a spacewalk, and "guest" cosmonauts from countries including Czechoslovakia, Vietnam,

Cuba, Mongolia, France and India. There were some tense moments. On three occasions, the crews proved unable to dock with or transfer into the space stations, and cosmonauts aboard Salyut 7 spent considerable time outside the vehicle patching up malfunctioning equipment.

In February 1985, ground controllers lost all contact with Salyut 7—which was unmanned at the time—and in June, a rescue mission was launched. Cosmonauts, finding the space station dead, cold and tumbling out of control, performed a tricky manual docking maneuver and then entered the vehicle wearing breathing masks and warm clothing, including woolen hats. They revived Salyut, and one cosmonaut, Viktor Savinykh, stayed aboard for 168 days. Salyut 7 received two more crews of cosmonauts before it was mothballed for the last time in 1986.

During their prolonged stays, cosmonauts typically spent much of their time operating various scientific, technical, biological and medical experiments: peering through telescopes, studying the Earth with remote sensors, monitoring heart rates and tinkering with furnaces that produce ultra-pure crystals for semiconductors. They also occasionally conducted spacewalks, allowing them to retrieve instruments and detectors and practice space construction techniques such as welding. The remainder of the time was spent in personal recreation—cosmonauts were allotted an hour a day for personal time—and exercising. To maintain muscle strength and cardiovascular condition, long-term Salyut residents hit the treadmill for at least two hours a day.

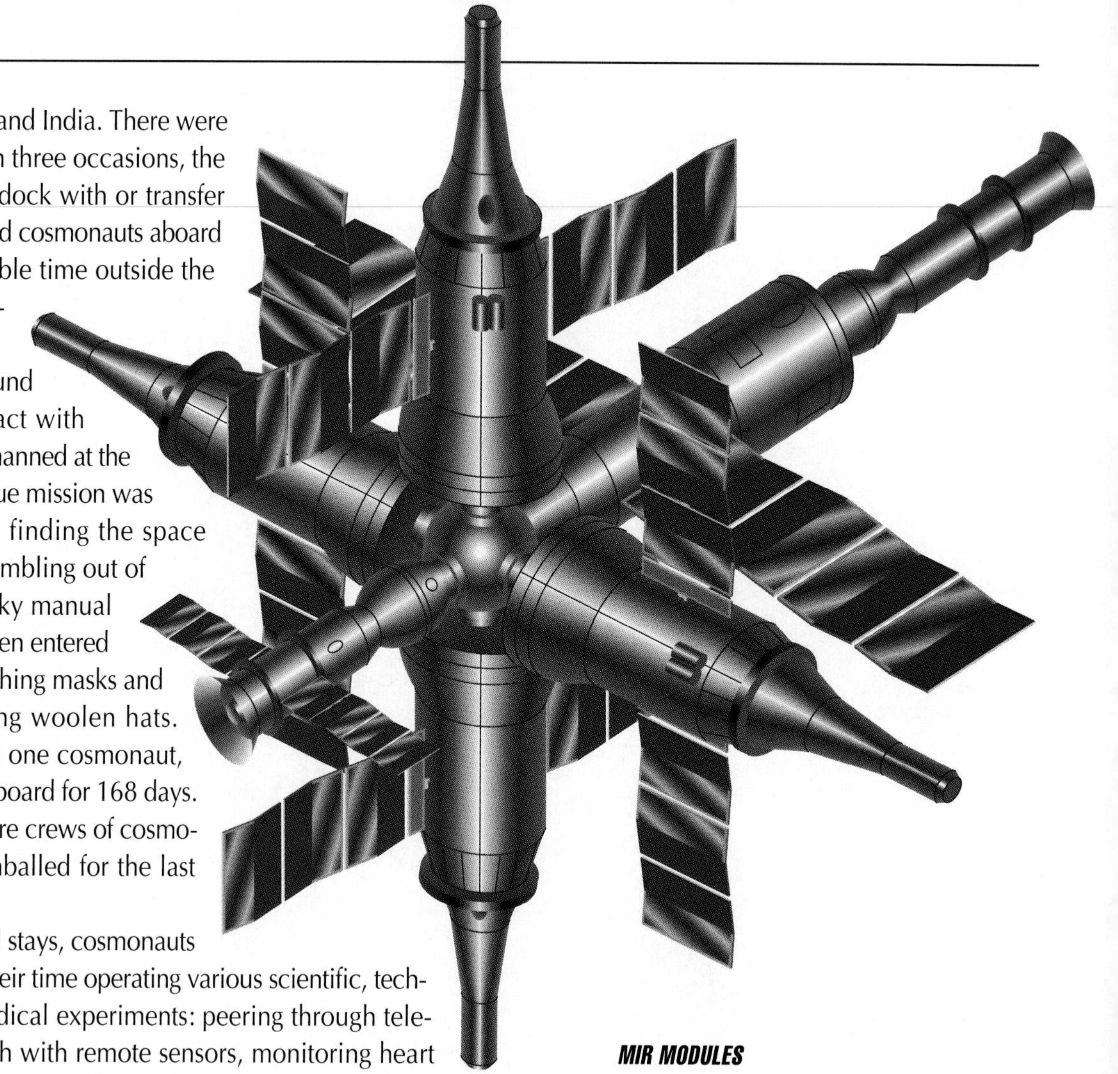

MIR MODULES

Mir's six docking ports allow the space station to be expanded by research and supply modules. The module's life-support system is connected to the central station's air ventilation system with flexible pipes laid through Mir's hatches.

The Salyut program set the stage for Mir, a more versatile space station with the same dimensions as the two previous Salyut stations—44 feet long and 14 feet in diameter. That size was determined by the dimensions of the launch vehicle, a three-stage version of the Proton rocket has been used to place all Soviet space stations in orbit. Sent aloft in 1986, Mir boasted an improved communications system, more electric power and a computer-control system that freed the crew from many tedious housekeeping tasks. Its most notable feature was a new front-end docking adaptor containing five ports, one along the main axis and four in a ring at right angles to each other. Including the aft port, Mir offers six sites where other vehicles can link up, providing unprecedented flexibility in attaching resupply and special-purpose modules.

In 1987, this potential was exploited for the first time with the launch of the 12-ton Kvant module—a year or more behind schedule—containing instruments for astrophysical experiments about the chemical and physical composition of celestial matter, gyroscopes for controlling the station's attitude and more advanced life-support systems. In late 1989, a much-delayed second module, the 20-ton Kvant 2 was added. It contained a shower and sink, improved water and oxygen equipment and an airlock and a rocket-propelled device, similar to the Americans' Manned Maneuvering Unit "jetpack," for use during spacewalks. In mid-1990, a third module, Kristall, joined the cluster; it weighed 22 tons and carried equipment for biomedical, astrophysics, Earth survey and materials processing research. Soviet officials hope to recoup part of the cost of the Mir program by producing ultra-pure crystals for the electronics industry. (A U.S. crystal-growth experiment package already has been carried on Mir and, in future, the station will support European materials research projects as well.) Two more modules, Spektr, a remote-sensing lab, and Priroda, devoted to environmental monitoring, are scheduled to be added before the end of 1992.

Mir has had its share of technical problems: Many of its instruments have not worked properly and crews have lost considerable time repairing equipment. Not only have the add-on modules been late, but docking has proved difficult. On its first attempt, Kvant sailed right by Mir. On the second pass, link-up was frustrated by a plastic trash bag full of hygienic towels and tissues caught in the docking mechanism. The crew was forced to don spacesuits and go outside to remove the obstruction. In general, putting a module station together in orbit has proved even more demanding than expected. And there have been some close calls: In September 1988, a crew sat trapped in their transfer vehicle for 26 hours when guidance problems twice forced them to abort reentry attempts. With their lives threatened by dwindling supplies of food and oxygen, they managed to overcome a faulty computer program, fire the Soyuz TM-5's retro engines and return safely to Earth.

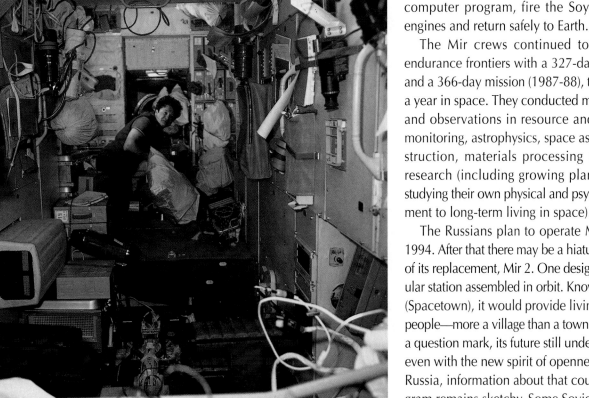

Cosmonaut Leonid Kizim floats near one end of the Mir space station, directly in front of the station's aft docking port.

The Mir crews continued to push back the endurance frontiers with a 327-day mission (1987) and a 366-day mission (1987-88), the first to exceed a year in space. They conducted many experiments and observations in resource and environmental monitoring, astrophysics, space assembly and construction, materials processing and biomedical research (including growing plants in space and studying their own physical and psychological adjustment to long-term living in space).

The Russians plan to operate Mir 1 until about 1994. After that there may be a hiatus until the launch of its replacement, Mir 2. One design calls for a modular station assembled in orbit. Known as Cosmograd (Spacetown), it would provide living quarters for 20 people—more a village than a town. But Mir 2 is now a question mark, its future still undecided. Moreover, even with the new spirit of openness, or *glasnost,* in Russia, information about that country's space program remains sketchy. Some Soviet space watchers

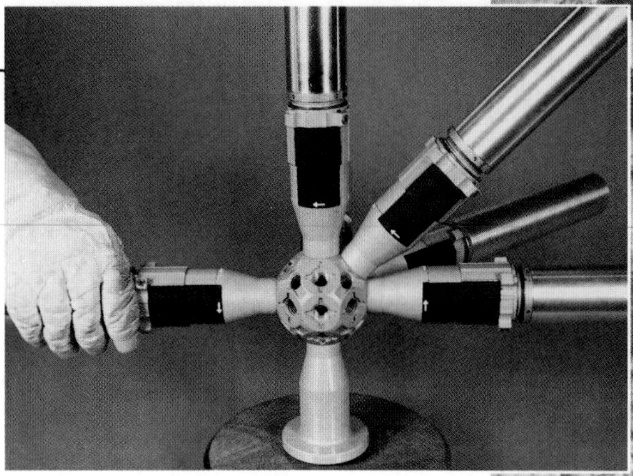

Each of Freedom's struts fits into a ball-shaped, grapefruit-sized joint. A quick twist of the wrist snaps it in place. The aluminum-coated struts are made of graphite fibers embedded in epoxy resin, producing a lightweight, anti-corrosion material that resists the effects of radiation and micrometeorites.

believe that Mir 2's design is contingent upon the success of Mir's material processing experiments—which still has not been ascertained. But before Mir 2's construction is complete, NASA should have finalized plans for America's first long-term home in space. Like Mir, it has been talked about—and dreamed about—since before the Space Age began.

THE BIRTH OF FREEDOM

Although the building of Freedom is scheduled to begin in the mid-1990s when astronauts start piecing together the space station 260 miles up into the heavens, its foundations were laid long ago on Earth. Decades before Skylab, decades before the technology even existed to lift a human into orbit, people dreamed of occupying a base that would orbit their home planet. The first such suggestions came in fiction. British author Arthur C. Clarke's vision of a gigantic wheel gently rotating in orbit enraptured filmgoers around the world when his story was turned into *2001: A Space Odyssey*. But it was in a work of nonfiction called *The Exploration of Space* that Clarke proved perhaps even more prescient. Published in 1951, the book contained a whole chapter devoted to space stations assembled in orbit by spacemen working with materials ferried up by spaceships. And once complete, Clarke predicted, they would serve as research bases that would expand the frontiers of scientific fields. More than four decades later, space station Freedom will demonstrate the clarity of Clarke's vision. Over a three-year period, 20 or so shuttle flights will haul aloft the building blocks that a cosmic construction crew will turn into NASA's dream home in the sky.

The ingredients for that home will consist of a single 476-foot horizontal scaffold, or truss; 4 habitable modules, each 43 feet long, where astronauts will live and work; a series of energy-producing solar panels so large that if placed side by side, they would cover more than half an acre; numerous externally mounted scientific instrument packages for observing the Earth and the stars; and a large, remotely controlled robotic system that will move around the truss, hauling supplies and performing periodic maintenance and repairs. The 290-ton station is expected to operate for 20 to 30 years, accommodating crews of 8 astronauts for 3- to 6-month stays.

In a speech to Congress in 1984 announcing Freedom's birth, President Ronald Reagan invited U.S. allies to participate in its construction. Later, agreements were signed to have Canada manufacture a robotic device known as the Mobile Servicing System, and Japan and the European Space Agency to provide two habitable lab modules. The U.S. will build the truss structure and two more modules, one

Perched at the end of the shuttle Atlantis' *remote manipulator arm, astronaut Sherwood Spring checks the joint of an EASE/ACCESS truss tower. The 45-foot-long structure was assembled by Spring and fellow astronaut Jerry Ross in 25.6 minutes from the back of the shuttle's cargo bay during a 1985 flight.*

for research and the other outfitted as crew quarters. In return for their contributions, the international partners will be able to use the space station as a research base and send up their own astronauts; they also will share operating costs.

During a shuttle flight in 1985, astronauts rehearsed the procedures required for the first part of constructing Freedom—assembling the truss structure that will form the structural backbone of the station. Consisting of interlocking triangles, a truss offers qualities of strength and rigidity that have long made it invaluable on Earth for bearing loads such as bridges and roofs. The astronauts used two experimental packages: EASE (Experimental Assembly of Structures in Extra Vehicular Activity) and ACCESS (Assembly Concept for Construction of Erectable Space Structure). EASE involved assembling and then breaking down a tetrahedron composed of half a dozen 12-foot beams. The procedure was repeated six times to test how well the cosmic construction crew adapted to working in zero-g, how their performance improved with learning and how quickly they tired. The ACCESS test involved assembling and disassembling a 45-foot-high truss tower.

Later the astronauts performed another series of tests with EASE and ACCESS in which they simulated space station construction techniques such as anchoring their feet with the shuttle's remote manipulator arm, attaching and removing the truss structure, lifting and rotating the truss by hand, and "repairing" a strut. These tests provided important data on the ability of astronauts to handle the onerous construction tasks required to build Freedom. Since then, however, serious concerns have been raised about the sheer amount of work that the astronauts might have to do, especially to maintain the station once it is assembled. While NASA originally estimated it would take about 130 hours a year, some scientists now suggest that a staggering 2,200 hours may be needed. The extensive use of robotics might alleviate the problem. At least two remote-controlled systems are expected to assist in assembling the station—a U.S.-built Flight Telerobotic Servicer that will sport camera eyes and three limbs for performing complex maintenance jobs, and Canada's Mobile Servicing System.

Because it will be used to help piece the space station together, the MSS will be one of the earliest pieces of equipment to be lofted by the shuttle during Freedom's assembly phase. Sitting on a sliding pallet, called the Mobile Transporter, that will carry it anywhere along Freedom's central truss, the 10,600-pound device will include a 58-foot-long manipulator arm (similar to the Canadian-built arm currently used by space shuttle astronauts) and two special-purpose "dexterous" manipulators, each 6.5 feet long. The longer arm will be used for heavy-duty activities, including station assembly, berthing the shuttle to the station and loading and unloading its cargo bay, hauling supplies and scientific equipment around the station and supporting astronauts during spacewalks. The smaller arms, which will have much greater manual dexterity, will do more delicate work such as cleaning surfaces and fixing or replacing malfunctioning equipment.

The MSS arms will have tactile sensors and a vision system that will allow them, in effect, to "feel" and "see" what they're doing, thus enabling them to perform many more tasks with a much finer degree of control than previous manipulator systems. In future, when the incorporation of artificial intelligence technology makes space robots even smarter, they will be able to accomplish more intricate tasks, performing many of them without human control. This should further reduce

The Perils of Space Garbage

No sooner had U.S. astronaut Michael Collins reentered his Gemini 10 spacecraft than he noticed something was missing. A chest-mounted Hasselblad camera had worked its way loose during a just-completed spacewalk and was now floating irretrievably through space.

For some onlookers, the 1966 event took on an air of quirky charm. The slip-up was a reminder that, despite the fact they worked in the heavens, spacemen were not gods. And the thought of an object as ordinary as a camera floating untethered through space was offbeat, even humorous.

There was, however, a more sober side: Collins' camera had become one more addition to an ever-growing pile of clutter orbiting the Earth, a garbage heap that poses a mounting threat to spacecraft. Since Sputnik became Earth's first artificial satellite in 1957, the catalog of space trash has included dead satellites, spent rocket stages, solar panels, rocket fairings, dropped tools, discarded clothes—even garbage bags. Today, an estimated 7,000 objects larger than four inches in diameter orbit the Earth.

But objects smaller than that evade detection. They include the nuts, bolts, springs, brackets, switches and other assorted remnants of collided objects and upper stage rockets that explode due to leftover fuel. Experts disagree about their numbers, but they do agree that it is at least double the 7,000 larger objects—possibly more. Then there are the minute particles of aluminum oxide from rocket fuel exhaust which could populate the heavens by the trillions.

Traveling at speeds of up to 17,500 miles per hour, even the smallest piece of orbiting debris packs a wallop that can threaten a spacecraft and astronauts. That fact was well illustrated by the post-flight examination of space shuttle *Challenger* in 1983. A paint fleck had collided head-on with the spacecraft, embedding itself in a windshield. Had the fleck been any larger, experts say, it might have shattered the windshield. An object as heavy as Collins' camera might have destroyed the shuttle itself.

All objects eventually fall from orbit depending on their altitude. In low-Earth orbit—150 miles up—for example, a piece of space garbage stays up for a few months or years; in geosynchronous orbit, 22,300 miles above the Earth's equator, the same object will remain aloft for centuries.

To ward off the small debris, space station Freedom will carry shielding supported several inches from its vulnerable surfaces. Objects larger than four inches in diameter will have to be sidestepped, with help from Space Command, a U.S. ground-based tracking station that monitors what is in orbit. But there are no guarantees. Says Dr. Drew Potter, chief of space science at NASA's Johnson Space Center, "There is a gray area; debris between one and four inches in diameter can't always be tracked, and this concerns us. We're still looking for a way to protect the station from this threat."

TRAVELING TRASH

Even space's outer reaches are falling prey to one of Earth's biggest problems: ever-increasing amounts of debris. In space, the most minute particles can stay aloft for years and, since they are traveling at great speeds, cause problems for spacecraft.

the need for astronauts to leave the safer environment inside the space station.

The habitable modules that will provide a "shirtsleeves" environment form the hub of the space station. Three of the four, including the European and Japanese modules, will function as scientific labs, and contain equipment for diverse studies on materials processing, technology development, Earth observations and environmental studies, biomedicine and life sciences, physics, chemistry, astronomy and many more.

The fourth module will provide living quarters for astronauts from all the participating countries. In an effort to make life in orbit more livable, this module will be outfitted with a refrigerator-freezer, microwave and conventional oven, a clothes washer-dryer and an improved shower with a cylindrical plastic stall that will produce an airstream to help the water fall down properly. The galley features a large picture window, so that crews can enjoy their favorite pastime—watching the Earth go by—as they eat their meals. In addition, each astronaut will have a 150-cubic-foot soundproof compartment, which can be decorated according to personal taste. These compartments will provide not only sleeping quarters, but also a private recreation area. They come equipped with TV set, video playback and stereo unit and a telephone/video system that will allow crew members to speak privately with friends and family back on Earth.

Freedom's laboratory module (top) *will contain test equipment stored in racks that can be tipped out easily for cleaning or replacement. Living in zero gravity will make even moving around the space station a novel experience as demonstrated in a module mockup* (bottom).

In the event of an emergency that threatens the integrity of the life-support system—for example, a fire or explosion, or penetration of the station's hull by a micrometeorites or space debris—the damaged area can be sealed off and the crew can assemble in one of two designated "safe havens" to decide what action to take. An Assured Crew Return Vehicle also will be stationed on board Freedom, allowing astronauts to return quickly to Earth. (It could take the shuttle up to 45 days to get to the station, at a cost of more than $100 million.)

As missions become longer and astronauts engage in more hazardous activities, such as construction and repair and maintenance outside the station, the likelihood of accidents, injuries and medical emergencies increases dramatically. Consequently, Freedom will be equipped with its own sophisticated medical clinic. Called the Health Maintenance Facility, it will take up about 60 cubic feet—the size of two telephone booths—and contain equipment and supplies to treat minor conditions such as sprains, colds and headaches, and moderately serious problems such as kidney stones, appendicitis, perforated ulcer, mild heart attack, tooth abscesses and some kinds of head wounds. The station also will have a compression chamber to treat astronauts suffering from the bends, a debilitating, potentially fatal condition caused by rapid depressurization. In the case of severe injuries, the major objective of medical treatment will be to stabilize the patient until rescue. At least one member of each crew will have some medical training.

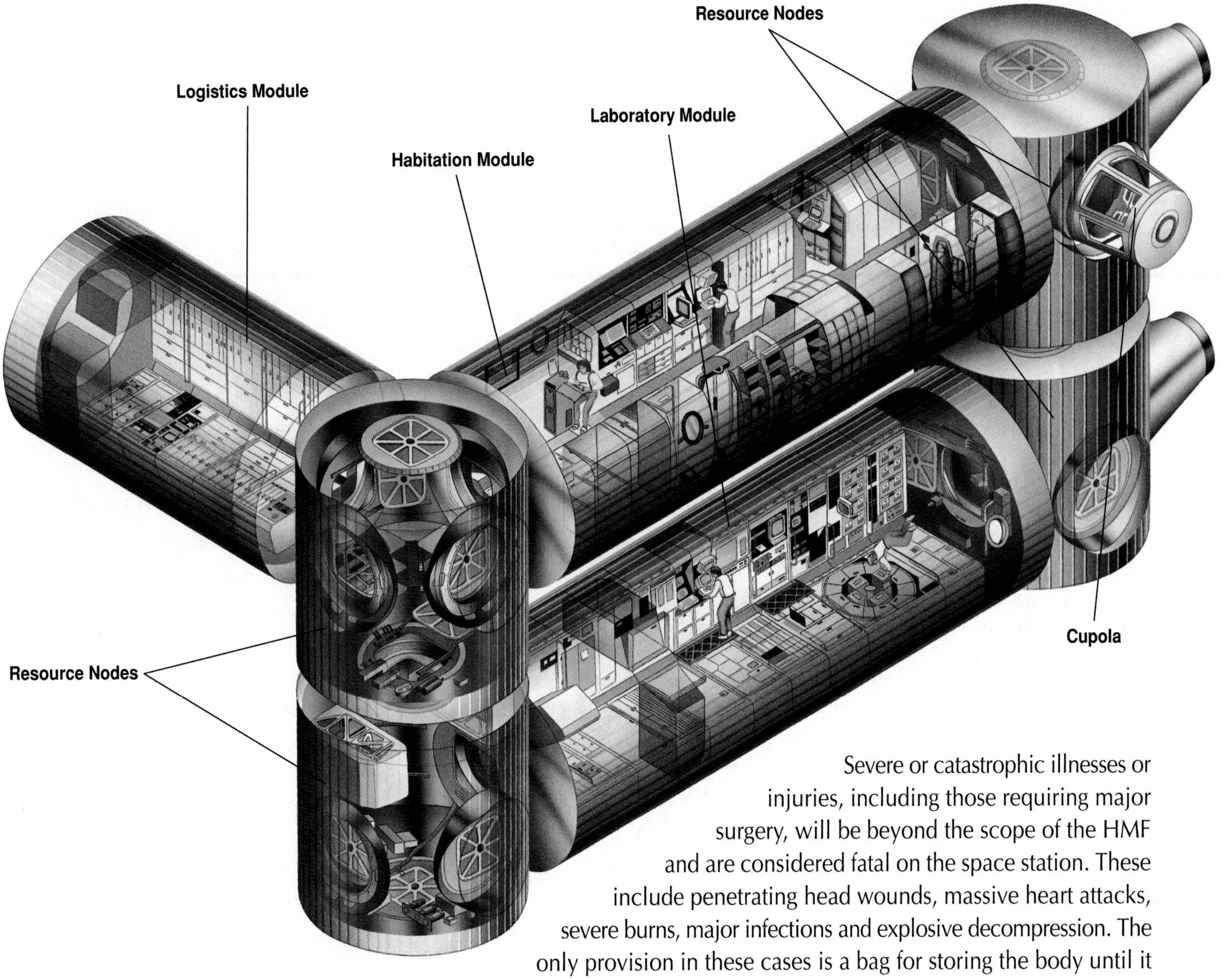
Resource Nodes
Logistics Module
Laboratory Module
Habitation Module
Cupola
Resource Nodes

SPACE STATION FREEDOM

Freedom's habitation and research modules will be connected by four "nodes," 18-by-15-foot cylinders that act as passageways between the modules and also serve as control centers for the station's propulsion, tracking and guidance systems. The cupola will serve as an observation deck, providing a panoramic view for scientific and operational observation. The logistics module, a glorified storage locker, will be used to transport experiments, supplies and perishable items to the station. When supplies dwindle, the shuttle will return it to Earth for replenishing and refurbishing.

Severe or catastrophic illnesses or injuries, including those requiring major surgery, will be beyond the scope of the HMF and are considered fatal on the space station. These include penetrating head wounds, massive heart attacks, severe burns, major infections and explosive decompression. The only provision in these cases is a bag for storing the body until it can be returned to Earth.

THE UPS AND DOWNS OF ZERO-G

Constructing a space station like Freedom in a hostile, airless void will tax American technological know-how in unprecedented ways. But no amount of engineering expertise can change the most important element in its success. The men and women who will live aboard this home in the sky will confront an inescapable factor that may profoundly influence humans' attempts to stay in space and reach for the stars—one that has been examined and analyzed by Russian and American physicians since before the days of Salyut 1 and Skylab.

For despite its marvelously resilient and adaptive abilities, the human body is the product of millions of years of evolution in a one-gravity environment. Forcing that body to exist for long periods of time in zero-g can create a catalog of ailments and disorders including space motion sickness, muscle deconditioning, changes in the heart, blood and circulation systems, shifting of body fluids, loss of bone calcium, weakening of the immune system, and finally, disorientation, perceptual illusions and changes in awareness of body position. Although many of these

Stranded in Space

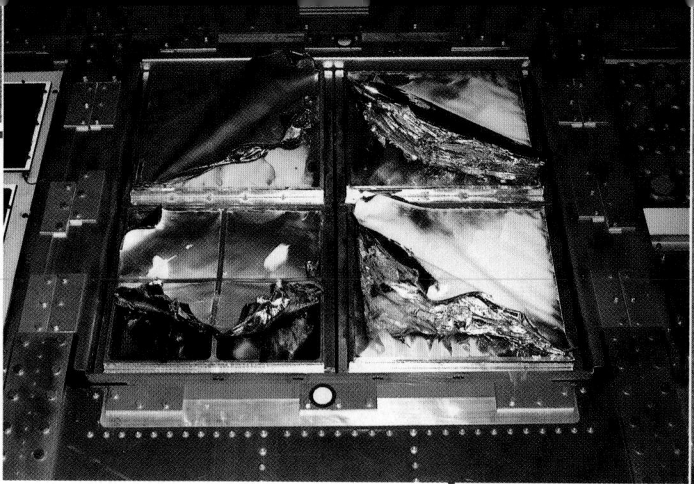

Sixty-nine months of exposure in space aboard the Long Duration Exposure Facility took its toll on these thermal covers. They left Earth flat and white, but returned tarnished and torn.

While most satellites and probes strut their stuff in space, snapping breathtaking photos, scanning the heavens or touching down on alien worlds, the Long Duration Exposure Facility did nothing but mind its own 260-mile-high orbital business. Launched in April 1984, LDEF awaited return to terra firma to prove its worth.

The goal of LDEF was simple—to expose various materials to the cosmic environment over an extended period of time. Bolted to the outside of the 22,000-pound satellite were special trays containing everything from future space station materials to tomato seeds (the latter, part of a student experiment) to see the effects of cosmic radiation, micrometeorites and extreme temperatures.

LDEF needed no intricate trajectory, boasted no message for extraterrestrials. It merely required surface area to spread its smorgasbord of materials before the hostile heavens. So NASA built LDEF as big as a bus and gave it a 12-sided cylindrical shape to convey 86 trays bearing 57 experiments.

LDEF also needed a safe ride home in order to reveal its cosmic scars. The space shuttle would fulfill that need by retrieving the facility 10 months after launch. But a year after it went into orbit, LDEF was still circling the globe, jilted by a shuttle program hampered with launch constraints. Two years later, LDEF was outright stranded as shuttle flights were grounded indefinitely following the 1986 *Challenger* explosion.

The cloud held a silver lining, however; longer exposure would provide further evidence of each material's ability to endure the rigors of space. But for how much longer? LDEF was capable of orbiting Earth for only six years before it would reenter the atmosphere and burn up.

Fortunately, shuttle flights were resumed in time to rescue LDEF in December 1989, just five months before its impending fiery demise. Scientists zeroed in on the many materials to assess the damage. Certain plastics (polymers) were seriously eroded, and in some cases completely destroyed, by the bombardment of oxygen atoms. Micrometeorite detectors were pelted tens of thousands of times by micrometeorites and man-made debris now littering space. However, space station materials such as anodized aluminum held out surprisingly well, as did the 12 million tomato seeds, which lived to yield normal-looking tomatoes in classrooms across America.

Since LDEF sported no attitude control thrusters, it was subjected to the lowest contamination levels of any spacecraft to date—an important factor in understanding the pure effects of space on earthly materials.

The panel of spacecraft coating samples at right was exposed for one year on LDEF and then automatically covered. Meanwhile, a canister bearing identical samples was left exposed for the entire duration. Back on Earth, scientists analyzed the differences in color to gauge the durability of the materials.

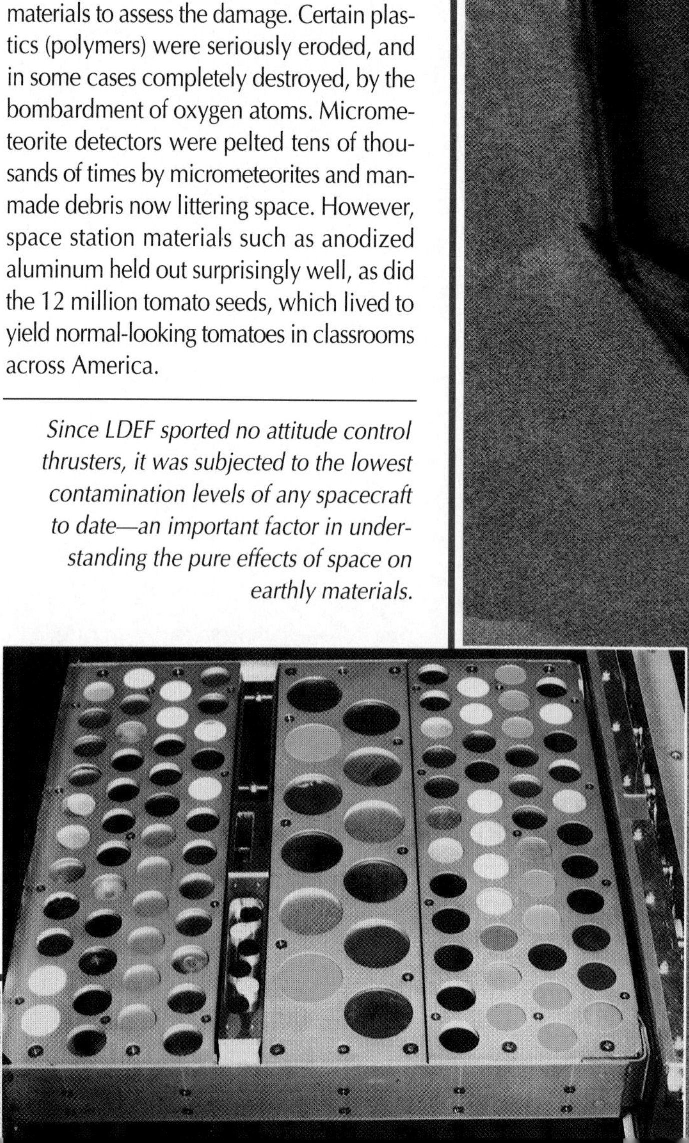

changes level out in space and reverse themselves back on Earth, some of them may pose health risks or cause operational problems during long-duration missions.

Space motion sickness has turned out to be surprisingly common—more than half the space workers have been afflicted—and difficult to predict, striking even experienced test pilots who perform aerobatic maneuvers on Earth without a twinge. Scientists are investigating the possible linkage of the nauseating ailment to the inner ear, where an intricate mechanism of tiny hairs, bones and fluid acts as an anatomical gyroscope to keep the body balanced. After a few days in space, the brain may learn to ignore the lack of gravity and confusing signals from the inner ear, but meanwhile, dizziness, nausea, sweating, fatigue and vomiting can occur. Astronauts and cosmonauts have at times been incapacitated for several days. Because it disappears in a few days, motion sickness poses less of a problem on longer missions, although it may continue to create risks if it occurs during critical operations such as docking or an emergency shuttle landing. Medication sometimes helps, but many sufferers simply have to wait out the malady. During this vulnerable period, susceptible crew members avoid sudden head movements or looking at another crew member while upside down.

Without the force of gravity compressing the spongy discs that separate the spinal vertebrae, astronauts actually grow an inch or two within a few days of entering space. The effects are temporary, as is the redistribution of fluids to the upper body that results in facial bloating and thinning of the lower body—what astronauts have dubbed "puffy face and bird legs." Less apparent and potentially more serious effects also occur: The body, suddenly sensing more fluid in the upper extremities than it considers normal, starts purging it through urination. Some scientists have linked this fluid loss to a reduction in the size of red blood cells, which carry life-supporting oxygen via the bloodstream throughout the body. Although this loss eventually levels off—and returns to normal on Earth—astronauts typically experience a drop in blood volume that could cause blackouts and faintness during reentry, when g forces build up and send blood rushing from the head to the feet.

In space, higher upper-body fluid levels also cause a chronic sensation of congestion (astronauts often feel like they have a persistent head cold) as well as a temporary increase in the size of the heart's chamberlike ventricles. Things stabilize after a few days—although heart size actually decreases during long flights—but it can take the cardiovascular system up to several weeks to re-adapt to one-g after a long mission. It is also difficult to maintain muscle tone in space; muscles simply do not have as much work to do in zero gravity as they do on Earth. Cosmonauts returning from long-duration flights, especially the early ones, were usually carried off in reclining chairs to lessen the physical exertion of returning to Earth and to prevent any injury. Valery Ryumin found a congratulatory bouquet of flowers as heavy as a sheaf of wheat after his 175-day mission. Under the influence of zero gravity, bones lose calcium and weaken. When cosmonaut Vladimir Titov docked with the Mir space station in 1987, he was cautioned not to offer a hug to his comrade Yuri Romanenko for establishing a new space endurance

Fatigued by the effects of 237 days aboard the Salyut 7 space station, cosmonauts Leonid Kizim, Vladimir Solovyov and Oleg Atkov rest in specially designed reclining chairs shortly after their 1984 landing in Kazakhstan.

record—more than 10 months in orbit. Soviet officials were worried that Romanenko's decalcified bones might fracture like dry sticks.

Although researchers are studying whether drugs and equipment might help alleviate some of these problems, they believe that intensive exercise in space is necessary to arrest zero-gravity deconditioning. At least two hours of exercise a day may be needed on long-duration missions. Whether exercise alone will be sufficient on very long-term missions remains an open question. Scientists currently are studying whether artificial gravity, which could be created by the centrifugal force resulting from spinning the spacecraft, might be necessary to maintain the physical condition of future crews.

Psychological well-being raises other concerns. Astronauts and cosmonauts are confined to close quarters for long periods of time in an isolated and dangerous environment, lacking privacy and personal contact with friends and family. No matter how motivated they are, they still have human emotions—not only the joy and excitement of spaceflight, but also anger, fear, loneliness, frustration, boredom and depression. Unhappy crew members are inefficient and potentially dangerous. The Soviets have put greater emphasis than the Americans on the psychological aspects of long-duration spaceflight. They do extensive pre-flight assessments, once sending a crew on a car trip across Siberia to see if they were compatible. A psychological ground support team observes and assists crews. They have also ferried mail and videotapes from home to the craft. One homesick cosmonaut watched a video of his daughter's birthday party when he felt lonely. Contact with friends and family is considered so important that cosmonauts are allowed to use the space station's two-way TV communication system for this purpose. In pre-*glasnost* Russia, crews' families were coached not to disclose any bad news and communications sessions included briefings from the Political Indoctrination Office; today's cosmonauts speak openly with their families and receive TV and newspaper items. Visiting crews of cosmonauts prove welcome company: "You wait for them like brothers and the joy of personal contact makes up for the difficulties," said Valentin Lebedev, veteran of a 211-day mission. Amenities are also important morale-boosters for spaceworkers: a shower for cleanliness; private bedroom cubicles for privacy; a large picture window to counter claustrophobia; variety in colors, textures and lighting—and individual control over these features in their personal space. Spicy food is keenly appreciated. And NASA scientists are developing a small greenhouse for growing vegetables hydroponically. This would relieve the technological environment and give crews something akin to gardening as a hobby. The plants also will play a role in regenerating the station's environment—performing a role in space that they first carried out on Earth millions of years before humans existed.

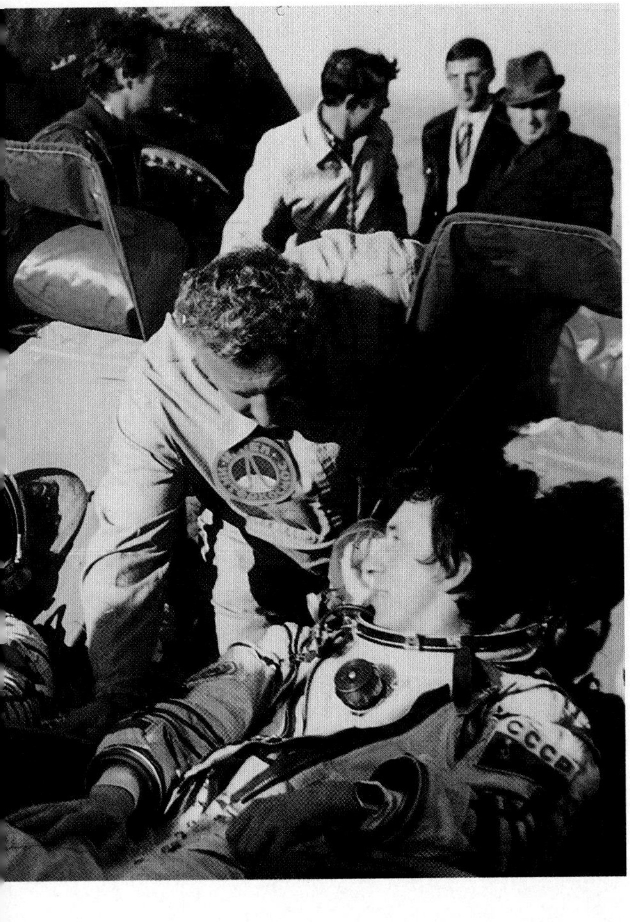
CCCP

If Freedom and Mir live up to their potential and provide more technical, biomedical and psychological knowledge and skills, earthbound scientists and engineers may gain the tools needed to venture ever-further afield. After thousands of years of roaming the Earth, humans are finally embarking on their biggest voyage yet, the exploration—and population—of the universe.

Martian Odyssey

The lure of the red planet remains undiminished, despite information from interplanetary probes and landers that it is almost certainly devoid of life. Even though a manned trip may be decades away, engineers already have begun serious studies on how it can be achieved. The far-reaching enterprise will demand a revolutionary rocket design. At its closest, the fourth planet is still about 35 million miles from Earth —more than 100 times the distance to the Moon. One proposal is for a nuclear thermal-powered design. A fission reactor at one end of the rocket would heat propellant stored in nearby tanks. The resulting gases, expelled through a nozzle, would provide the necessary thrust. The crew quarters would be situated at the opposite end of the rocket structure to protect the crew from radiation. Once the spacecraft arrived in Martian orbit, its speed could be reduced by using the drag provided by the thin Martian atmosphere. Known as aerobraking, means that fuel would not have to be expended firing retrorockets to ease the spacecraft into orbit around the red planet.

Whatever the design, engineers and scientists seem to agree that a Mars-bound rocket cannot be launched from Earth. The launch machine required would have to be enormously powerful. Space station Freedom, however, could provide a convenient assembly platform for a so-called Mars Transfer Vehicle. The return trip likely will take from one-and-a-half to three years.

One of two trajectories is likely: the conjunction-class mission, which involves taking off when Mars is in conjunction with Earth (on the opposite side of the Sun from the Earth); or the opposition-class mission, involving a flight designed to land astronauts when Mars and Earth are closest together. Both have their advantages and disadvantages: The former takes twice as long to complete; the latter allows only a few weeks of exploration time on Mars.

In this artist's conception, a thermal-nuclear rocket nears Mars following a trip from Earth. The spacecraft is based on technology once developed for a program called Nuclear Engine for Rocket Vehicle Application.

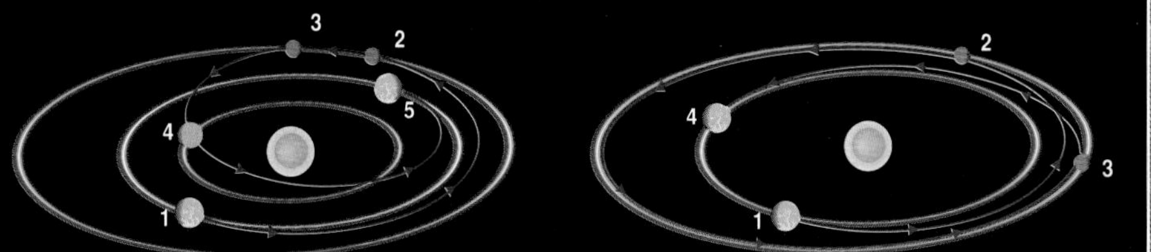
3
2
5
4
1
2
4
3
1

TWO POSSIBLE ROUTES TO MARS

Opposition-class trajectory
Return Trip: 580 days

1. Leave Earth
2. Land on Mars
3. Leave Mars
4. Venus Flyby
5. Return to Earth

Conjunction-class trajectory
Return Trip: 1,050 days

1. Leave Earth
2. Land on Mars
3. Leave Mars
4. Return to Earth

The first steps on Mars probably will not be taken by a human, but by some form of unmanned robotic device. One design on the drawing boards is the so-called Walking Beam shown above. It consists of a collapsible, seven-legged T-beam structure. Traveling at a slow-but-steady 300 feet per hour, the beam's telescoping legs will allow it to climb over obstacles five feet high. Onboard sensors and computers will help the machine avoid hazards. It will be equipped with scientific instruments to collect and test soil samples.

Later, when humans land (President Bush has proposed a mission that will plant a U.S. flag on Mars in 2019—50 years after the first lunar landing), a rover will become a necessity to permit extended sorties. The vehicle show at right would sustain two astronauts on a 14-day 180-mile round trip. With numerous storage compartments for equipments and samples, fold-down beds and robotic arms, the rover would be a virtual spacecraft on wheels.

Since any Martian excursion would undoubtedly include Extra Vehicular Activities, the rover would include an airlock, much like the one used on the shuttle *(page 106)*. It also would feature a "rumble seat," allowing an astronaut to ride outside the rover between EVAs, thereby minimizing the time-consuming task of depressurizing and repressurizing the airlock. Although the rover would be capable of traveling at 12 miles per hour, its average speed would probably be a more sedate five miles per hour. Should the rugged Martian surface ensnare the vehicle, millions of miles from the nearest tow truck, a motor-driven winch could help put it back on course.

Before humans set foot on Mars, a robotic device like the walking-beam design above may range over diverse terrain. The pressurized rover at right would provide a shirt-sleeves environment for two astronauts.

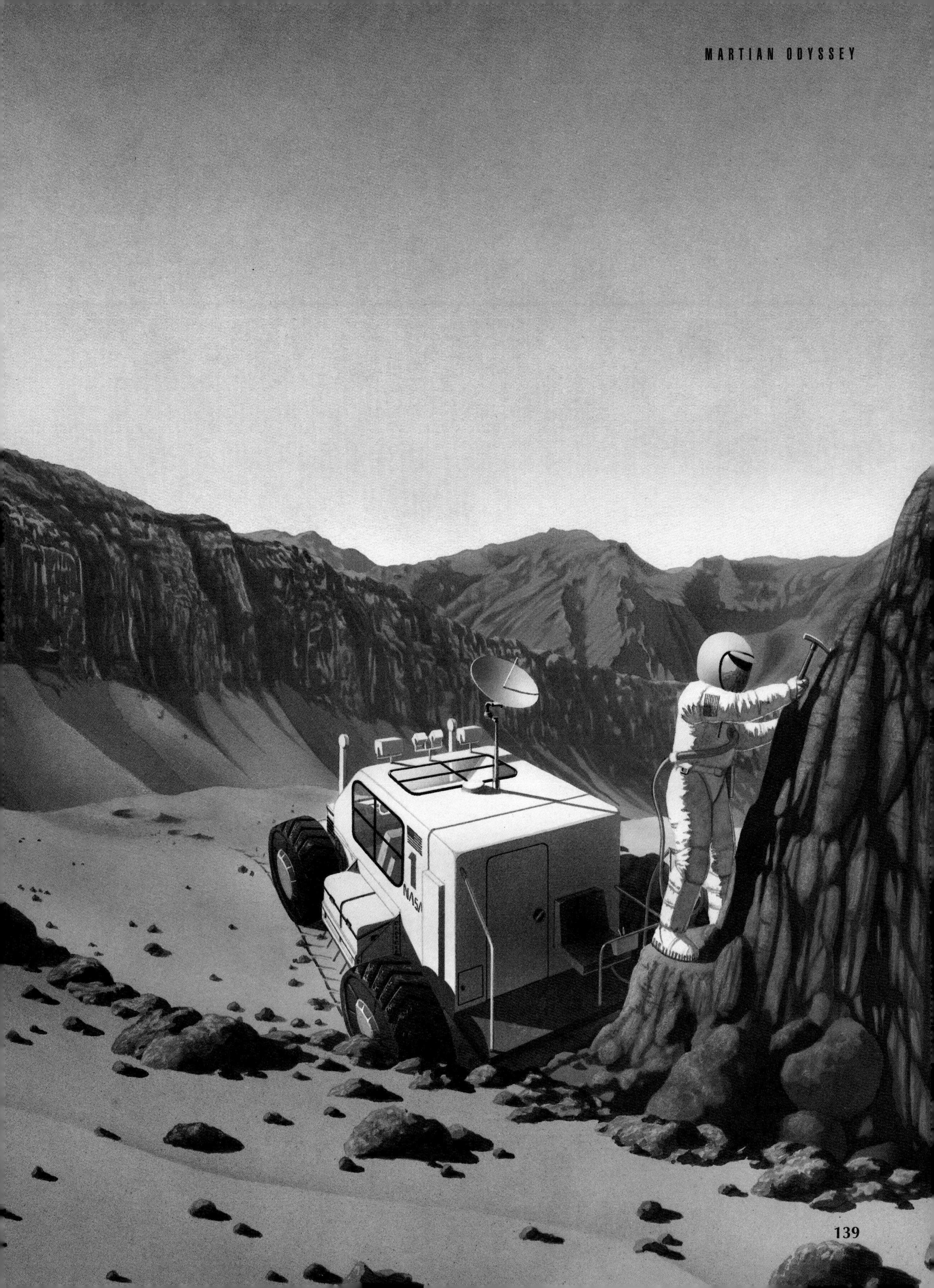
1
NASA

Index

Numerals in *italics* indicate an illustration of the subject mentioned.

S

T

U-V

W-X-Y-Z

PICTURE CREDITS

Multiple credits on a page are read left to right, top to bottom, divided by semicolons.

Cover courtesy NASA.

6,7 Smithsonian Astrophysical Obesrvatory; NASA (3). 14,15 Roger Ressmeyer/Starlight.16 Chris Grajczyk; Courtesy Kevin Pang. 17 California Institute of Technology. 21 Kim Steele. 23 G. Jacoby/NOAO. 24 Tim Fuller. 25 Courtesy NRC/Dominion Astrophysical Observatory (2). 29 NRAO/AUI. 30,31 Doug Johnson/SPL/Photo Researchers. 32,33 Tom Wolff (2); Courtesy Zeiss Jena. 36 NASA. 40 Courtesy EOSAT (2). 42 Philip C. Jackson with the kind permission of The Weather Network. 43 NASA. 44,45 Courtesy Spot Image Corporation; © Peter B. Kaplan (3). 46 Courtesy Hughes-Danbury Optical Systems; NASA. 50,51 Philip J. Griffiths/Magnum Photos. 52,53 Courtesy G.E. Astro Space. 55 NASA; NOAO. 57 Museum of Science, Boston. 58,59 TASS/Sovfoto; Richard Haynes. 60 Philip C. Jackson, courtesy Merril Collection of Science Fiction,© 1939, Ziff-Davis Publishing. 62 NASA. 63 Jet Propulsion Laboratory. 64,65 David Harvey/© National Geographic Society; Courtesy National Astronomy and Ionosphere Center/Cornell University/NSF; Jet Propulsion Laboratory (2); NASA. 68,69 Jet Propulsion Laboratory; Chad Slattery. 70,71 NASA. 76,77 Courtesy Martin Marietta Manned Space Systems; Courtesy Rocketdyne; NASA. 78,79 Courtesy Thiokol Corporation (3). 80 NASA/Photo Researchers. 81 Novosti. 82 NASA (2). 86,87 NASA (3). 88 NASA. 89 NASA (3). 90 NASA. 91 NASA. 92,93 NASA (3). 94 NASA. 95 NASA (2). 96,97 NASA. 99 NASA. 100 NASA. 104 NASA (2). 106 NASA. 108 NASA. 111 NASA. 112,113 NASA; NASA/Photo Researchers; Courtesy Spar Aerospace. 114 NASA. 120,121 NASA (3). 125 Tass/Sovfoto. 126,127 NASA (2). 128,129 NASA (background). 130,131 Courtesy Boeing Alabama; NASA. 132,133 NASA (3). 134,135 Tass/Sovfoto.

ILLUSTRATION CREDITS

8-13 François Chartier. 19 Alain Longpré. 20 Guy Charette. 26-7 Sam Montesano. 34-5 Robert Monté. 40-1 Josée Morin. 49 Luc Normandin. 73 Alain Longpré. 84, 85 Josée Morin. 108-9 Alain Longpré. 118,119 Courtesy McDonnell Douglas Space Systems. 129 Sam Montesano. 131 Claude Lafrance. 136,137 Paul DiMare. 138-9 Luc Normandin.

ACKNOWLEDGMENTS

The editors wish to thank the following:
Scott Bleisath, NASA Lyndon B. Johnson Space Center (MOD), Houston, TX; Joe Boyce M.D., NASA Lyndon B. Johnson Space Center, Houston, TX; Tom Branigan, Martin Marietta Manned Space Systems, New Orleans, LA; Pierre Chastenay, Planetarium Dow, Montréal, Qué.; Mikhail Chernyshov, Novosti Press Agency, Moscow; Geoff Chester, Albert Einstein Planetarium, Smithsonian Institution, Washington, DC; Phillip Clark, London, England; Jean W. Clough, NASA Langley Research Center, Hampton, VA; Kevin Corbley, EOSAT, Lanham, MD; Louis D'Amario, NASA Jet Propulsion Laboratory, California Institute of Technology, Pasadena, CA; Jim D'Andrade, ILC Dover, Inc., Frederica, DE; Ray Del'Osso NASA Lyndon B. Johnson Space Center, Houston, TX; Raleigh Drake, Kitt Peak Observatory, Tucson, AZ; European Space Agency, Public Relations, Paris, France; Mark Eustis, EOSAT, Lanham MD; Randee Exler, NASA Goddard Space Flight Center, Greenbelt, MD; Dr. James Faller, JILA-NIST, University of Colorado at Boulder, CO; Delma C. Freeman, Jr., NASA Langley Research Center, Hampton, VA; Mike Gentry, NASA Lyndon B. Johnson Space Center, Houston, TX; John Gustafson, California Association of Research in Astronomy, Oakland, CA; Emma Hardesty, NOAO, Tucson, AZ; Ed Harrison, NASA John F. Kennedy Space Center, Cape Canaveral, FL; Scott S. Hildreth, Astronomical Society of the Pacific, San Francisco, CA; April Hiller, Kitt Peak Observatory, Tucson, AZ; Jane A. Hutchison, NASA Ames Research Center, Moffet Field, CA; George Jacoby, Kitt Peak National Observatory, NOAO, Tucson, AZ; William H. Kinard, NASA Langley Research Center, Hampton, VA; James D. Lawrence Jr., NASA Langley Research Center, Hampton, VA; Steve Lawson, Thiokol Corporation, Brigham City, UT; Frank C. Lepore, Jr., National Oceanic & Atmospheric Administration, Washington, DC; Robert J. Lessels, George C. Marshall Space Flight Center, Huntsville, AL; Dr. Erwin G. Loewen, Milton Roy Co., Rochester, NY; Jon Lomberg, Honaunau, HI; Robert MacMillin, NASA Jet Propulsion Laboratory, California Institute of Technology, Pasadena, CA; Gail Macnaughton, SPAR Aerospace Ltd., Weston, Ont.; J. Campbell Martin, NASA Langley Research Center, Hampton, VA; Kerry M. Masson; Martin Marietta Astronautics Group, Denver, CO; Nicola McAlister Noll, SPOT Image Corp., Reston, VA; Anthony F.J. Moffat, Département de Physique, Université de Montréal, Montréal,Qué.; Museum of Science, Boston, MS; NASA Goddard Space Flight Center, Greenbelt, MD; National Research Council of Canada, Dominion Astrophysical Observatory, Victoria, BC; Jerry Nelson, W.M. Keck Observatory, Mauna Kea, HI; Major Thomas Niemann, U.S. Space Command, Colorado Springs, CO; William O'Leary, NASA Goddard Space Flight Center, Greenbelt, MD; Carol Petrachenko, Bionetics Corp., Hampton, VA; David Pine, NASA Headquarters, Washington. DC; Gwen Pitman, NASA Audio-Visual/Broadcast Services, Washington, DC; R. Stephen Price, Martin Marietta Astronautics Group, Denver, CO; E. Brian Pritchard, NASA Langley Research Center, Hampton, VA; R. Robert Robbins, University of Texas at Austin, TX; Duane Ross, NASA Lyndon B. Johnson Space Center, Houston, TX; Paul Seiler, NSI Technological Service Corp., Greenbelt, MD; Albert R. Schallenmuller, Martin Marietta Astronautics Group, Denver, CO; Carol A. Schmidt, General Electric Astrospace Division, Princeton, NJ; Jim Shali, NASA George C. Marshall Space Flight Center, Hunstville, AL; Peter J. Shelus, McDonald Observatory, University of Texas at Austin, TX; Mike Simmons, NASA George C. Marshall Space Flight Center, Huntsville, AL; Alda D. Simpson, NASA Goddard Space Flight Center, Greenbelt, MD; Andrei V. Stulov, USSR Embassy, Ottawa, Ont.; Joe Talbot, NASA Langley Research Center, Hampton, VA; Chris Talley, Martin Marietta Astronautics Group, Denver, CO; Michael G. Thorton, Martin Marietta Astronautics Group, Denver, CO; Caprina Tomlinson, MétéoMédia Inc., Montréal, Qué; Carol S. Toole, ILC Space Systems, Houston, TX; Pat Troutman, NASA Langley Research Center, Hampton, VA; Dr. Kosta Tsipis, Massachusetts Institute of Technology, Cambridge, MA; Jurrie van der Woude, NASA Jet Propulsion Laboratory, California Institute of Technology, Pasadena, CA; Dr. James (Ox) van Hoften, Bechtel National Inc., San Francisco, CA; Lisa Vazquez, NASA Lyndon B. Johnson Space Center, Houston, TX; Edward Weiler, NASA Headquarters, Washington, DC; Brian D. Welch, NASA Lyndon B. Johnson Space Center, Houston, TX; Frank H. Winter, National Air & Space Museum, Smithsonian Institution, Washington, DC; Michael Withey, ILC Space Systems (EVA Engineering), Houston, TX; Dieter Wolff, Lisle-Kelco Ltd., Mississauga, Ont.; Alan Wood, NASA Jet Propulsion Laboratory, California Institute of Technology, Pasadena, CA; Richard N. Young, NASA John F. Kennedy Space Center, Cape Canaveral, FL; Yuri Zaitsev, Institute of Space Research, USSR Academy of Sciences, Moscow.

The following persons also assisted in the preparation of this book:
Stanley D. Harrison, Jenny Meltzer, Shirley Sylvain.

This book was designed on Apple Macintosh® computers, using QuarkXPress® in conjunction with CopyFlow™ and a Linotronic® 300R for page layout and composition; StrataVision 3d.®, Adobe Illustrator 88® and Adobe Photoshop® were used as illustration programs.